AIDS AND THE BODY POLITIC

In this masterful study, Waldby offers crucial new insights into the relationships between biomedical discourses, the sexual politics of citizenship, macro- and micro-bodies and the processes of normalisation. This challenging and thought-provoking work is essential reading for anyone interested in biopolitics, sexual difference, queer theory and critiques of science.

Moira Gatens, University of Sydney

AIDS and the Body Politic traces the fascinating and disturbing shape of how culturally desirable is the clean, self-identical and sharply bounded (male) body, protected against infection, and how culturally horrifying are open, permeable, uncontrolled (female and gay male) bodies, prone to collecting and proliferating infection. This work is an important and fresh analysis of how cultural material informs biomedical and epidemiological models and measures.

Emily Martin, Princeton University

Why have women and gay men become the targets of AIDS education, while heterosexual men are exempt? *AIDS and the Body Politic* addresses the relationship between medical discourse and the sexual politics of AIDS.

Catherine Waldby's informative study draws on feminist theory, cultural studies, the philosophy of science and gay and lesbian studies to problematise the factual scientific discourse about AIDS and interpret it as a political discourse. Waldby argues that much AIDS discourse relies on an implicit and unconscious equation between sexual health and heterosexual masculinity. Biomedical discourse sets out the heterosexual male body as normative ideal, which renders other kinds of bodies inherently pathological.

Drawing upon examples of preventative policies from Australia, Britain and the USA, Waldby investigates the concept of public health and questions whose interests are represented in a 'healthy society'. *AIDS and the Body Politic* demonstrates the extent to which established ideas about the virus, the immune system, the HIV test and the epidemiology of the disease, rely upon unexamined, conservative assumptions about sexual identity and sexual difference.

Catherine Waldby currently teaches in the Communications and Cultural Studies programme and the Women's Studies programme at Murdoch University, Perth, Western Australia.

WRITING CORPOREALITIES
Series Editor: Elspeth Probyn

This series seeks to encourage innovative writing about corporealities. It takes as a leading premise the fact that writing and studying embodied forms of sociality are intricately mutually informing. The type of work presented under the rubric of this series is therefore engaged and engaging, as it understands that writing itself is an embodied and social activity. The range of theoretical perspectives privileged may be wide but the common point of departure is a certain *parti pris* to study the materiality of contemporary corporeal processes and realities. Beyond discrete description, through different forms of writing, bodies, discourses, forms of power, histories and stories are put in play in order to inform other relations, other corporeal realities.

AIDS AND THE BODY POLITIC

Biomedicine and sexual difference

Catherine Waldby

London and New York

First published 1996
by Routledge
11 New Fetter Lane, London EC4P 4EE

Simultaneously published in the USA and Canada
by Routledge
29 West 35th Street, New York, NY 10001

Typeset in Times by Routledge
Printed and bound in Great Britain by Clays Ltd, St Ives PLC

British Library Cataloguing in Publication Data
A catalogue record for this book is available from the British Library

Library of Congress Cataloguing in Publication Data
A catalogue record for this book has been requested

ISBN 0–415–14129–X (hbk)
ISBN 0–415–14130–3 (pbk)

CONTENTS

FIGURES

ACRONYMS

ACT-UP AIDS Coalition to Unleash Power. An activist organisation formed originally in New York, to raise public awareness about AIDS and to lobby government bodies for better funding. ACT-UP is known for its highly sophisticated graphics, street performances and radicalism. Groups now exist throughout the world.

AIDS Acquired Immunodeficiency Syndrome. In strict biomedical usage, the term 'AIDS' is only used to refer to the later symptomatic stages of HIV infection, and when the T cell count has dropped below a certain level. In this book, however, I have used the term 'AIDS' to also designate the general social field of the disease. I use the term 'HIV' in a more specific sense to refer to the virus and viral processes, e.g. HIV infection and transmission.

CDC Centres for Disease Control. The US public health agency responsible for national disease surveillance.

ELISA Enzyme-Linked Immunosorbent Assay. A laboratory test used for the detection of antibody. The HIV seropositive test to determine if a person is infected with HIV consists of two ELISA tests and one WB test.

HIV Human Immunodeficiency Virus. The aetiological agent understood to cause AIDS.

MSM Men Who Have Sex With Men. A term coined by public health bodies to apply to men who have sex with other men but who do not identify themselves as gay.

PLWA Person Living With AIDS. Term used by AIDS activists to describe people who are HIV seropositive and their friends, carers and supporters.

WB Western Blot Test. Part of the procedure of the HIV seropositive test.

ACKNOWLEDGEMENTS

This book is based on my doctoral dissertation, so my first debt of gratitude goes to my supervisors, Helen Pringle at the University of New South Wales, and Bev Thiele and Zoe Sofoulis at Murdoch University, for their generous and encouraging support, both practical and intellectual. I was extremely fortunate to have three generous examiners whose helpful comments encouraged me to see this project through. Thanks to Elspeth Probyn, Moira Gatens and particularly to Thomas Laqueur, who took on the difficult task of examination at extremely short notice.

I owe a great debt to the staff at the Australian National Centre for HIV Social Research, Macquarie University, who provided various forms of institutional and intellectual support for the early part of my work on this thesis. In particular I would like to thank the director, Susan Kippax, for her remarkable intellectual open mindedness in a difficult political climate, and for her friendship.

I would also like to acknowledge the support of the School of Humanities at Murdoch University for financial support in the preparation of this text. Tracy Reibel proved extremely helpful with the frustrating task of document preparation. My thanks to her.

Numerous friends and colleagues have contributed to the ideas I have tried to formulate here, through conversation, comments on previous drafts and long sessions on the Internet. I would like to thank Tim Carrigan, Bob Connell, Rosanne Kennedy, Genevieve Lloyd, David McMaster, Carol Vance, John Kaldor, Elizabeth Grosz, Cathryn Vasseleu, Alec McHoul, Deborah Lupton, Celia Roberts, Anna Gibbs, Carole Pateman, Frazer Ward, Elizabeth Wilson, Peter Aggleton and John Ballard. If I have forgotten anybody, please forgive me.

My family, Valerie, David and Gavan Waldby, all deserve thanks for their encouragement through difficult times and for their belief in my right to intellectual activity.

My greatest thanks must be to my partner, Mark Berger, without whose kindness, critical engagement and financial support this book would not have been written. I dedicate it to him.

ACKNOWLEDGEMENTS

I would like to thank the British Health Education Authority for permission to reproduce their 'How Far' advertisement; The Commonwealth Department of Human Services and Health, AIDS Campaign for their permission to reproduce 'If it's not on...'; and the Australian National Centre in HIV Epidemiology and Clinical Research for permission to reproduce the 'Notification of AIDS Form' and the Australian HIV Surveillance Report.

1

INTRODUCTION
Total war

Declarations of epidemic are declarations of war. In the biomedical imagination, epidemics are crisis points in the Darwinian evolutionary struggle between the microscopic, inhuman world of bacteria and viruses, and human populations. The microscopic world is on a mission to colonise the human, to render the human body an extension of bacterial and viral interests. This apocalyptic mission, favourite theme of science-fiction cinema and horror fiction, also motivates the rhetoric of the most sober microbiological and immunological textbooks which, like the text cited below, regularly evoke a vision of genetic colonisation in their opening paragraphs.

> We live in a potentially hostile world filled with a bewildering array of infectious agents of diverse shape, size, composition and subversive character which would happily use us as rich sanctuaries for propagating their 'selfish genes' had we not developed a series of defence mechanisms at least their equal in effectiveness.
>
> (Roitt 1991: 1)

Infectious disease is the product of successful microbial propagation in a particular body, when a viral or bacterial population overtakes a single body's population of healthy cells. Epidemic is declared when, according to biomedicine's determinations, *too many* bodies succumb to this colonisation, when nature inundates culture. Declarations of epidemic are not merely quantitative determinations, however. They also involve qualitative decisions regarding the kind of threat that particular diseases represent. Viral infectious diseases represent not only a practical, but also an ontological threat. They are a practical threat because, unlike bacterial diseases, antibiotics are ineffectual against them. They are an ontological threat because they challenge the status of the human, because viral infection involves the colonisation of human genetic identity with viral genetic identity. Viruses are understood to replicate themselves through their annexation of the reproductive apparatus of human tissue cells, forcing the human cells to manufacture alien viral cells, forcing human identity to participate in its own infectious defeat. Viral epidemics signal the mobilisation of extraordinary

1

medical effort to contain the spread of infection and to regain lost evolutionary ground on behalf of the human.

This book is about the declaration of the AIDS epidemic and about the kind of war this declaration has unleashed. A glance at the rhetoric which circulates in the field of AIDS can leave no doubt that war has been declared. From the scientific characterisation of the behaviour of HIV in the infected body to the writings of AIDS activists and theorists, the language of militarism prevails. Warfare analogies, concepts of attack and retreat, triumph and defeat, infiltration and discovery, are drawn upon to describe the machinations of the virus at every level of scale, from the microscopic to those of community and nation. Edelman enumerates the motives for this proliferation of warfare analogies, their multiple applications to the biopolitical situation specific to AIDS.

> Because the syndrome itself attacks the body's mechanisms of defence; because once it does so science as yet can offer no defence against it; because in the West it has appeared primarily among groups already required to defend themselves against the toxic intolerance of the dominant order; because the scientific establishment . . . feels called upon to defend their professional prestige against the questioning of medical authority that has been occasioned by the disease; because individuals and groups have sought to defend themselves, often with appalling acts of violence, against any contact with 'AIDS' or those they construe as embodiments of it.
>
> (Edelman 1994: 81)

If military metaphor is general to AIDS discourses, there is, as Edelman's words imply, little agreement between them about where the battlelines are drawn. Within the terms of biomedical representation, for example, scientific knowledge and technology occupy one side of the AIDS war and the virus occupies the other. Biomedical research scientists and public health officials commonly refer to the various educative, clinical and research efforts mobilised in the name of the virus as 'the war on AIDS', or the 'effort to combat AIDS', and regard themselves as the shocktroops in this heroic battle. Scientists, according to *Scientific American*, 'have almost unanimously welcomed the call to arms' occasioned by the advent of AIDS (*Scientific American* 1987). Scientists regard themselves as the true opponents of the virus because only they command the necessary knowledge and technology required to fight it. It is science's capacity to visualise the virus at the molecular and cellular level which secures its claim to wage war at the appropriate level of scale. One biomedical scientist stated that we face 'an impending Armageddon of AIDS, and the salvation of the world through molecular genetics' (cited in Treichler 1988a: 62).

Conversely the virus is represented, even in the most technical biomedical literature, as an enemy alien, a 'foreign antigen' or the 'AIDS agent' which invades the sovereign state of the body and subverts from within its conventional defence force, its immune system. The HIV virus is, for example, imaged as a spherical 'grenade' on the cover of one issue of *Scientific American*, Treichler notes (1988a). It is the virus's capacity to 'disable' the body's defences, rather than engage in honest warfare with the immune system like lesser infectious agents, which leads biomedical science to characterise itself as the substitute army on behalf of the body. According to *Scientific American*'s editorial, 'Science and the citizen', in its special issue on AIDS (January 1987: 50), the mounting of a properly researched and scientifically rational war on AIDS has worked to pre-empt even more serious conflicts. It has prevented social disintegration, perhaps even civil war, which might otherwise have developed in reaction to AIDS.

> Without such reassuring [scientific] achievements the AIDS outbreak might conceivably have triggered a severe degree of publicly sanctioned discrimination and widespread physical violence.
>
> (*Scientific American* 1987: 50)

It suggests in other words that scientific knowledge has drained away the potential for political conflict from the field of AIDS, successfully containing warfare to its two proper sides, science versus the virus. Science has prevented nature from contaminating culture, and so stopped us reverting to a state of nature, the war of each against each.

From the perspective of those whose bodies are implicated in the disease, however, no such neat containment of violence and conflict is in evidence. Rather, metaphors of warfare are seen to carry well beyond the fields of biomedicine's technical capacities in what Treichler (1988a) has dubbed an 'epidemic of signification'. Military metaphors infect the entire AIDS body politic, and imply a quite different position for biomedicine within this political field. The AIDS war from this point of view involves numerous and heterogeneous sites of social conflict. The primary casualties in this conflict are, Watney argues, not the viruses themselves but people who are infected with the virus.

> The 'war against AIDS' . . . concerns the power of the State to define 'the public good', frequently in terms of 'public health'. From this perspective the systematic denials of adequate health care, and the directions of international research make perfect, coherent sense. For the 'war against AIDS' has *never* principally targeted HIV, or its multiple tragic consequences in the lives of individuals or communities. On the contrary, from the perspective of the State, it has been precisely and skilfully targeted against those of whom any AIDS diagnosis is held to reveal a far more deadly threat that reaches to the very heart of the epistemology of modernity, and the compliant identities it lovingly nurtures within the strict categories of gender, race and sexuality.
>
> (Watney, Introduction to Michaels 1990: 16)

So biomedical science understands the 'war on AIDS' as war on the virus, but Watney and many other commentators[1] understand it as a war on People Living With AIDS (PLWAs) and on those identity categories which feature in AIDS discourse. For AIDS activists, in other words, the biomedical battle with the virus has extended itself to include those who are infected with the virus, and those who are simply *associated* with the virus, the future infected, in the biomedical imagination. By virtue of this infection or association they have passed irrevocably over onto the side of the inhuman, the side of the virus, the side of death, and have thus become the enemies of the medical campaign to contain viral spread.

Declarations of war allow the deployment of legitimate violence, and the suspension of normal civil rights. From the point of view of PLWAs and of those caught up in the various medical strategies involved in the management of the epidemic, biomedicine often does its work through the wielding of violence, cast in terms of preventative, therapeutic or diagnostic practices. My use of the term 'violence' here clearly differs from, or more accurately exceeds, its familiar usage. Eric Michaels, writing in the diary he kept of his own death from AIDS, conveys the double sense with which I refer to biomedical practice as 'violent' when he describes his medical examinations.

> I have just today returned from two nights spent in the Infectious Diseases Ward....Mama, you wouldn't believe how people treat you there! It's not the rubber gloves or facemasks, or bizarre plastic wrapping on everything. It's the way people address you, by gesture, by eye, by mouth. And yet, done with the tests, I walk out in the street, go to work, and assume a comparatively normal interactive stance and distance....I imagine the diary-keeping might serve to keep another set of definitions going against the quite barbaric ones that were inflicted in these last few days, through the rubber gloves, facemasks, goggles....What begins here is a process of labelling, a struggle with institutional forms, a possible Foucauldian horror show, which must be resisted, counteracted somehow.
>
> (Michaels 1990: 25)

Michaels describes his submission to the empirical violence of the examination; he is manipulated and humiliated, subjected to tests and procedures, treated as infectious matter. He also suffers violence of a less literal but no less painful kind, which he terms the barbaric inflicting of definitions. His description is useful for my attempt to open out the term 'violence' because it implies that the literal pain of his ordeal is an *implementation* of his new classification as 'AIDS case'. To cast my argument in broad theoretical terms, it implies that the empirical violence involved in biomedical practice arises from a prior classificatory violence, the violence of a rational knowledge which forces its objects to conform with its logic in order that they might be rendered knowable.

The violence of biomedical practice in the field of AIDS is the concern of this book. I have elected to investigate biomedical discourse rather than other forms of knowledge which constitute the political field of AIDS (the law for example) because biomedicine has successfully established its right to represent the *real* of the disease, its irreducible materiality. Biomedical knowledge has the greatest legitimacy in the field and can effectively set the terms that other discourses must observe. As Patton states,

> For the most part, science serves as the master discourse that administers all other discourses about AIDS....Knowledge is perceived to arise from science and filter out into the social [world]...the [various] knowledges of the epidemic arise and compete (most visibly in the policy arena) but it is the logic of *science* that anchors the power relations which determine *whose* knowledge counts as 'real', as 'objective'.
>
> (Patton 1990: 53)

The legitimacy of biomedicine's therapeutic and preventative strategies depend upon this claim to represent the real. The success of this claim can be gauged by the extent to which activist groups and critics of AIDS policy accept the truth of AIDS science even as they contest particular public health policies.[2] It is this legitimacy which I want to call into question through a demonstration of the complicity between biomedical knowledge and non-scientific systems of thought. Biomedical knowledge cannot, I will argue, be quarantined from general ideas operative in the culture, even when it understands its concepts to be carefully and directly deduced from the factual evidence of the body. Despite, or perhaps because of, biomedicine's assertion of its own innocence of historical and political meaning, it constantly absorbs, translates and recirculates 'non-scientific' ideas – ideas about sexuality, about social order, about culture – in its technical discourses.

This permeable relationship between medical and social knowledges implies that biomedical discourse can be treated, at least in part, as a discourse of culture. In this interpretative framework, the legitimacy of the violence associated with many of its practices can be called into question. It is important to point out here that biomedicine can only work as a practice because it has technologies which provide it with ways to work directly upon bodies, ways to intervene in and transform them. Violence, in the sense of transformative force, is in other words a condition of biomedicine's efficacy, a condition of its power to heal and treat to the same extent that it is a condition of its power to administer and govern. My contention then is not with this *necessary* violence as such, but rather with instances where it is deployed in a political fashion, where the power to govern is presented as the power to heal.

The configuration of these technologies and procedures is, in turn, informed at a general level by what I will term the 'biomedical imagination'. This term refers to biomedicine's speculative and explanatory universe, the kind of propositional world that it makes for itself. In the case of AIDS, and of illness

5

more generally, this imagination is preoccupied with the establishing of distinctions between the normal and the pathological.

It is at this point, the adjudication of the normal and the pathological, that biomedical discourse is necessarily caught up in broader cultural narratives and power relations. This is so because, as I shall discuss in detail in the next chapter, *the normal is always normative*, always involved in the assertion of particular social values. In a highly politicised field like that of AIDS, determinations between the normal and the pathological are prone to contamination by other determinations, between the clean and the unclean, the innocent and the guilty, the (sexually) normal and the perverted, and so on. Under these circumstances the violence of biomedical practice can be interpreted as a form of political violence, concerned with the maintenance of various kinds of social power relationships.

In this book I will discuss the particular forms of violence perpetrated upon PLWAs, the kinds of clinical violence so graphically evoked in Michaels's diary. However, I will be more concerned with another aspect of its classificatory violence: the discursive practices used by biomedicine and public health policy to reconfigure sexed bodies since the advent of AIDS.

My argument is that biomedicine has inculcated new and compelled forms of medicalised sexual 'identity' as a primary means of government of the epidemic. The surveillance practices of AIDS epidemiology have effectively (re)classified the sexual identities of whole national populations, according to its understanding of HIV transmission processes, in its allocation of 'risk categories'. I am referring to epidemiology's utilisation of the idea of 'high risk' and 'low risk' groups, where these groups coincide with specified sexualities. AIDS epidemiology relies upon these categorisations to locate HIV infection in the social fabric and to organise its preventative strategies. It also relies upon several other axes of 'identity', those of 'intravenous drug user' (IVDU), haemophiliac, and various configurations of race, but these categories will not be addressed here, except in passing, because my focus is upon sexual power relations.[3]

Biomedical discourse has forcibly reorganised the significance of the binaries of sexual differences, those of masculine/feminine and straight/gay, to bring them into line with its understanding of AIDS pathology. This claim clearly rests upon a reversal of the usual understanding of the relationship between biomedical knowledge and sexual difference, wherein medicine is simply the scientific description of biologically given bodies. I am suggesting a far more dynamic process here, in which the morphologies of sexual difference, the ways that differences are lived and represented, are constituted in part by biomedical knowledge and practice. This claim clearly locates my work within the feminist theoretical trajectory which contends that the binaries of sexual difference are produced in cultural practices rather than biological givens. Within this trajectory these binaries are treated as relational terms, which mutually constitute each other, and which are open to various kinds of historical transformation and negotiation. From this perspective biomedical discourse can be recast as a highly privileged part of the process of production of sexual difference, privileged precisely because the body is generally understood as biological and given. Biomedicine's claim to represent the real of AIDS largely derives from its more general claim to know the real of sexed bodies, the irreducible processes associated with the biology of sexual differences. It is this global claim which facilitates its interventions in bodies and its right to adjudicate them, to produce them in various ways.

In what follows I will demonstrate the extent to which biomedical knowledge is contaminated by everyday, conservative assumptions about the meanings of sexual difference. This contamination infects biomedical representations of the real, it *makes the real mean* in particular ways. It is these assumptions which it seeks to implement in the clinical and public health practices associated with AIDS, an implementation which 'targets' the bodies of the infected and those associated in varying degrees with infection. Biomedical practices can thus be understood as political practices, seeking to enforce compliance with conservative regimes of sexuality.

HIERARCHIES OF PATHOLOGY

If biomedical discourse involves corporeal violence, declarations of epidemic provide optimum conditions for the exercise of this violence. Biomedical knowledge gains its greatest legitimacy under conditions of epidemic, allowing it to take extraordinary measures, command extensive social resources and mobilise entire populations in the interests of disease management. As Singer (1993) observes, conditions of epidemic legitimate an escalation in various *dirigiste* bodily practices on the part of medicalised institutions.

> An epidemic emerges as a product of a socially authoritative discourse in light of which bodies will be mobilised, resources will be dispensed, and tactics of surveillance and regulation will appear to be justified ... the construction of an epidemic situation has a strategic value in determining the configurations of what Foucault calls 'bio-power', since the epidemic provides an occasion and a rationale for multiplying points of intervention into the lives and bodies of populations.
>
> (Singer 1993: 117)

Singer argues, following Foucault, that the control of sexual epidemic legitimates even more detailed forms of intervention and demands for self-discipline, because sexual epidemic presents a double threat to the bio-social order, a threat to both general health and the processes of sexuality. According to Foucault (1979, 1980a) the sexual capacities of bodies represent the most dense and productive point of connection between individual bodies and the capacities of population, bearing upon reproduction, the formation of familial units, the reproduction or disruption of racial and ethnic divisions, and so on.

7

Implicit in these threats, although unremarked in Foucault's work, is the tendency of sexual epidemic to sharpen certain conflicts over the power relations constructed around sexual difference. Under conditions of sexual epidemic each sex and sexual orientation becomes a disease threat to the other, exacerbating existing tensions between masculinity and femininity, hetero-sexuality and homosexuality.[4]

Consequently, the strategies addressed to sexual epidemic are of a different order of complexity from those of other epidemics. As Singer argues,

> The construction of sexual epidemic ... provides an optimum site of intersection between individual bodies and populations. Hence sexual epidemic provides access to bodies and a series of codes for inscribing them, as well as providing a discourse of justification.
>
> (Singer 1993: 117)

A list of *dirigiste* bodily strategies associated with the AIDS epidemic might include widespread HIV testing, the mounting of a vast number of research projects into the sexual practices of various sectors of the population, increased government regulation of prostitution, strategies to change intra-venous drug use habits, transformations in infection control procedures within medical institutions, a mobilisation of the old surveillance and restraint techniques associated with notifiable diseases, and the creation of new ones. Sexual practices are rechoreographed at the behest of AIDS education campaigns and, as Singer (1993) points out, the commodification of women's bodies is intensified around strategies to control their cleanliness and hence suitability for sexual relationships and maternity.

Underpinning and organising these techniques, however, is the prior division of the populations of the first world democracies into various categories of 'risk group', graded from high to low, or more recently 'transmis-sion category'. These categorisations will determine who is to be 'targeted' and by what strategy. This categorisation process derives from biomedicine's understanding of HIV transmission processes, which then forms the basis for the design of preventative measures.

The important feature of this categorisation process for my argument is its vertical ordering. As Patton observes, division of the population into risk categories effectively sets up a hierarchy where 'high risk groups' are posi-tioned as threats to 'low risk groups'. This hierarchy in turn determines the kinds of education and public health attention which the two groups receive.

> There is a hidden ethical structure underlying information-giving models of health education which directs different strategies at what are perceived as 'high' and 'low' risk groups. Even though each group receives 'facts', the 'public' is given information on the assumption that they have a *right to know*, that is a right to 'protect' themselves, while [risk

groups] are educated on the assumption that they have an *obligation to know* and protect the 'public'.

(Patton 1990: 103)

In these hierarchies of risk the lower represents a threat to the health of the higher, and hence the lower becomes the object of measures to control contagion. It is in the creation of these hierarchies, and the 'targeting' of those at its lower end, that the violence involved in epidemiological classificatory practices becomes evident. In the case of the risk categories organised by sex or sexuality, 'targeting' maps itself onto the hierarchy already implied in the binaries of sexual identity, so that women are treated as threats to men, and homosexuals as threats to heterosexuals. 'Targeting' involves the pathologisation of sexuality, the inculcation of a sense of responsibility for potential transmission to others, the adoption of a disciplined sexual practice. It may involve an encouragement of HIV testing, and various kinds of epidemiological and clinical surveillance. In other words, to be 'targeted' involves the internalisation of a sense of one's sexed body as potentially deadly, and the adoption of a different sexual choreography and sense of bodily limit as a consequence.

The organisation of risk hierarchies thus involves the privileging of certain bodies and sexualities at the expense of others, the protection of some through the disciplining of others. The management of epidemic is never a politically neutral affair, but is rather always enmeshed in particular power relationships and involved in the defence of a particular social order. The stakes in the AIDS epidemic are high, involving issues of sexual identity and practice, of illness and mortality, and for these reasons the struggles over management of the disease expose interests that might otherwise remain implicit and tacit.

What kind of social order do the struggles around AIDS management make visible? I will argue in this book that the shape of 'official' AIDS discourse, of biomedical knowledge and public health policy, is complicit with a phallocentric social order. This order holds that only the heterosexual masculine is fully equivalent with the human and the normal. It readily represents other sexed interests as allies of the viral and the pathological. My evidence for this claim is drawn from two sources. The first of these is the empirical position of heterosexual masculinity within the epidemic. 'Heterosexual men' is the sexual category which has remained largely unmarked by a 'risk' status within the epidemic. This exemption of heterosexual men from the demands for a disciplined sexuality was brought to my attention very forcibly when in 1987 I began work on a feminist AIDS research project into sexuality and prevention among heterosexual women. A cursory examination of the Australian federal government's education programmes addressed to the 'general population', that is to 'heterosexuals', indicated to me that men and women occupied asymmetrical positions in this discourse. While 'men' were never addressed as a 'group' within general population rhetoric, 'women' were repeatedly singled out. They were nominated in policy documents as a 'group' requiring special education on various grounds, and they were also the 'group' to whom nominally heterosexual safe sex education messages were addressed. So, for example, in the policy discussion document *AIDS: A Time to Care, a Time to Act* women were said to require special education on the grounds of their interpersonal and sexual passivity.

> There is a need to identify the range of sexual, social and economic factors which place women at risk of infection. One such factor is a lack of assertiveness in interpersonal or social relations. Education programs need to encourage women to develop skills in negotiating sexual and drug use situations and in communicating their decisions to others.
>
> (Commonwealth Department of Community Services and Health 1988: 146)

In the mid-1990s there were seven AIDS education programmes addressed to heterosexual women in New South Wales, the most populous state in Australia, and none addressed to heterosexual men.[5] However, despite this alleged tendency to passivity and need for education, the burden of enforcing safe sex practice in heterosexual relations has been placed squarely on women's shoulders. In Australia the national 'If it's not on, it's not on' advertisement, designed to encourage women to ask their partners to use condoms, made quite explicit the assumption that women must act as the guardians of socially responsible sex, while the actual wearers of condoms are not addressed (Figure 1.1). Similar forms of advertising have been used in British education campaigns (Figure 1.2). Clearly the question 'How far will you go before you mention condoms?' is addressed to the woman, and practical advice is offered about the appropriate point in the evening when she should enforce her partner's compliance.

In this way education campaigns addressed to 'heterosexuals' throughout the 1980s effectively addressed their demands for the new prophylactic disciplining of sexual practice solely to women, while those other denizens of the category, heterosexual men, remained unmarked, the unspecified force which women are asked to control, the force against which they need protection.

So in the first instance my evidence for the complicity of official AIDS discourse with phallocentric interests derives from this empirical privileging of heterosexual men within the epidemic. By remaining the only unmarked category within the terminologies of sexual risk, heterosexual men effectively occupy the position at the top of the hierarchy. As the only group exempted from direct address by public health discourse, they are freed from internalising the idea of their bodies as dangerous or infectious, relying instead on the willingness of heterosexual women to undertake such internalisations. Heterosexual men are thus allowed to maintain the (imaginary) position of the clean who are threatened by infection from below and elsewhere, and are not

Figure 1.1 'If it's not on, it's not on'
Source: Commonwealth Department of Human Services and Health (1988)

required to consider themselves as possibly infectious for another. This privileged, unmarked status for heterosexual men is of course not exclusive to the field of AIDS, but characterises many social domains where discourses of 'disadvantage' are implicitly constructed around the presumed but unarticulated 'advantage' of heterosexual masculinity. Nor is the masculine exemption from a self-conscious or responsible sexual practice exclusive to the field of HIV/AIDS but arguably characterises many aspects of heterosexual erotic negotiations, particularly the deployment of contraception. The exemption of heterosexual masculinity from HIV responsibility is, in this sense, continuous with the more general equation between sexuality and freedom that Pateman (1988) identifies as the particular political right of men in our homosocial order.

The full political significance of this equation between heterosexual masculinity and cleanliness becomes evident when compared to the corollary status of gay men within the epidemic. As Patton (1990) repeatedly points out, and as I shall demonstrate in detail, gay masculinity has been so intensely medicalised and so closely associated with the AIDS epidemic that gay men are

11

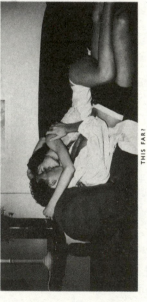
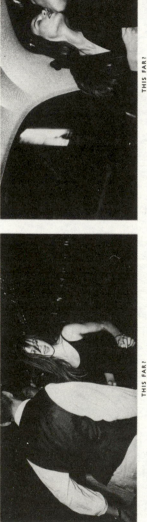

Figure 1.2 'How far will you go before you mention condoms?'
Source: Health Education Authority, UK

effectively treated by much public health discourse *as if they themselves were the virus,* the origins of infection. Gay men and heterosexual women have been made to bear the burden of infected sexual identity that heterosexual men have refused.

While I take this heterosexual male privilege as evidence for my overall argument, I will treat it as symptomatic of a phallocentric order rather than the substance of that order. It seems to me important to maintain a distinction between heterosexual men as subjects and phallocentric privilege, because not all men who may define themselves as 'heterosexual' will reliably benefit from this privilege, nor may they wish to do so. As I demonstrate in the discussion of the HIV test in Chapter 5, while the *category* 'heterosexual' is privileged in AIDS discourse, this category is residual, protected by a string of qualifiers which may work to disqualify many men who identify as 'heterosexual'. In other words, while the category is privileged, administrative technologies of identification, rather than self-identification, determine admission in the final instance.[6]

So the sexual privilege of heterosexual men is, I will argue, not the product of a homosocial political conspiracy but rather a somewhat erratic effect of the circulation of certain normative concepts within AIDS discourse, concepts which determine the distinction between the normal and the pathological. In other words heterosexual masculine privilege is maintained indirectly, through knowledge practices which often seem to have no bearing on this question, or any relationship to sexual difference. As Irigaray suggests (1985), it is in precisely the most neutral scientific concepts that phallocentric privilege is inscribed.

My second order of evidence for this phallocentrism is a reading of these knowledge practices for the ways in which they indirectly enshrine the cleanliness and authority associated with the heterosexual masculine body. This interpretation involves tracing some of the textual moves through which biomedicine both incorporates and disavows its debt to general cultural understandings about sexual difference, particularly the ways that it con-structs its concepts of causality, and the kinds of image systems through which it maintains the coherence of its imaginary universe. In this way I demonstrate that certain key scientific understandings about the nature of the HIV virus, of the disease and of its transmission rely upon an unconscious idealisation of the phallic body, against which the infectious threat of other bodies is measured. The biomedical understanding of HIV transmission is focused around bodily boundaries and bodily permeability, whereas the idealised phallic body is effectively a prophylactic device. It is an immunologically perfect body without orifices, whose individuality cannot be compromised, the body which neither takes nor gives infection.

This healthy body is of course impossible to attain at the level of lived corporeality, but, I argue, it is nevertheless *taken to be the heterosexual masculine body for the purposes of creating hierarchies of AIDS pathology.* This confusion is possible because of the extent to which the phallic status of the heterosexual masculine body organises its general cultural representation. This status is shored up, I have argued elsewhere (Waldby 1995), through the elision of any representation of anal receptivity from the dominant imago of heterosexual masculinity. To the extent that aspiration to a phallic status organises the heterosexual masculine body, it must suppress its capacities for passivity and anal and oral receptivity, capacities which are then projected onto the bodies of women and gay men. In other words, the permeability of the heterosexual male body is suppressed in dominant forms of cultural representation, and this general suppression enables the confusion in AIDS discourse between the normative ideal and particular heterosexual masculine bodies.

Despite this enabling confusion, however, the way in which this idealised imago is taken up betrays marks of anxiety about the impossibility of being that body. The heterosexual male body can remain unmarked by pathologisation because of its alleged resemblance to the immunologically perfect body, but it is in practice as vulnerable to HIV infection as any other. It is here that the public health measures to control HIV infection can be seen to work from the point of view of the masculine body and its protection. The allocation of a 'risk' status to all other forms of sexuality and corporeality places demands upon these subjectivities to actively control the spread of infection, so that the heterosexual body remains unthreatened. There is too an anxiety generated around the way that the immunologically perfect body works in AIDS as the sign of 'non-homosexuality', at a time when the idea of 'immunocompromise' is taken in biomedicine to typify the 'homosexual patient'.[7] The status of the immune system has become caught up in the figuring of masculine heterosexual/homosexual difference, a dynamic which donates additional anxiety to the question of body boundaries.

So in this book I will argue that the figuring of body boundaries and their transgression is a central representational strategy in the way that biomedicine imagines and sexes the distinction between the normal and the pathological in HIV transmission. The discursive manipulation of bodily boundaries also carries an additional burden of significance in the determination of the sexual politics of AIDS. This is so because of the privileged part played by concepts of corporeal boundary in the figuring of the HIV-infected Body Politic.

I am referring here to another 'enabling' confusion which is evident within AIDS biomedical discourse, a confusion effected between the body as society or nation, and the nation as a body. As we will see, epidemiology habitually conceptualises social order as analogous to organic order, while the technical discourses of the physiological body (immunology, endocrinology) figure it as a social microcosm. This confusion has a long history and many variations, but within the historical and cultural particularity of the AIDS Body Politic the sexuality and ascribed boundaries of bodies take on particular political significance, determining who is and is not a threat to the 'public health'.

Here I am working from some of the propositions made in Douglas's (1984) work concerning the peculiar power of body boundaries to signify social systems, particularly the fragility of social systems, their openness to a dangerous outside. Douglas remarks that 'the body is a model that can stand for any social system. Its boundaries can represent any boundaries that are threatened or precarious' (Douglas 1984: 115), a proposition which Butler elaborates upon in the age of AIDS.

> Permeable bodily boundaries present [dangers] to the social order as such ....Douglas suggests that all social systems are vulnerable at their margins, and that all margins are accordingly considered dangerous. If the body is synecdochal for the social system *per se* or a site in which open systems converge, then any kind of unregulated permeability constitutes a site of pollution and endangerment.
>
> (Butler 1990: 132)

Part of the process of imagining an AIDS epidemic involves thinking the whole social order as itself an infected body, or more precisely a body threatened by infection which biomedicine must localise in order to treat. Hence the surveillance strategies and infection control procedures used in both clinical and epidemiological medicine are conceived on the same model. The same idea of infection presides over both the particular body and the social order, and the HIV-infected person is thus assimilated to the position of the virus in the body politic. Similarly the bodies of 'risk groups', with their dangerous permeability, are assimilated to the position of fluid transmission points for the virus's progress through the body politic. Only the phallic body can stand unproblematically for the intact body of the nation.

The constitution of this relationship between particular bodies and the body politic is, I argue, made possible through the deployment of various imaging and diagnostic technologies. These technologies fulfil biomedicine's panoptic aspirations to simultaneously visualise the macroscopic and the microscopic, and to propose relations between them. The HIV antibody test is an exemplary technology for making linkages between infection in particular bodies and the body politic, through its ability to mark the infected, to prevent their 'passing' as clean.

ORGANISATION OF THE TEXT

The next chapter sets out the interdisciplinary encounters and epistemological critiques necessary to the book. It first considers how biomedicine can be understood as a cultural practice, particularly in relationship to its conceptualisation of sexual difference and the biological facts of bodies. It analyses the ways in which general cultural ideas become implicated in scientific reasoning, the extent to which biomedicine relies upon familiar analogies, speculative proposals and propositional logic to think itself. I term this implication the 'biomedical imagination' in order to emphasise the speculative, 'fictional' dimension of the medical enterprise. This reliance on other cultural domains makes any clear distinction between biomedical knowledges and other forms of knowledge impossible to sustain. It enables the importation of social narratives into biomedicine's technical narratives.

This chapter then considers in what sense sexed bodies can be interpreted as forms of cultural practice, and the nature of biomedicine's relationship to this practice. This involves a discussion of recent feminist and poststructuralist literature addressed to this question, particularly as it is framed around the concept of the 'imaginary anatomy'. I use this as a term which can be made to account for both the cultural significance of fleshly bodies and the various representational practices which constitute them, by doubling the word 'anatomy' to signify both body and medical representation. The distinctions between normal and pathological bodies in biomedicine are considered as forms of imaginary anatomy, which then form the basis for the normalisation of sexed bodies in the field of AIDS. This chapter demonstrates the extent to which the biomedical imagination utilises models of social order and disorder to constitute its imaginary anatomies, models which have direct consequences for the ways that the bodies so imagined are positioned in the social order.

The next three chapters each take a particular biomedical subdiscipline – immunology, epidemiology and serology – and examine the particular ways that these disciplines inscribe ideas of sexual difference in their discursive practices and conceptual repertoires. Each of these discourses concerns itself with mapping the anatomy of AIDS at a different level, either its micro-anatomy at the level of cells and viruses or its macro-anatomy, the distribution of infection in the nation. While each chapter takes one particular discourse, they also each investigate ways that homologies are set up between these different levels of scale, so that the micro- and macro-anatomies of AIDS achieve congruence and help to naturalise each other.

Chapter 3 examines the representation of normal and HIV-infected bodies within the medical subdiscipline of immunology. Using a combination of popular, textbook and journal texts it considers the micro-anatomy of AIDS, the way that biomedicine conceptualises infection at the level of the cells and genetic structure of the immune system, the bodily system that HIV infects. The immune system is a crucial device for the representation of sexual difference in relation to HIV infection, because the microscopic activity of the system is understood to constitute the boundaries of the organism, its self/other distinction. This task inevitably implicated immunology in the determination of relations between boundary, infection and sexual identity, in so far as genital permeability links all three instances in the age of AIDS. Consequently this chapter examines in detail the representation of this microscopic activity in AIDS immunology and the kinds of transformations in both activity and body boundaries associated with HIV infection.

AIDS immunology tends to be organised through military metaphor, where the healthy, 'immunocompetent' body appears as a kind of nation-state, threatened from without by 'foreign' infection and protected by the defence activity of the immune system cells. The centrality of this metaphor in the conceptualisation of healthy immunological activity carries gendered implications at both the level of the cells and the level of the body's boundaries. The chapter focuses particularly on the representation of the T cells, understood to be both the 'commanders' in the immunological hierarchy and the cells infected by the HIV virus. HIV infection involves both the violation of the rigid impermeability of the nation-state body and the subversion of the 'command' masculinity of the T cells. In this way the HIV-infected 'immuno-compromised' body narrativises biomedicine's understanding of the gendered consequences attendant on boundary violation, whether it be at the level of the particular body or the level of whole populations.

This chapter also performs a close reading of one particular popular immunology text and considers its textualisation of the process of HIV infection in some detail. I utilise this account of infection as a kind of 'primal scene' for AIDS immunology, an explicitly sexual 'causal' scene which is normally suppressed in immunological discourse, and which helps to make sense of many of its assumptions. At the same time I utilise the notion of the primal scene as a critique of the teleological nature of biomedical concepts of causality.

The fourth chapter investigates the macro-anatomy of AIDS as it is elaborated in the discourse of AIDS epidemiology, the biomedical discipline which maps the social distribution of disease. It does this through a discussion first of all of the risk group/general population binary which has historically organised AIDS epidemiology, and considers the ambiguous position of women in this division. I argue that the borders of the 'general population' are variable but that the only denizens of this group that are *never* excluded by it are those in the category 'heterosexual men'.

The chapter then discusses the relationship between the term 'general population' and the rhetoric of the 'public health', which I argue is indicative of the extent to which the nation is conceived on an organic model, a unified organism which can be considered to have a singular state of health. Drawing on feminist theorisations of the sex of the body politic, I propose that sexual epidemic is a circumstance in which the health of the body politic and its implicitly masculine sex are simultaneously at stake. Under these circumstances the health of the heterosexual masculine body, which is taken to stand for the 'public health' in a general way, becomes the ultimate object of the protective strategies of public health policy. To demonstrate this proposition I look at models of infectious process in AIDS epidemiology which implicate permeable and receptive bodies as infectious rather than infected.

Chapter 5 discusses the HIV test as a technology of the body politic, a technology which can mark and track infection in both the particular body and the nation as a whole. It is an exemplary confessional technology in the

Foucauldian sense, one which conjoins the truth of sexual identity with immanent signs of pathology, and which marks the subject in a manner compatible with the demands of governance. Utilising queer theory's concept of 'passing' as a critique of identity politics, I argue that the test is ultimately concerned to pre-empt the ability of the infected to 'pass' as uninfected, by marking them with the sign of the virus. At the same time it allocates the infected person a position within epidemiological hierarchies of pathology through its identification of their sexual identity.

While this determination of sexual and viral identity is presented as a simple combinatory procedure, I demonstrate that the results of the HIV antibody test are not reducible to a simple positive/negative opposition. The results are relative determinations and remain uninterpretable without the additional knowledge of the person's sexual categorisation. The technology of the test is organised through concepts of 'risk populations' and ambiguity in the results cannot be interpreted without a knowledge of the person's placement within the discourse of risk. At the same time, a person diagnosed as HIV antibody positive is highly unlikely to be classified as a low risk 'heterosexual', because the classificatory logic of the administrative form is such that this category remains the most residual. Men are highly susceptible to classification as 'bisexual' which aligns them with 'homosexual' in the test's logic. In this sense I argue that the test works to protect the *category* 'heterosexual' as clean, even as it sacrifices individual men and women to its logic.

The concluding chapter reframes the relationship between AIDS biomedicine and sexual 'identity' politics that has been investigated in the book, considering it this time as a historical relationship. The body of the book demonstrates the power of biomedicine to intervene in and shape the field of sexual politics, particularly in conditions of epidemic emergency. This chapter speculates about certain transformations in both feminist and gay politics as responses to this biomedical intervention. In particular it considers the emergence of queer theory, whose critique of identity politics gains part of its impetus from the pathologisation of sexual identity that has taken place as a result of the domination of AIDS by biomedical discourse. It seems possible that one of the forces that has contributed to the emergence of Queer derives from the way that biomedicine has been able to exploit concepts of sexual 'identity' in its explanatory logic and its infection control strategies. Queer politics advocates notions of provisional rather than absolutely stable sexual identity, a position which has arguably emerged as a response to this exploitation. This chapter also extends the discussion, developed throughout, of the idea of the body politic, and the particular ways in which biomedical discourse contributes to the constitution of this body politic.

2

THE BIOMEDICAL IMAGINATION AND THE ANATOMICAL BODY

AIDS and the nature/culture distinction

I suggested in the introduction that from the biomedical point of view, the battle to control epidemic is a battle to control the nature/culture distinction. Epidemic occurs when the virulent natural world flows across the distinction into the proper domain of culture and the human. The mission of biomedicine is then to re-establish the prophylactic function of the distinction, to render it impervious to infection.

Within the terms of science's self-representation and of liberal social theory, the nature/culture distinction describes a given arrangement, a set of objective referents. The natural world is considered to provide a foundation, upon which culture can erect itself on condition that it finds ways to keep the forces of nature in check. The 'human' is generally understood to coincide with the location of culture, but under conditions of epidemic the distinction between the natural and the human becomes blurred in biomedicine's understanding. The infected appear as a human locus for the viral, hybrids who occupy an indeterminate position between nature and culture.

All infection is imagined as hybridisation in biomedicine, because bacteria or viruses are understood to use human bodies as sites for self-multiplication. They colonise the human body and human subjectivity, making them amalgams of the microbial and the human. For several reasons HIV infection represents a particularly serious and extreme form of this marriage of the viral and the human. First, it is a lifelong infection, so that the virus is understood to be perpetually integrated into the human body it occupies. Integration occurs at the genetic level, where, as I described earlier, the virus's genetic 'identity' replaces the human genetic 'identity' of the cells it infects, utilising the previously human cells to further its own replicative interests. I do not use the term 'identity' gratuitously here. The present status of genetic codes in the life sciences is such that these codes are considered to be the irreducible essence of the organism and its species, its repository of self-information, which, if properly communicated, determines the self in its entirety. Given this premise, viral colonisation readily appears like literal species colonisation, a humiliation to the claimed transcendental status of the human.

Second, the virus can only exist within human bodies and some simian

19

species. Unlike many other micro-organisms which can continue to live in soil, for example, the HIV virus has no other functional domain.[1] It must seek human bodies to live. Third, because the virus cannot live outside the body, infection can only occur as a result of the infected body's action on another body, an 'exchange of body fluids' which may involve sexual relations, breast feeding or a sharing of needles. So the agency of the infected subject is always involved in transmission, irrespective of their knowledge of their own infection. This circumstance can make the infected subject appear as the ally of the virus, one who, wittingly or unwittingly, furthers its interests. Fourth, HIV infection inflicts a painful death upon its host, often after a long asymptomatic latency period. The HIV infected are subjects who publicly bear witness to the mortality of us all, and to the inability of medicine to find a cure for this ultimate encroachment of nature upon culture. In summary, HIV infection involves a permanent and indissoluble form of lethal hybridity, where virus and host cannot be functionally separated.[2]

Consequently, biomedicine's strategies to control the AIDS epidemic and reassert the division between nature and culture do not 'target' the virus alone, but rather 'target' the person as viral agent. They inscribe themselves upon the bodies and desires of the infected and the potentially infected. It is at this point – the characterisation of certain bodies as hybrids caught on the threshold between nature and culture – that biomedicine can be understood as a political practice. My argument is that, in the case of HIV/AIDS and elsewhere, biomedicine exploits the nature/culture binary in ways which create hierarchies of pathology along the lines of sexual identity. It uses unexamined and naturalised notions of sexual identity, of male and female, and of heterosexual and homosexual, to 'explain' and thus to control the transmission of natural virulence into culture. As I shall describe, AIDS biomedicine maps the flow of infection from its 'reservoir' in the gay male body, through the transmission bodies of bisexual men and heterosexual women to the ultimately 'cultural' body, that of heterosexual masculinity.

In other words, biomedicine maps the flow of infection according to a successive positioning of these sexual identities across the threshold of the nature/culture division, where departures from the heterosexual masculine are represented as departures from the fully human. In so doing it recapitulates a whole history of the association of the nature side of the division with the feminine,[3] an association which has formed the basis for women's exclusion from the sphere of politics and the public world (Pateman 1988). In the case of AIDS, however, codification as feminine is not restricted to the designation of the body of woman, but also marks certain non-phallic masculine bodies, that is gay male bodies or male bodies that engage in sexual relations with other men. Under conditions of epidemic the association between nature and the feminine is readily conjured into an agentic alliance, where the feminine becomes the ally of the virus. Bodies coded as feminine are understood to *lend themselves* to viral hybridisation, because they are already on the side of the natural.[4]

AIDS is, as Altman (1992) puts it, 'the most political of diseases'. Over the course of its short history it has precipitated multiple episodes of political contestation between the various 'AIDS constituencies' – gay men, sex workers, feminist women concerned about the positioning of women in the epidemic – and public health authorities, over sexual practice, discrimination, access to experimental drugs and a variety of related issues. This contestation has been crucial and often highly effective in mitigating more authoritarian tendencies evident in biomedical proposals for management of the epidemic.[5]

However, it seems to me that any attempt to account for the sexual politics of AIDS which fails to address the multiple effects generated by the nature/culture distinction will fall into a tautology. AIDS activism has generally mapped itself onto the same categories of sexual identity, particularly those of gay masculinity and heterosexual femininity, that biomedicine utilises in its explanatory discourses. In both cases these sexual categories are treated as if they were stable, given entities, who are naturally vulnerable to (or responsible for) HIV infection. These identity categories then form the starting point for AIDS politics, which is generally conceptualised on the model of anti-discrimination and defence of the civil rights of these categories.

But if my argument is correct, the biomedical reliance upon and deployment of these identity categories as explanatory devices in its technical discourse about HIV/AIDS already carries political significance, which sets out beforehand the terms for the 'proper' sexual politics of AIDS, in the arenas of social contestation. As I shall demonstrate, the biomedical 'explanations' for how AIDS works and what it is cannot be extricated from its highly conservative, phallocentric conceptualisations of the essential distinctions between gay and straight, between man and woman. Such concepts of sexual identity organise not just AIDS epidemiology, where biomedicine makes pronouncements about actual categories of person, but also the medical sub-disciplines which conceptualise the virus (virology), the operations of the immune system (immunology) and the design of the HIV anti-body test (serology).

Biomedicine uses ideas about the 'natural' relations between the sexes and sexualities to think the 'nature' of the virus and the disease itself. And in the process it inscribes sexual identity as explanation at the level of viruses, cells, genes and immunological communications. Biomedicine's nomination of sexual identity categories in AIDS discourse is in a sense a result of this saturation of its entire conceptual field with such explanations, of the sexual codification of its most apparently neutral aspects. HIV infection appears to have a 'natural' relation to certain sexual identity categories because *AIDS has been conceptualised through these categories from the start*. There is no point at which a sexually neutral explanation of the microphysiology of AIDS is wilfully grafted onto these categories of sexual identity. Rather it is sexual identity 'all the way down'.

Accounts of the sexual politics of AIDS which fail to address the nature/culture distinction necessarily remain blind to these naturalising processes. And this blindness is a feature of the majority of sociological and political accounts,[6] because such accounts are themselves meshed in the nature/culture distinction which organises academic knowledges into knowledges of the natural world (the sciences) and knowledges of the social and cultural world (the social sciences and the humanities). Hence these studies tend to treat the *disease* AIDS as an entity separable from the politics of AIDS. The scientific 'facts' of AIDS are treated as events located in nature, that nevertheless have social implications which can be described in social scientific discourse. Such accounts implicitly assume the scientific knowledge of AIDS, including its irreducible reliance on concepts of sexual identity, its absolute inability to think *without* these categories, as their foundation.

Consequently any study of the sexual politics of AIDS seems to me to require a *denaturalisation* of these identity categories as they are exploited in biomedical discourse, and a more general denaturalisation of the nature/culture distinction itself. It requires what Butler, following Foucault, calls a genealogical critique,

> [which] investigates the political stakes in designating as an *origin* and *cause* those identity categories that are in fact the effects of institutions, practices, discourses with multiple and diffuse points of origin.
>
> (Butler 1990: xi)

A genealogical critique is concerned not only with demonstrating the constructed nature of sexual identities but also with investigating the configuration of power relations enabled by their construction. In relation to AIDS politics the question then becomes, what are the political stakes involved in treating sexual identity categories as though they formed a natural basis of explanation for HIV transmission? What kind of power does this configuration of the nature/culture distinction deliver over to biomedical knowledge and what kind of social order does it help to naturalise?

As with all conceptual dichotomies, the nature/culture distinction asserts an exhaustive opposition between its two terms, dividing up the world in a particular way. One way to think about the power relations it enables is to consider what shape this division gives to our conceptual processes. What kinds of ideas does it enable and what ideas does it constrain, how does it condition processes of representation and the kinds of questions that can be asked of AIDS and sexual politics? First, it effectively organises the distinction between what counts as a self-evidently social matter, hence subject to legitimate political contestation, and what appears to be biologically fixed and immutable. Contemporary sexual politics, both feminist and gay, has typically involved disputation over the *location* of the distinction rather than its legitimacy per se. Disputes of this kind involve a contestation over where the limits of biomedical expertise can be drawn, whether it has the right to define a particular matter as a medical, natural matter, or whether it can be considered available for social transformation. Nature/nurture debates typify this kind of contestation and their recurrence, for example around the question of the 'gay gene', indicates the efficacy of the nature/culture distinction in placing limits on the kinds of questions that sexual politics can ask of scientific knowledge. In this case it shapes the debate so that it is generally restricted to the question 'does a gay gene exist, or is gayness a matter of socialisation?' Biomedicine's *desire* to 'explain' sexual identity in terms of genetics is not itself generally interrogated, nor are its concepts of identity, 'genes' or 'causality', generally unpacked.

A second way to think about the political implications of the nature/culture distinction is to consider how it organises the institutions of knowledge, the disciplinary borders of the academy. As I noted earlier, it determines what kinds of objects are considered appropriate to what kinds of knowledge practices, so that 'natural' objects are studied in the sciences, and social and cultural objects in the social sciences and the humanities. Consequently, any knowledge production which observes these disciplinary boundaries can only reiterate the division in various ways. The nature/culture division sets out in advance the ways that particular objects or categories can be investigated, and excludes or delegitimises other approaches. It gives biomedical knowledge unlimited fiat to make pronouncements about the 'natural' aspects of sexed bodies and the sexual identities which it extrapolates from them, while effectively pre-empting other knowledge practices.

In both these conceptual effects, the peculiar legitimacy donated to biomedical knowledge can be seen to derive from the mutual exclusivity of the division. It alleges that the natural world is impervious to culture and its implications, and is governed by its own laws that only scientific knowledge can determine. The nature/culture distinction is thus treated as an absolute and mutually exhaustive distinction, which in turn generates its own mutually exclusive forms of knowledge.

It is for this reason that both feminist and non-feminist intellectual strategies designed to undermine the absolute claim to legitimacy made by biomedical discourse have done so through demonstrations of precisely the permeability of the distinction, its dynamic and relational mode of constitution. These strategies, some of which are drawn upon here, could be broadly characterised as 'deconstructive', in the sense that they are concerned to disturb the power relations enabled by the dichotomous logic of the nature/culture distinction. Grosz (1989) describes the power relationship specific to conceptual dichotomies in the following terms:

Within [the structure of dichotomous logic] the opposed terms are not equally valued: one term occupies the structurally dominant position and takes on the power of defining its opposite or other. The dominant and subordinated terms are simply positive and negative versions of each other, the dominant term defining its other by negation . . . the positive term gains its privilege only by disavowing its intimate dependence on its negative double.

(Grosz 1989: 27)

Cast in these terms, the power relations specific to the nature/culture distinction derive precisely from the unacknowledged, indeed the actively repressed, implication of each term's meaning in that of the other.

While the strategies for displacing the truth effects of the nature/culture distinction discussed in this chapter do not conform to a rigorously deconstructive practice, what they have in common is a sensitivity to the exploitative economies operating in dichotomous logic. They explore some ways in which the nature/culture distinction provides a rhetorical *resource* to those discourses which appeal to the natural either as their limit or their object. In various ways they demonstrate that the distinction fails, and that the very usefulness and efficacy of the distinction *depends* on just such an unacknowledged failure.

Central to this argument is the recognition that biomedical knowledge is a discursive practice, involving the *production* rather than the simple *discovery* of meaning. Hence its determination of the natural is always and necessarily made within culture, the domain of meaning-making practices. The specific content of the category 'nature' is open to cultural reinvention, while nevertheless appearing as the origin of itself. As Butler points out, this apparently self-originating significance of the natural world is always a feminist issue, because it involves an implicit exploitation of the 'feminine' as explanatory principle.

> The binary relation between culture and nature promotes a relationship of hierarchy in which culture freely 'imposes' meaning on nature, and hence renders it into an 'Other' to be appropriated to its own limitless uses . . . nature/culture discourse regularly figures nature as female, in need of subordination by a culture that is invariably figured as male, active and abstract . . . this is yet another instance in which reason and mind are associated with masculinity . . . while the body and nature are considered to be the mute facticity of the feminine, awaiting signification from an opposing masculine subject . . . . The sexual politics that construct and maintain this distinction are effectively concealed by the discursive production of a nature, and indeed a natural sex that postures as the unquestioned foundation of culture.

(Butler 1990: 37)

Butler's words suggest that naturalisation and feminisation can both be considered in the light of rhetorical ploys, which help to secure certain kinds of explanations against others. Recourse to the natural and the feminine as causative principles in biomedical AIDS discourse can thus be interpreted as polemic, a politically interested discourse which asserts a point of view.

So what political interests are involved in the particular itinerary taken by the nature/culture division as it traverses the field of AIDS? In what follows I want to set out some interpretive strategies that will be useful in demonstrating the political stakes involved in posing naturalised sexual identities as explanations for AIDS. This demonstration requires a prior denaturalisation of both sexual identity and biomedical discourse, and in what follows I will develop a methodological and theoretical framework through which this denaturalisation might be perused.

First I will discuss ways that biomedical discourse can be read as a (very particular kind of) textual practice rather than a transparent and referential science. Then I will consider how sexed bodies, the loci of naturalised ideas of sexual identity, can be located in historical processes, both subject to social transformation and the subjects and objects of historical contestation. Finally I will reconsider the relationship between biomedicine and sexed bodies as a political practice through a consideration of the normalising function of the biomedical distinction between health and illness, and the powers of corporeal intervention this gives to biomedicine.

AIDS AND SCIENCE FICTION

I have already commented briefly on the ways that the nature/culture distinction presides over the organisation of knowledges. In his essay on the nineteenth-century formation of professional forms of knowledge and discipline boundaries, Weber elaborates upon the significance of an idea of the 'natural' in the ordering of scientific and other professional knowledges.

> The professional disposes over a body of systematic, esoteric knowledge, inaccessible to the layman and yet in itself coherent, self-contained, reposing on founding *principles*. These principles form the cognitive basis of laws, rules and techniques, which constitute a *discipline*....Although a specialised branch of knowledge, such a discipline is regarded as comprising a coherent, integral, and self-contained domain, based on an equally self-contained 'natural' state of things. 'Nature' here designates above all the objective referent, the *fundamentum in re* which guarantees the legitimacy of particularised knowledge and the efficacy of its applications.
>
> (Weber 1987: 27)

This claim to an exclusive knowledge of the natural referent is intrinsic, Weber suggests, to the social authority wielded by such knowledges. A fiat is established over a specific part of the world, and the object of knowledge is considered to circumscribe the field of the discipline itself.

25

The stabilising and defining object of the biomedical sciences is the human body considered as a unified physical, material entity. Located as a naturally given scientific object, human bodies are understood by biomedicine as organic 'matter', as stuff whose form and behaviour are determined by natural processes of evolution and decay. This relegation of human bodies to the status of matter demands that other less fixed bodily meanings be actively refused. Grosz comments on the way that the natural sciences drain the possibility of historically mutable, unstable or subjective meanings from human bodies, in order to render them coherent objects for systematic forms of scientific knowledge.

> As an organism, the human body is [regarded by science as] merely a more complex version of other organic ensembles. It is not qualitatively distinguished from other types of existence....The body's sensations, activities and processes become 'lower order', natural or animalistic functions of the human subject, tying it to nature. It becomes one part of an interconnected chain of organic forms.
>
> (Grosz 1987: 5)

This model of the body is clearly situated within a rationalist mind/body split, where the mind, proper subject of literature, history and philosophy, is the site of meaning production. The body on the other hand means only what medicine discovers about it, through its diagnostic and observational techniques. The meaning of the body is located in the laws of nature, and only biomedicine is able to determine these laws.

For the most part biomedicine, unlike some relativised domains of the physical sciences, utilises a model of knowledge based on a simple subject/object distinction,[7] whose concept of adequate knowledge presupposes 'both the *separation* of thought from its object and the *priority* of the latter over the former', as Weber (1987: ix) puts it. Its concern is to generate a transparent knowledge of the body which adequately reflects that body in its givenness. For this reason Foucault nominates the central epistemic device in the formulation of modern medical knowledge to be what he terms the 'clinical gaze'. This gaze is distinguished by its commitment to a pure perception of the logic of the body's organisation. Medical discourse is merely the description of what this pure gaze perceives in its analysis of the body, its recognition of bodily systems. The clinical gaze is 'pure of all intervention' and generates 'only the syntax of the language spoken by things themselves in an original silence' (Foucault 1975: 109).

The clinical gaze is the intermediary device that permits the exact description of the body as thing-in-itself. It acts as the guarantee of the referential status of biomedical knowledge, its capacity to accurately represent the materiality of the body and its diseases. In other words it enables a practice of perfect representation, a one-to-one correspondence between the thing described and its description. The scope of this gaze is not limited to direct face-to-face encounters between doctor and body but extends itself through the large repertoire of visualising technologies specific to biomedicine. Clinical devices like the X-ray and the endoscope, and laboratory technologies like the microscope and the assay, can all be considered extensions of the clinical gaze, ways for it to see the microscopic interior processes of bodies that the everyday gaze cannot envisage.

It is precisely the transparency of this gaze and the discourse which it generates which has fallen under suspicion. Biomedical science's claim to represent its objects unproblematically is being challenged from a number of directions which hold in common the position that scientific discourse has no greater claim to referentiality, a transparent relation to a stable referent, than any other form of knowledge. Instead these critiques position scientific discourse in the order of representation, where the images and texts it produces can be regarded as active processes of cultural production, which have problematic relations to the entities described.

In his study of medical knowledge, Armstrong (1983), for example, suggests that the apparent stability of medicine's referent, the human body, is an effect, rather than the cause, of its representation as stable matter in biomedical texts and knowledge practices. He describes his personal certainty of the descriptive accuracy of the anatomical atlas when, as a medical student, he first dissected corpses. 'In dissecting and examining bodies I had come to take for granted that what I saw was obvious', he writes (Armstrong 1983: 2). His study proposes this certainty as index of the success of anatomy's 'reality-effect', its organisation of the medical gaze along particular lines, so that it sees what it is instructed to see. To the untutored gaze, the spectacle of dead flesh is alarming and uninterpretable, but the anatomical atlas provides reassurance that an organic order can be discerned if one looks with professional eyes.

> The anatomical atlas directs attention to certain structures, certain similarities, certain systems, and not others and in so doing forms a set of rules for reading the body and making it intelligible. In this sense the reality of the body is only established by the observing eye that reads it. The atlas enables the anatomy student, when faced with the undifferentiated amorphous mass of the body, to see certain things and ignore others. In effect what the student sees is not the atlas as a representation of the body but the body as a representation of the atlas.
>
> (Armstrong 1983: 2)

This conclusion, that the body under the medical gaze acts as a representation of the anatomical atlas, rather than the reverse, might however be a little too hasty, propose too simple a reverse causality. This is a question I will return to a little later in this chapter. For the moment I want to investigate some other implications of the proposition that biomedical knowledge is a form of representational practice, a kind of 'science fiction'.

This proposition implies that biomedical texts are, like all scientific and non-scientific texts, dependent upon the ambiguities and connotative forces of language. Biomedicine derives its authority from the claimed transparency of its relation to its object, and this transparency is in turn shored up through the reduction of its language to a technical 'precise' status. The function of this language is to denominate and describe as economically as possible the implicit logic of bodies, a logic which is held to pre-exist both the clinical gaze and the description which it enables. But this claim to transparency is unsustainable, because biomedical language, like all language, is figurative. It works through metaphor and other kinds of trope to think itself and to make itself intelligible. As Treichler puts it, it is impossible to 'look through language' for the real, even in the case of something so demonstrably real as fatal disease. Referring to the name 'AIDS' she writes:

> *AIDS* is not merely an invented label, provided to us by science... for a clear-cut disease entity caused by a virus. Rather, the very nature of AIDS is constructed through language and in particular through the discourses of medicine and science; this construction is 'true' or 'real' only in certain specific ways – for example in so far as it successfully guides research or facilitates clinical control over the illness. The name *AIDS* in part *constructs* the disease and helps make it intelligible. We cannot therefore look 'through' language to determine what AIDS 'really' is. Rather we must explore the site where such determinations *really* occur and intervene at the point where meaning is created: in language.
>
> (Treichler 1988a: 31)

The metaphoric texture of scientific discourse has been demonstrated in a wide range of studies. Emily Martin's (1987) study of medical representation of the female hormonal system for example points out that it is consistently described as an hierarchically organised system of communication, whose workings are modelled on telecommunications technologies. Haraway (1991), Montgomery (1991) and Martin (1994) all examine the use of military metaphors in the figuring of the immune system, a metaphoric system which I also investigate in the following chapter.

What then does this figurative necessity imply about scientific discourse? Within biomedicine's self-understanding, the recurrence of figurative language is generally understood to serve two related functions. It is either pedagogical, providing a familiar analogy to the novitiate to help in their induction into the unfamiliar, or it is illustrative of an essential, complex idea.[8] In both cases biomedicine casts metaphor as the 'expression' of an essential idea, the economical representative of a thought which has its existence prior to language.[9] This relegation of metaphor to an illustrative or derivative status, attendant on a real meaning situated elsewhere, helps shore up biomedicine's claim to deploy language transparently, unencumbered by the ambiguities of fictional language. As Vasseleu puts it, scientific discourse both proceeds through figurative language and disavows its reliance upon figurative language.

> In the very manufacture of metaphors, images, models, diagrams and analogies, and their simultaneous dismissal as just substitutes for or illustrations of the essential thing, science effaces itself as a figurative practice.
>
> (Vasseleu 1991: 60)

This relegation of metaphor to an illustrative status works, as Derrida (1982) points out, on the assumption that metaphor is simply a rhetorical tool, whose deployment and significance is subject to perfect authorial control. Furthermore it assumes that metaphor is a provisional hermeneutic device which can be disposed of once it has facilitated the expression of its guardian idea. But the figurations traceable in scientific texts can be interpreted as precisely the failure of these claims. Their recurrence indicates the absolute indissociability of figurative from technical language, the impossibility of controlling its connotative force, the irreducible operation of the metaphoric in scientific textual practice. Processes of analogy, the use of one image or system as a propositional model for another, are essential to the production of scientific work, as both Hesse (1963) and Latour and Woolgar (1986) have demonstrated in different ways. Hesse argues that the process of scientific research is *analogy driven*, in the sense that research is oriented towards determining the extent of positive or negative analogy between the thing to be explained and some kind of model. Research, she says, consists of determining to what extent gas molecules behave or fail to behave like billiard balls, for example. This systematic analogisation is indispensable for scientific thought because it is the means whereby a scientific theory can come into being as a proposition and subsequently extend, modify or extinguish itself.

> A theory in its scientific context is not a museum piece, but is always being extended and modified to account for new phenomena . . . [in] the kinetic theory of gases [the] billiard-ball model of this theory played an essential part in its extension . . . [because] without the analogy with a model, any such extensions will be merely arbitrary.
>
> (Hesse 1963: 4)

Latour and Woolgar's ethnography of scientific practice, *Laboratory Life* (1986), provides a day-to-day account of the research process in a biomedical technology laboratory which also indicates the extent to which scientists rely upon analogical and propositional discourse as modes of thought. They argue that it is precisely these aspects of the research process which are erased from fact production, at the point at which the laboratory formally presents its discoveries in the public domain. Their study documents the slippage between various kinds of analogic intuitions, vague proposals and circumstantial considerations in the research process as they observed it, and the presentation of the process in professional journals as logical, deduced from the logic of the object that has been 'discovered'. The rhetoric of 'discovery' effectively involves a kind of fetishisation of the object, where it gradually takes on the qualities attributed to it by scientists, and finally turns into a 'fact'. In this process of fetishisation 'statements', unsecured but potentially productive proposals made by scientists, are stabilised into 'facts' through forms of authorisation, through references to the literature, experimental testing procedures, the status of the proposer and so on. They write:

> Once the statement begins to stabilise [it] . . . *becomes a split entity*. On the one hand, it is a set of words which represents a statement about an object. On the other hand it corresponds to an object in itself which takes on a life of its own . . . . Before long, more and more reality is attributed to the object and less and less to the statement *about* the object. Conse-quently, an inversion takes place: the object becomes the reason why the statement was formulated in the first place. At the onset of stabilisation, the object was the virtual image of the statement; subsequently, the statement becomes the mirror-image of the reality 'out there'.
>
> (Latour and Woolgar 1986: 176–7)

What then is at stake for scientific discourse which leads it to try and erase its dependence on metaphorical language, to stabilise its statements in this fetishistic manner? The short answer to this question is, the authority of scientific discourse, and the epistemological claims upon which this authority rests. I am referring to the claims already outlined, those of the transparency of language and the derivation of its knowledge in a direct sense from the naturally given object.

This precise correspondence between object and knowledge legitimates biomedicine's power to diagnose and manipulate its objects, to undertake clinical practices like surgery and public health practices like screening which require the trust and at least tacit consent of its patients and potential patients. Explicit displays of metaphor in scientific texts can be interpreted as endan-gering these claims, acting as vulnerable points in its system, because metaphor is both excessive and ambiguous. Metaphors form connotative chains of analogy which travel across system boundaries in ways that are not control-lable. As Treichler (1988a) puts it, metaphors are 'contagious'. They infect each other, forming chains of association which can link different texts and narratives together in complex ways without regard for the nature/culture distinction. They create intertextual relations which complicate the simplicity of referential claims, and assimilate the authoritative discourse of science towards the less certain status of literature.

The irreducibility of metaphor in scientific text points towards the debt that scientific thought owes to its cultural 'outside', to non-scientific narratives and to the ambiguity and density of language. Le Doeuff's (1989) propositions about the operation of metaphor in philosophical texts also apply to scientific texts. She suggests that the recurrence of such imagery marks the points of difficulty in the drive to systematise a learned text. They mark the impossibility of sustaining a purely rational hermetic discourse, without recourse to analogy, or to the familiar, everyday world which also provides the text's historical context. Images recur within a logical system because, she writes, 'they sustain something within the system which the system cannot itself justify, but which is nevertheless needed for its proper working' (Le Doeuff 1989: 3). Metaphors are simultaneously functional for a system and excessive to it. Le Doeuff goes on to suggest that metaphoric performance within a learned text is, at least to some extent, complicit with what she calls the discourse's 'theoretical enterprise', its projects, its attempts to secure its authority and shape the world in its own image. But such metaphoric performance is, as we have seen, also the text's point of vulnerability to an irreverent reading. Consequently she uses these points of vulnerability to interpret particular philosophical imagery as historically specific, symptomatic of the historical relationship between systematic knowledges and their social context.

This historical specificity is crucial to my utilisation of metaphoric language to interpret the politics of biomedical AIDS discourse. My reading of this metaphoric language attempts to specify what I have termed the biomedical imagination. At a general level this term refers to biomedicine's speculative universe, its ways of proposing relationships and processes, of imagining the world according to its own requirements and interests. I have elected to use the term imagination in order to stress its fantasising, imagic qualities, the qualities it is at greatest pains to repress. The aspect of this imagination which I focus on is the ways in which it imagines social order and its historical transformations, the ways that it converts these imaginings into the 'technical' language and imagery of science. It seems to me that biomedicine must necessarily assimilate historical changes in this way because it is so deeply enmeshed in the social order.

A concern for historical specificity thus determines which metaphoric systems I have decided to work and which to leave unexamined. This is always and necessarily a political decision, because in a sense no aspect of biomedical discourse, no matter how technical, is free of metaphoric resonance. That which seems most self-evidently 'metaphoric' in a scientific text might simply be indicative of the most recent 'problem', the as yet unassimilated trace of an attempt to conceptualise some new social phenomenon and systematise its discourse in some new way.

Consequently I have focused on those metaphoric systems which seem to me more complicit with the contemporary sexual politics of AIDS than others. These are metaphoric systems which figure sexual differences (often implicitly) as analogues of viral or bodily processes. The biomedical imagination is, as I demonstrate throughout the book, a phallocentric and homosocial imagination, one which uses metaphors of the feminine to designate weakness, infectiousness, virulence, and which tries to order the world according to this principle.

I have argued that scientific discourse can be read as a textual and intertextual rather than a referential practice. It can be considered as a narrative among other narratives, in that it both uses and produces mythologies, analogies and figurations in a fashion not dissimilar to literary production. Like literary production, science draws on culturally available meanings to 'make things up'. But what status does this fabrication have with regard to biologically specified bodies?

This returns me to the problem of the reversal of the real/representation dichotomy proposed by Armstrong (1983) to explain the relationship between the anatomical atlas and the body. He stated that, 'in effect what the student sees is not the atlas as a representation of the body but the body as a representation of the atlas'. This way of understanding the efficacy of biomedical representation seems to me to be problematic, because it equates the power of representation with the power of illusion, and locates its operation only in the field of vision. On this analysis biomedical representations of bodies are significant only because they organise the doctor's gaze in a particular way, which the blank facticity of the body simply allows.

But I want to argue that the power of biomedicine to 'make up' bodies is less totalising and more complex then this reversal suggests. I want to take the phrase 'biomedicine makes things up' quite seriously, and move it into a double register. On the one hand it creates narratives and on the other it *realises*, or struggles to realise, these narratives through their embodiment. It *anatomises* its narratives in the sense that it orders its images of bodies according to their logic, but it also anatomises them in the sense that it reads them into lived bodies in ways that are constitutive of important aspects of corporeality itself. As Vasseleu puts it, 'Scientific practice *is* writing. It makes things up. Its figurative strategies are constitutive of the objects whose essence they describe' (Vasseleu 1991: 60). The coherence of the biomedically specified body is not simply 'discovered' or represented, but to some extent engendered by biomedical practice.

This claim involves a further challenge to the nature/culture distinction, because it is based on the proposition that bodies can be located in the domains of history and cultural practice, rather than contained in the stability and inertia of the natural. It is based on the proposition that, as Grosz puts it,

> Bodies must take the social order as their productive nucleus. Part of their own 'nature' is an organic or ontological 'incompleteness' or lack of finality, an amenability to social completion, social ordering and organisation.
>
> (Grosz 1994: xi)

In what follows I will argue that biomedical knowledge is always a discourse about social order, worked out in bodily terms. Its clinical and public health practices can be interpreted as its means of anatomising this order on the bodies of populations, both at the level of particular bodies and that of the body politic. It is precisely because bodies are, as Grosz puts it, 'amenable to social completion' that biomedicine can be efficacious, both in its own terms as an ameliorator of illness, and as a force for certain kinds of social order. In this sense biomedical practices are constitutive of, although not determining of, a historical and political field which directly implicates sexed bodies. In the next section I want to make some proposals about how both biomedical representations and sexed bodies can be regarded as historical practices, and about how the relationship between these practices can be thought.

HISTORICAL ANATOMIES

If medical knowledge works itself out in cultural terms, then this knowledge is necessarily sensitive to transformations in culture. Nonetheless, while biomedical narratives and images owe a demonstrable debt to other non-scientific narratives, they are also specific discursive formations, meeting the qualifications for scientific as opposed to other forms of statement and image. How then does the biomedical imagination translate cultural arrangements into its own practices, what transformations do they undergo?

I have already suggested that biomedicine 'anatomises' culture. What I mean by this is that biomedical knowledge constructs its representations of bodies according to ideas about social order. The term 'anatomy' is peculiarly suggestive of what I am trying to get at in this statement because it carries a double significance. On the one hand it designates the biomedical practices of bodily mapping, of producing both cartographic and narrative representations of the body's physiology and micro-physiology, the medical subdiscipline known as 'anatomy'. On the other hand it is a term often used to designate the factitious or 'biological' body, the body as given flesh. When I say that biomedicine 'anatomises' culture I want to explore the historical implications of this statement in both registers of the anatomical, as both a knowledge practice and as designating the fleshly body. How can these two senses of the anatomical be interpreted as subject to historical process?

The first sense of the anatomical, anatomy as biomedical representation, has been the subject of a number of feminist historical studies which demonstrate the ways that biomedicine literally incorporates the social questions of its time, particularly into the anatomical representation of the body of woman. In her elaboration on philosophical metaphorics and figurative language Le Doeuff (1989), for example, examines the complicity between eighteenth-century biomedical and philosophical discourses in their representation of the body of woman, the way that, as she puts it, the former *realises* and hence naturalises the latter's pronouncements. She focuses her argument on one Enlightenment medical text, *Système Physique et Moral de la Femme*, which renders the Rousseauian philosophy of sexual difference into physiological terms. In particular it renders anatomical the Rousseauian proposition that every aspect of Woman, her lack of reason, incapacity for politics, sensitivity to sensation and mobility of emotion, is determined by her sex(uality). It creates a pansexual physiology of Woman, where the entire body is modelled on the maternal and the gynaecological.[10] The great success of Doctor Roussel's text, she argues, derived from this capacity to realise the ideas of its age.

> Roussel concentrates in woman's body a number of representations developed in various other sectors of the age's encyclopedia, within the general space of letters which that period termed philosophy. Roussel *realises* (in the strongest sense of the word) his century's theoretical creations, he projects onto the female body the Enlightenment's conceptual products, and thereby invents a physiological image, an anatomical compendium of the new normativity which has been (or is still being) constructed in anthropology, aesthetics, the philosophy of history.
>
> (Le Doeuff 1989: 141)

Schiebinger's (1987) study of the process of production of skeletal anatomies in the eighteenth and nineteenth centuries also demonstrates this pansexualisation and its relationship to particular social questions of the day. She documents the new specification of the female skeleton around the functions of maternity on the one hand and the alleged intellectual deficiencies of women on the other, a skeleton which displayed a wider pelvis and smaller skull than that of the male skeleton. The question of the size of women's skulls compared to that of men's was, Schiebinger argues, both provoked *as a question* in anatomical research by the nineteenth-century controversies over women's right to education and participation in the public sphere, and then used as biological evidence in the various arguments. Representations of the skeleton played a particularly authoritative part in these debates because it was thought to act as the foundation of the body. Consequently sex differences in the skeleton formed the basis for sex differences everywhere else.

Schiebinger's history also provides a second sense in which the anatomical can be historicised. It is not just a question of certain social issues or questions being transformed into anatomical questions, but also of the process of production of skeletal images themselves. Schiebinger's study, and also Daston and Galison's (1992) study of the concept of 'objectivity' in the production of nineteenth-century anatomical images, indicates the extent to which anatomical images are produced as 'ideal types' of the object they wished to represent. Schiebinger reports the extent to which the Enlightenment anatomists were influenced by current aesthetic ideals of physical beauty in their production of anatomical drawings, ideals which were of course quite different for men and women. Describing the work procedures of one particular anatomist she writes,

Sommerring strived . . . for exactitude and universality in his illustrations. He made every possible effort to 'approach nature as nearly as possible'. Yet, he stated, the physiologists should always select the most perfect and most beautiful specimen for their models. In identifying and selecting the 'most beautiful specimen', Sommerring intended to establish norms of beauty. According to Sommerring, without having established a norm by means of frequent investigations and abstractions, one is not able to decide which cases deviate from the perfect norm. Sommerring chose the 'ideal' model for his illustration of the female skeleton with great care: 'Above all I was anxious to provide for myself the body of a woman that was suitable not only because of her youth and aptitude for procreation, but also because of the harmony of her limbs' . . . . Anatomists of the eighteenth century 'mended' nature to fit emerging ideals of masculinity and femininity.

(Schiebinger 1987: 62)

Schiebinger implies in her argument that this utilisation of aesthetic 'ideal types' was prompted by a generalised sexism on the part of anatomists, a wilful reading of masculine and feminine stereotypes into their practices. Daston and Galison's study of similar processes of production of anatomical atlases demonstrates however the extent to which the utilisation of such ideals was not just prompted by habit, sexism or misplaced aesthetic concerns. They argue that the recourse to ideals was bound up with a major epistemological problem for biomedical representation, a problem which still has important implications for any consideration of current biomedical representations of AIDS. This is the problem of the 'representativeness' of the anatomical image, its claim to be typical of a class of phenomena.

The purpose of anatomical representation, they argue, is precisely the standardisation of phenomena, the generation of images which could claim a general representativeness *exactly because* they do not succumb to the infinite idiosyncrasy of naturally occurring objects. Procedures for the standardisation of images of, say, body organs, are irreducible in the production of biomedical knowledge because the practitioner, whether researcher or clinician, cannot work without a knowledge of the exemplary, healthy organ and exemplary manifestations of particular diseases.

All sciences must deal with the problem of selecting and constituting 'working objects', as opposed to the too plentiful and too obvious natural objects. . . . Working objects can be atlas images, type specimens, or laboratory processes – any manageable, communal representatives of the sector of nature under investigation. No science can do without such standardised working objects, for unrefined natural objects are too quirkily particular to cooperate in generalisations and comparisons.

(Daston and Galison 1992: 85)

This necessity for selection and standardisation then raises the question of criteria for deciding 'typicality'. Daston and Galison identify two variant means of making such selections, the 'ideal' and the 'characteristic'. The 'ideal', which they associate more strongly with enlightenment anatomical practice, works on the assumption that an archetypic image, one which depicts the 'best pattern in nature', acts as representative for all lesser natural variants. Here the purpose of the anatomical image is to depict the metaphysical order implicit in particular natural objects, an order which cannot be adequately represented by the flawed particularity of any natural object. This mode of reconciling the particular with the general is employed by the anatomists whose work is described in Schiebinger's text. Classical aesthetic ideas of masculine and feminine beauty, with their quite different sets of connotations, are utilised to solve the problem of the exemplary.

The 'characteristic' mode of image production, on the other hand, locates the typical in an individual specimen or object. The selection of particular objects is nevertheless made on criteria of typicality, that is on some claim to represent the majority of objects in the class of objects in question. So Daston and Galison point out that the choice of a typical object for anatomical representation was made on the basis of a prior knowledge of the range of 'normal' variation, and a judgement about at what point variation became deviation. These two variations on the process of selection of images persist despite the advent of photography and its biomedical variations, the X-ray, microphotography and so on. While specific photographic images are readily used throughout medical textbooks, they are *always* coupled with drawings and graphs which present standardised and simplified versions of the phenomena under discussion, and which in effect act as guides to the interpretation of the messily particular tissue sample or X-ray.

So in both cases anatomical forms of representation involve standardisation along particular lines which allow the single image to stand for a class of objects. Standardisation in turn can only be made outside the frame of the representations themselves, in the sense that no purely quantitative, statistical process can average out, in the sense of flatten out, morphological idiosyncrasy. There can be no neutral process whereby all natural variation can be condensed into a single image, or even a series of images. Condensation always involves judgements about what counts as normal, judgements which precede the process of condensation itself. So both the characteristic and the ideal bases of anatomical representation are caught up in the specification of a concept of perfection, as a way of solving the problem of the representation of health.

Here I am drawing on Canguilhem's (1989) demonstration of the impossibility of reducing the question of the norm in biomedicine to a simple expression of average or type. While an average expresses the probability of recurrence of a particular morphology, the likelihood that a group of persons will be a certain height for example, it cannot solve the problem of the distinction between normal and pathological variation from the average. This

36

distinction involves questions of value, which must be made outside the representational space of the series. And as Daston and Galison's study indicates, anatomical representation is concerned above all with finding ways to depict this distinction, the distinction between physiology, the normal body and various pathological variations.

It is for this reason that anatomical representation, and the clinical practice it enables, can *never* be disentangled from a culturally and historically specific normativity, an ideal of perfection. As Canguilhem demonstrates, it is impossible to have a science of the pathological without a science of the normal, the physiological. Pathology can only be figured as various kinds of departure from a concept of the healthy functioning of bodies. While this distinction is generally expressed in quantitative terms in biomedical discourse, as deficit or excess of physiological function, it *always* involves a positive, qualitative concept of health.

> Excess or deficiency exist in relation to a scale deemed valid and suitable – hence in relation to a norm. To define the abnormal as too much or too little is to recognise the normative character of the so-called normal state. This normal or physiological state is no longer simply a disposition which can be revealed and explained as a fact, but a manifestation of attachment to some value.
>
> (Canguilhem 1989: 57)

How then are positive, exemplary images of health arrived at? According to my argument so far, *positive images of health can only be arrived at in biomedical practice through successive conjectures about the ideal organisation of the body.* These conjectures, the speculative processes central to the biomedical imagination, then form the basis for the technical discourse of physiology and the graphic condensations of anatomy. The question then becomes, by what procedures are these conjectures made? How do conjectural statements meet the formal requirements for acceptance as properly scientific?

There are both positive and negative poles of biomedical conjecture about the healthy organisation of the body. To take the negative first, Canguilhem points out that in biomedical practice the specification of normalcy is necessarily posterior, at least in its detail, to the specification of pathology. The description of the pathological failure of organs or processes precedes the description of their normal operation.

> In biology it is the *pathos* which conditions the *logos*....It is the abnormal which arouses theoretical interest in the normal. Norms are recognised as such only when they are broken. Functions are revealed only when they fail.
>
> (Canguilhem 1989: 208–9)

In other words, one of the starting points for conjecture about the healthy organisation of the body derives from the understanding of pathological failures. So any operative concept of health is enmeshed in and partially derived from current descriptions of pathology. This suggests to me that whatever concepts of health are dominant at a particular historical moment can be read as a negative registration of whatever forms of pathology are salient at that moment. The healthy body projected out of a concern with heart failure (slim, athletic) will be quite different from a healthy body projected out of a concern with tuberculosis (plump, rosy), for example. Similarly the healthy body projected out of a concern with a sexually transmitted viral illness which destroys the immune system will be qualitatively different from that suggested by other kinds of disease which have no bearing on sexual practice.

The positive pole of conjecture is related to the negative, and also takes us back to the question of analogy in biomedical discourse. Dominant concepts of health involve the ordering of the body both against dominant pathologies and according to positive understandings of optimum function, maximum communication, system maintenance, and homeostasis, where all parts of the body cooperate in an organic harmony and return to optimum states after temporary departure. The healthy organism is the result of its appropriate organisation, and for this reason positive conjectures about health are habitually made on analogies of ideal social order in biomedical discourse. Anatomy as the proper ordering of the body is repeatedly expressed in terms of an ideal social order.

There is extensive evidence of the habitual use made of this kind of analogy in biomedical discourse, which will be drawn upon throughout this book. A few examples will suffice here. Canguilhem (1989) documents the consistency with which the positivist physiologists of the nineteenth century, particularly Comte, drew comparisons between pathology in the organism and revolutionary change in the social order, or as he referred to it, the social organism. These were analogous because both pathology and revolution demanded vigorous intervention to return the organism to homeostasis. Both states exceed the self-regulating capacities of the organism.

Martin's (1987) study of biomedical metaphor in the conceptualisation of birth and reproductive process details numerous similar instances. She cites instances where the body's processes are likened to economic processes, spending, saving or balancing its energy resources, for example. She provides a particularly graphic instance of analogy between the working of the body and that of a city, made by Frederick Gates, an important figure is US public health in the early twentieth century.

It is interesting to note the striking comparisons between the human body and the safety and hygienic appliances of a great city....The body has a network of insulated nerves, like telephone wires, which transmit instantaneous alarms at every point of danger. The body is furnished with the most elaborate police system, with hundreds of police stations to which the criminal elements are carried by the police and jailed. I refer to the great numbers of sanitary glands, skilfully placed at points where viscous germs find entrance.

(cited in Martin 1987: 36)

The recurrence of these kinds of global comparisons between bodies and social units in the history of biomedical discourse suggests that the biomedical imagination is deeply enmeshed in the same kinds of bodily representations described by Douglas (1984) in her cross-cultural study of pollution taboos, *Purity and Danger*. Douglas proposes that bodies stand for social systems and social systems for bodies in many, if not most, societies. Various orderings of bodily attributes, particularly through pollution rules, help to anatomise social order, to render it corporeal.

> I believe that some pollutions are used as analogies for expressing a general view of the social order. For example, there are beliefs that each sex is a danger to the other through contact with sexual fluids....I suggest that many ideas about sexual dangers are better interpreted as symbols of the relation between parts of society, as mirroring designs of hierarchy or symmetry which apply in the larger social system....The two sexes can serve as models for the collaboration or distinctiveness of social units. So also can the processes of ingestion portray political absorption. Sometimes bodily orifices seem to represent points of entry and exit to social units, or bodily perfection can symbolise an ideal theocracy.
>
> (Douglas 1984: 3–4)

In the case of biomedical representation in our own society, however, these kinds of global analogies between bodies and social order tend to remain immanent. The potential for explicit comparison is maintained through the process of negative conjecture which I described above, where concepts of healthy functioning are proposed out of specific kinds of organ failure. This negative conjecture maintains a strong relationship with positive forms of social analogy, however, because both healthy functioning and pathological deterioration tends to be thought of through comparison with various social sub-units. What I mean is that specific bodily functions are generally modelled in contemporary biomedical discourse on particular social technologies and hierarchies. The brain is likened to the body's computer, the hormone production 'system' is modelled on a hierarchically organised system of communications, the eyes are the body's camera, and so on.

Global social analogy can be readily mobilised by assembling these various technological sub-units into an integrated social universe, as does the quote from Frederick Gates. Both these levels of analogy, between body part and social sub-unit and between body and society, are thus instances of biomedicine's power to 'anatomise' culture. It is evident, however, that biomedicine does not simply operate with received ideas about appropriate forms of social

39

order, but rather builds up its imagos of both the healthy and the diseased body around *particular concepts* of social order, concepts which tend towards the centralised, the hierarchical and, as we shall see, the phallocentric.

Furthermore it seems plausible to me that conditions of epidemic present a particularly urgent provocation to such analogies, because in the biomedical imagination epidemic is *a pathology which operates at the level of the entire social order*. Under conditions of epidemic the representation of the body as a social microcosm is fully mobilised, because the control of epidemic demands that biomedicine rethink its concept of social order in relation to its under-standing of epidemic pathology. Epidemics, particularly epidemics like HIV for which there is neither vaccine nor cure, tend to be thought of as effects of poor social order, which must be brought under control through a social reordering.

It is for this reason that biomedicine's representations of AIDS can be read simultaneously as, first of all, a description of a disease process, a viral pathology of the immune system that is transmitted through an exchange of body fluids. Second, it can be interpreted as the negative imprint of an ideal concept of health and hence an ideal body, a body whose immune system is perfectly self-replicating and defensively mobilised and which is resistant to bodily exchanges. Third, it works as a narrative of social order and its failures, figured both at the level of the anatomical body and the body politic, the social order conceived on an organic model. Because AIDS is understood to be a sexually transmitted disease, and associated with particular sexualities, the anatomies and discourses of AIDS pathology can be seen to imply certain concepts of an ideal sexual ordering, both of particular bodies and of social relations.

In the following chapters I argue that the crucial aspect of biomedicine's figuration of the distinction between health and pathology in the case of AIDS is its representation of bodily boundaries. The normative ideal of health which circulates implicitly in AIDS discourse, and which is explored in detail in this book, can be summarised as a seamless, impermeable, individuated body, a body inimical to infectious processes. Increasing degrees of risk are associated with bodily openness and a confusion of individuation.

There is historical evidence to suggest that this figuration of the normal and the pathological is not exclusive to AIDS discourse, but is rather general to concepts of infectious disease. Both Foucault (1979) and Corbin (1986) relate the nineteenth-century rise of individualism, the concept of the proper body as a singular, self-contained and self-possessed entity, in part to concerns with the control of epidemic disease. The discourse of hygiene which was addressed to the control of infectious disease strived for an individuation of bodies, their separation in space and their self-containment, because infection was under-stood to take place when bodies exceed their proper borders and mingle with each other in various ways.

This hygienic individuation involves the pathologisation of bodily orifices and body fluids, points of permeability and fluid excess that confuse the distinction between the body's inside and outside. Nettleton's (1992) history of dentistry indicates, for example, that the mouth became the object of anxiety about infection during the late nineteenth and early twentieth centuries, after the ascendancy of germ theory.

> An examination of the public health literature of this time reveals that 'points of contact' were of particular significance. The mouth was conceived as a vulnerable region or 'boundary' between the internal body and external sources of pollution ... the significant interface between the internal body and all that lay beyond it.
>
> (Nettleton 1992: 26–7)

If the pathologisation of bodily thresholds and confusions of singularity are general to biomedical figurations of infectious disease, however, the figuration of sexual infection concerns itself specifically with genital thresholds and the sexual fluids which traverse them. These thresholds are also of course the sites for the determination of sexual 'identities' in AIDS discourse, for the assertion of coherent, predictable and stable relationships between sex, sexual object choice, sexual practice and subjective identity. It is at this point that biomedical specifications of normal and pathological processes can be seen to enter into the field of sexual identity and sexual politics.

The logic of contagion in AIDS discourse maps itself onto different risks associated with various genital practices, and the 'sexual identities' they are said to denote. The most virulent sexual practice is both receptive and penetrative anal sex between men, which is taken to denote homosexual identity. This is followed by a combination of anal receptivity and vaginal penetration, taken to stand for bisexual male identity, which is in turn followed by indiscriminate vaginal receptivity which stands for 'promiscuous' femininity, and so on.[11] In this way biomedical normativity can be seen to both postulate and moralise sexual identities along particular lines. It simultaneously assumes a relationship between genital capacity and subjectivity, and orders this capacity into a hierarchy of pathology. But what consequences does this normalisation have for the bodies of subjects nominated in this way? What kinds of political effects are set off through the circulation of these medical imagos of the normal and the pathological?

BODY BOUNDARIES AND THE ANATOMY OF THE FLESH

Canguilhem maintains that the function of biomedical normativity is to modify and transform the subjectivity of the patient. The concept of health works for medical practice by making demands upon bodies.

> Strictly speaking a norm does not exist, it plays its role which is to devalue existence by allowing its correction. To say that perfect health

41

does not exist is simply saying that the concept of health is not one of an existence, but of a norm whose function and value is to be brought into contact with existence in order to stimulate modification.

(Canguilhem 1989: 77)

In other words the normativity of biomedical representations derives not only from certain kinds of representational constraints, limits and processes, but also from the need for a certain kind of efficacy. Norms of health exercise transformative effects on the imperfect bodies with which they are brought into contact. This transformative effect, Canguilhem seems to suggest, derives precisely from the impossibility of achieving the normative ideal in the lived body. The unobtainable norm functions to galvanise the subject's investment in regaining health along particular, prescriptive lines by proffering an impossible vitality and bodily perfection.

This brings me back to the second sense in which I want to consider the term 'anatomy', and its relationship to the idea that biomedicine 'anatomises' culture. I observed earlier that the term 'anatomy' is used to designate both the graphic practices of biomedicine and the putatively natural organisation of the fleshly body. In the previous section I proposed some ways in which graphic anatomical practices render cultural and social concerns into biomedical narratives and images. In this section I want to explore the proposition that biomedicine anatomises culture precisely through its historical organisation of fleshly bodies along certain normative lines.

To do this I want to move both senses of the anatomical into the register of 'imaginary anatomies', a term coined by Lacan and taken up within current feminist theory as a means of thinking through the proposition that bodies are historical entities. I have already demonstrated the sense in which biomedical anatomies can be understood as 'imaginary anatomies'. They are the products of the biomedical imagination, arrived at through processes of selectivity, idealisation, utopian speculation and analogy, fictional products in the sense that they are *fabricated* within the constraints of biomedical discourse. But in what sense can fleshly anatomies be understood as 'imaginary', and what role does biomedical normativity play in their fabrication?

The term 'anatomical body' carries with it connotations of overall bodily order, the terms of coherence and the relation between parts which make up the whole. Here I am referring back to a now anachronistic meaning of the term 'anatomy', used during the seventeenth and eighteenth centuries to describe any specification of relations between parts and the whole, any analytic enterprise.[12] On the scientific model this bodily order is given and natural, an ordering intrinsic to the body's identity as an organism. The term 'imaginary anatomy' as it has been developed in feminist theory, however, proposes that this order, and the different kinds of order involved in marking sexual difference, is socially produced, and intrinsic to the process of subjectification.

Lacan generated the term 'imaginary anatomy' to help account for the 'somatic compliance' of hysterical symptoms, their incarnation of ideas about bodily functions and boundaries which exist in a given culture. Interestingly hysterical symptoms, for example eating disorders, are defined by Lacan as anatomically 'naive'. They are expressive of certain cultural fantasies, say of causal relationships between eating and pregnancy, but are nevertheless eccentric with regard to properly biomedical, anatomical understandings of how bodies work.[13]

The imaginary anatomy refers then to what might be called a psychic mapping of the body, the subject's creation of a kind of narcissistic imaginary schema of their own body. This schema, Grosz argues, is a condition of embodied subjectivity as such.

> The subject's relation to its body is always *libidinal*: that is a necessary condition of its ability to identify the body as *its own* . . . the body and its various organs and orifices are always psychically or libidinally mapped, psychically *represented*, as a condition of the subject's ability to use them and to include them in his or her self-image.
>
> (Grosz 1987: 8)

The subject's anatomy is 'imaginary' then in the sense that its coherence, the relations between parts and its overall assemblage, is fantasised as a (pre-)condition of its achievement at any moment. Just as all communities must, as Anderson (1991) argues, imagine their terms of coherence as soon as they exceed a very low level of spatial complexity, so too must subjects imagine the coherence of their bodily form in order to successfully inhabit and perform them. They must function as objects in space and for others, but can never be just objects to themselves. So imaginary anatomies come about through the necessity that subjects be able to choreograph themselves in space, that they be able to negotiate self/other relations, and that they be able to identify themselves with a singular bodily assemblage.

There are two features of the imaginary anatomy as lived body which are crucial for my argument. One is the idea that it is unstable and hence open to reconfirmation and reorganisation. Grosz, drawing on cases of disintegration of the imaginary anatomy in psychic disturbance as her evidence, suggests that the subject's grasp upon stable unified being is fragile, open to perturbation and disturbance. The coherence of the imaginary anatomy demands considerable psychic investment for its maintenance. It can only be operative on the condition that it be continually reiterated.

> The stability of the unified body image, even in the so-called normal subject, is always precarious. It cannot be simply taken for granted as an accomplished fact, for it must be continually renewed, not through the subject's conscious efforts but through its ability to conceive of itself as a

subject and to separate itself from its objects and others to be able to undertake wilful action.

(Grosz 1994: 44)

This open-endedness, this susceptibility to partial (and sometimes total) disintegration, and to social forms of reconfirmation seems to me to be the aspect of corporeality which allows biomedical practice the kind of direct efficacy that Canguilhem ascribes to it. As was described earlier, he argues that the function of biomedical normativity is to make a demand upon the sick person's body, to 'stimulate modification'. If we reconsider these words in the light of my brief excursus on the imaginary anatomy, they suggest that biomedicine's deployment of its own normative bodily schemata work in the clinical sense because bodies are susceptible to normative reconfirmation. States of illness involve a partial fragmentation of the bodily subjective order involved in health, and clinical biomedicine intervenes to reconstitute this order along its own particular lines. In the case of public health, too, its discourses involve a strategic destabilisation of the sense of health of particular 'target groups'. Public health preventative discourse, which conceives of itself as educative, seems to work through an inducement of a surplus anxiety about the body's everyday habits and workings, as a precondition for the installation of some new demand for bodily reconfiguration, or adoption of new habitual practices.

The second relevant feature of the concept of the imaginary anatomy for my argument is its normativity, the extent to which it conforms to general cultural understandings of bodies and what is appropriate to a proper body: its mode of relations, its choreography, its posture and the way that it enacts its sex. Subjective imaginary anatomies are not generated through erratic isolated fantasies but share to some extent in a common cultural imaginary about bodily processes, meanings and limits. The susceptibility of hysterical symptoms to 'fashion', to cultural and temporal specificity, is evidence for this, as is the body's susceptibility to the temporary adoption of changeable bodily 'styles' of health and beauty. Gatens lists some of the historical and cultural constituents of normative imaginary anatomies.

> The surprising homogeneity in the expression of the hysterical symptom, such as anorexia nervosa, within a given culture, signals the social character of the imaginary body. The imaginary body is socially and historically specific in that it is constructed by: a shared language; the shared physical significance and privileging of various zones of the body (e.g. the mouth, the anus, the genitals); and common institutional practices and discourses (e.g. medical, juridical, and educational) on and through the body.
>
> (Gatens 1983: 151–2)

This suggests to me that in addition to the kinds of direct clinical practices of normative modification described by Canguilhem, biomedical anatomies are also taken up in subjective imaginary anatomies in a more diffused sense. This is so because biomedical 'imaginary anatomies' play an important part in generating the general regime of regulatory images which constitute our culture's available repertoire of bodily practices.

I am not suggesting that subjective imaginary anatomies arise from some detailed knowledge of biomedical anatomy. However, biomedical images of and explanatory schemata about bodies still form the last court of appeal as it were on what constitutes a 'normal' body and bodily functioning. Biomedicine has the power to arbitrate upon other regimes of regulatory images.[14] In a more diffuse way it seems plausible that biomedically specified elements are taken up into the everyday living of subjective imaginary anatomies in various ways, particularly around concepts of bodily health and fitness, sexual 'normalcy', the body's proper conformation and co-ordination, and so on. Medicalised concepts of bodily order circulate in the institutions of education, sport, fashion, childcare and innumerable other social sites which generate our ideas and practices about bodies. This point is well made by Diprose in her study of biomedical ethics. She writes:

> Biomedicine is not just a practice which works directly on bodies. It is also one of the discourses which make up the world in which we ordinarily dwell....Furthermore, biomedicine is not just one among many fields of knowledge which regulate bodies in the name of the so-called common good: it holds a privileged place in disseminating knowledge about what a body is, how it functions and the nature of its capabilities. And, in this, biomedical knowledge does its own social dichotomising in delineating the normal body from the abnormal. So it is possible not only that biomedical science is involved in the restoration and expansion of bodies upon which it practices, but that as a field of knowledge it may play a part in the constitution of those bodies prior to any alienation [in illness].
>
> (Diprose 1994: 124)

These two features of imaginary anatomies, their open-endedness to clinical intervention and their susceptibility to social normativity, suggest that bio-medical anatomies can exercise strong specificatory powers over bodies as they are lived, in both health and illness. So if Lacan distinguishes hysterical symptoms from organic symptoms on the basis of their 'anatomical naivety' I suggest that this can never constitute an absolute basis for distinction. It cannot be absolute precisely because the 'normal' non-hysterical body is already enmeshed in a naive form of anatomical specification as an important element of its subjective animation, while more technical forms of anatomical specification also specify the organic symptom. In other words if both subjective and biomedical anatomies are produced through imaginary processes and help to specify each other, then distinctions between hysterical and organic symptoms are relative rather than absolute.

This relativity is in a sense acknowledged in many areas of clinical practice when dealing with diseases which seem irrelevant to any concept of body image. I am referring to symptomless diseases like certain forms of cancer to which subjects have no sensory access and hence which cannot have psychic significance prior to their (often accidental) diagnosis. Once diagnosis has occurred clinicians increasingly use the practice of 'imaging' as a therapeutic process, where the patient is provided with ways of imagining their cancer and their immune system fighting it, using models, graphics and computer games, for example. It seems to me that this brings the cancerous body part into the patient's imaginary anatomy, in order to stimulate some modification in that part, to psychically invest it in ways that might promote health. In other words virtually any aspect of the body's functioning as it is understood through biomedical anatomy can be interpolated into subjective imaginary anatomy, prompted by the experience or fear of illness.

Now if I can bring all of this to bear on the imaginary anatomies generated in AIDS biomedicine and the general social conditions of sexual epidemic, it seems to me that the object of normative concern is precisely the bodily boundaries lived out in subjective imaginary anatomies. I have already argued that body boundaries, and the internal structures which determine them in biomedicine's understanding, are the most important ways that infection and contagion are anatomically figured. The public health programmes around the control of HIV/AIDS transmission are concerned above all to remap the boundaries between bodies and the terms of their exchanges along lines which guard against contagion. The highly contested political nature of this attempt to reconfigure the imaginary anatomies of whole populations derive however from the extent to which the specification of body boundaries is always sexed, both with respect to the distinction between masculine and feminine and between heterosexual and homosexual. In what follows I want to briefly outline some elements of the relationship between sexual identity and body boundary, and then make some concluding remarks about the circulation of biomedical imaginary anatomies.

BOUNDARY, ABJECTION AND CONTAGION

The adoption of certain boundary formations is a crucial part of sexed subjectification, in the sense that body boundaries help to organise both the significance of sexual identity and the modes of relationship between sexes and sexualities. Quite different protocols of permeability, limit and potential for relational confusion set the terms of sexual difference and naturalise certain kinds of power relationships between masculinity and femininity, and hetero-sexuality and homosexuality.

To take the question of the masculine/feminine distinction first, this binary

46

is associated with other binaries which specify boundary, those of imperme-able/permeable and active/passive. As Gatens notes, these binaries are crucial to the genital imaginary anatomies of sexual difference. She observes that the representation of the act of heterosexual intercourse, as it appears both within psychoanalysis *and* biology, plays out these binaries *as if* they were essential attributes of sexual difference.

> The man actively penetrates the passive vagina. However, and this is the role of cultural and historical specificity, it is not given *a priori* that the penis is active, the vagina passive. This concept has to do with the imaginary anatomy, where the vagina is conceived of as a 'hole' or 'lack' and the penis as a 'phallus'. One could just as well, given a different relational mode between men and women, conceive of the penis as being enveloped or 'embraced' by the active vagina.
>
> (Gatens 1983: 152)

As Gatens's words imply, the connotative chains which link together these binaries, which make masculinity associate with activity and penetration and femininity with passivity and penetrability, make sense from, and so betray, a phallocentric point of view.

The term 'phallocentrism' is, in one of its aspects, a general term to describe dominant forms of sexed imaginary anatomy in our culture. As the word itself implies, phallocentrism is a form of homosocial thought which places the phallus at the centre of bodily signification. It specifies sexual difference as absolute, mutually exclusive difference, figured around the possession or lack of a penis, taken to be a phallus.[15]

Phallocentrically specified imaginary anatomies also tend to read a certain representation of genital difference out onto the whole morphology of the sexually differentiated bodies that the genitals are said to determine. Here I am following Butler's (1993) reading of Lacan's propositions about the (implicitly) masculine imaginary anatomy which figures the body as a controllable unity. This imaginary anatomy is bound, integrated and hierarchically controlled through its organisation around the possession of a penis, hypostasised as a phallus.

Butler argues that in the constitution of the masculine imaginary anatomy as it is analysed in several of Lacan's seminars, the fantasised, idealised penis-as-phallus works as a synecdoche through which the entire masculine body can be idealised, postulated on phallic lines. Butler writes:

> [the male genitals] function as both the site and token of a specifically male narcissism. Moreover, in so far as these organs are set into play by a narcissism which is said to provide the structure of relations to the Other and to the world of objects, then these organs become part of the imaginary elaboration of the ego's bodily boundary, token and 'proof' of its integrity and control....One might be tempted to argue that in the

course of being set into play by the narcissistic imaginary, the penis
becomes the phallus.

(Butler 1993: 77)

So according to this argument, within a phallocentric representational
order[16] bodies which 'possess' a penis are subjectified through an idealised,
phallic imaginary anatomy. In other words boundary difference is displaced
outwards from (imaginary) genital difference. The fantasy of the always hard
and ready penis/phallus characterises the entire surface of the male body,
whose stable borders, internal hierarchy and integrity correspond to a certain
social status. These borders confer capacities for activity, self-control and self-
possession, the capacities that Pateman (1988) demonstrates are associated
with the 'individual', the implicitly masculine subject of modern political
discourse, and with the claims of sovereign subjectivity. The phallic anatomy is
the anatomy of 'Man'.

These phallically constituted borders correlatively imply a feminine imaginary anatomy constituted through an absence of these capacities. As Butler
states, imaginary anatomies anatomise not only the bodies they connote but
also this body's Other, the other from which it seeks to distinguish itself and
also the other which it desires. In this sense imaginary anatomies are always
relational constructs. Within a phallocentric representational order the feminine body always appears as more or less abject, as lived out in the absence of
proper border or self-control. As Grosz (1994) argues, and as I shall demonstrate at length in this text, the phallocentric imaginary associates the feminine
body with an engulfing lack of boundary and a kind of fluid permeability
which places it in a marginal position in relation to individuated, sovereign
models of subjectivity.

What is disturbing about the viscous or the fluid is its refusal to conform
to the laws governing the clean and proper, the solid and the self-
identical, its otherness to the notion of an entity – the very notion that
governs our self-representations and understanding of the body. It is not
that female sexuality... resembles an inherently horrifying viscosity.
Rather it is the production of an order that renders female sexuality and
corporeality marginal, indeterminate, and viscous.

(Grosz 1994: 195)

On the phallocentric model male homosexuality is also produced as abject.
The gay male body appears from this point of view as a site of permeability and
potential leakage, because it is connoted through a cloacal and non-phallic, or
not exclusively phallic erotics, that of anality. This abjection of sexual bodies
which cannot lay claim to phallic specification has multiple effects in the
negotiation of power relations between men and women and between heterosexual and homosexual. An extensive feminist and gay/queer literature
examines these effects, which I can only gesture towards here.[17]

What I wish to stress however is the immense political weight which is attendant on the representation of body boundaries. This weight could be summarised as their power to confer or deny subjectivity *as such*, or at minimum to heavily qualify the status of subjectivity. According to the logic of abjection, proper subjectivity is signified by the body's containment within culturally specified boundaries. Anything excessive to this boundary aligns the body with natural processes, with decay, contagion and death, draining away its claims to sovereign self-control, to proprietal individualism, and the political status these claims shore up. Bodies which do not conform to these protocols of subjectivity thus appear to be in need of social intervention and regulation.

Consequently, if the biomedical understanding of contagion works through its own representation of normative bodily boundaries, and maps itself onto the body boundaries lived out in subjective imaginary anatomies, it enters into, and contributes to, a highly politicised field. Any attempt to refigure boundaries along normative lines necessarily touches upon all of the power that body boundaries have to create social hierarchy and to set the terms for kinds of exchange and relationality. At the same time the biomedical understanding of contagion is, I shall demonstrate, deeply complicit with the phallocentric order of representation which attributes abject status to non-phallicised bodies. Abjection *is* contagion in the biomedical imagination, an equation I shall investigate at length in the next chapter. Biomedicine's determination of contagious bodies recapitulates phallocentric anxieties about the threat posed by such bodies to its own founding repressions, its eliding of body fluids or permeability from its self-representation. Furthermore the protocols and phobias around contagion may be one of the most important ways that abjection is instituted and lived out. The sense of boundary and phobias of encroachment and engulfment by the bodies of others involved in the anxiety of contagion are arguably instances where biomedicine institutes individuated subjectivity through abjection. As I suggested earlier, biomedically specified anatomies may be taken up as important elements of our day-to-day imaginary anatomies, and it seems to me that contagion anxieties are an important way that this relationship is enacted. The complicity between the biomedical concept of contagion and the psychoanalytic concept of abjection provides a productive point of investigation for my analysis of the politics of AIDS subjectivity.

CONCLUSION

I began this chapter by considering the increased weight of significance placed on the nature/culture distinction under conditions of lethal epidemic, and the conceptual limits this distinction places on any attempt to rethink the sexual politics of the AIDS epidemic. The distinction serves to shore up biomedicine's power to determine what AIDS *really* is, to draw a line separating the real immutable facts of AIDS from those aspects of AIDS which can be politically contested. It drains off the possibility of interpreting biomedicine's explanatory deployment of concepts of sexual identity as politically interested, as enmeshed in some concept of social order. So in this chapter I have introduced some conceptual methods of destabilising the nature/culture distinction, as it pertains to biomedical knowledge and to anatomical bodies, in order to reconsider both of these as historical and political matters.

I introduced the problem that the ambiguity and metaphoricity of language posed for biomedicine's claim to correspond accurately and referentially to its pre-existing object, the human body. The operation of analogy and narrative is irreducible in scientific practice, and offers points of non-systematicity through which cultural readings of biomedical texts can be introduced. Analogy is a crucial element in the kinds of idealisation and standardisation through which biomedical representation produces its anatomical objects, and biomedicine's specifications of the normal and the pathological are always enmeshed in normative social analogies. In this sense biomedicine can be understood as an anatomisation of culture, a rendering of concepts of social order into anatomical terms. I termed this process of reframing cultural concerns in anatomical terms as the biomedical imagination.

This anatomisation of culture takes place not only at the level of formal biomedical knowledge production but also through its privileged relationship to the specification of normal and pathological bodies. Drawing upon recent feminist conceptualisations of the imaginary anatomy I argued that, in both its clinical practices and its general social power to describe bodily operations, biomedicine helps to engender the social coherence of bodies. In the case of AIDS this power of anatomisation is exercised in a complex and contested field of sexual politics, because AIDS biomedicine is concerned above all with the regulation of body boundaries, boundaries which are already highly politically invested.

In the following chapters I will discuss some of these proposals in greater detail in relation to both the micro-anatomies and macro-anatomies of the normal and the pathological as they are posed in AIDS biomedicine. The next chapter addresses the micro-anatomy of AIDS as it is specified in immunology, the biomedical sub-discipline which conceptualises the body's immune system. The iconography of the immune system provides biomedicine with complex representational resources through which to figure its social concerns, particularly its concerns with sexual order. AIDS is understood to be a pathology of the immune system, and as we shall see this *location* of the infection provides biomedicine with a multiplicity of ways to narrate and represent its phallocentric understandings of the consequences of sexual epidemic.

3

THE PRIMAL SCENE OF IMMUNOLOGY

Political philosophy seems to dominate biological theory.

Georges Canguilhem

I have argued that any biomedical representation of disease can be read at least three ways. It can be read first of all as straightforward technical description, as a positive representation of a bodily pathology. Second, it can be interpreted as the negative registration of a particular concept of health, and hence of normative perfection, against which its pathology is determined. Finally it can be considered as an immanent narrative of social order. These subtextual narratives can be opened out to interpretation through a consideration of the kinds of analogy which biomedicine draws upon to determine distinctions between the normal and the pathological in particular diseases. In this chapter I want to follow these last two lines of interpretation in relation to the micro-anatomy of AIDS, in order to demonstrate the untenability of the first.

The representation of AIDS falls under the provenance of certain biomedical sub-disciplines, particularly those of virology, immunology and epidemiology. The first two of these are microscopic[1] anatomies, concerned with the cellular and molecular relations between the virus and the body's inside and surface. The third is a macro-anatomy, concerned with relations between the virus, the body's surface and the social 'organism'. This chapter is concerned with the immunology of HIV infection, although it will also draw upon some virological representations of the virus.

The immune system is the bodily 'system' understood to be attacked by the virus, its site of colonisation. Viruses rely upon the host cells of other organisms to reproduce themselves, and HIV 'targets' particular cells of the human immune system as its means of replication. The immune system is considered to be the body's means of guarding against and ridding itself of infection. HIV infection is understood to involve the progressive weakening of the immune system, through both the simple 'killing' of cells and through various disturbances to their functioning and their communication with each other. The weakened immune system results in increased susceptibility to all kinds of infections. The disease AIDS is not strictly speaking a disease, but a series of infectious diseases contracted by the person as a result of HIV infection, diseases which eventually kill the host.

From this brief account,[2] it is evident that the 'immune system' is a system of biomedical representation that is crucial in the figuring of both AIDS pathology and the assumed bodily normalcy which infection is said to disrupt. In this chapter I want to examine the representational work performed by this way of figuring infection, and in particular its consequences for the conceptualisation of sexual difference. Following my argument about the operation of metaphor in scientific texts, my focus will be upon the kinds of social analogies the immune system draws upon to compose itself as a system, and the kinds of sexual power relations these analogies both assume and help to *realise*. What aspects of culture do these analogies help to naturalise and make seem inevitable?

In particular I am interested in the recurrence of what might be called 'biomilitary'[3] metaphors in figurations of the immune system. In the introduction I commented upon the ubiquity of the language of warfare in a number of different AIDS discourses, and as we shall see the immune system is habitually and comprehensively figured through military metaphor. Metaphors of warfare organise its technical lexicon, so some lymphocytes (immune system cells) are termed for example 'Killer T cells', and viruses are known as 'foreign antigens'. Such metaphors also preside over its concepts of organisation and action, where lymphocytes are said to practise surveillance and to 'kill' other cells, for example.

Certainly this body of metaphor does not exhaust the metaphoric possibilities presented by the immune system. Two other very important tropes which contribute to its concepts of activity and 'systematicity' are those of communication and visual recognition. These would seem more benign activities if they were not so readily put to the service of warfare, made to appear as 'military communication' and 'military surveillance'. And, of course, as I observed in the previous chapter, there is really no end to the metaphoricity of biomedical discourse. All the most fundamental categories and objects, that of cell, of reflex, of organism, of system, and of life itself, can be subjected to this kind of cultural interpretation.[4] However, while this analysis will raise some of the consequences of the idea of the 'cell' and 'organism', for example, I will focus on biomilitary metaphor, including its communicative and visual aspects, because it seems to me to have a privileged relationship to the figuring of HIV infection, and to the ways that particular bodies are positioned in the political field generated by AIDS.

Consequently this chapter concerns itself first of all with the kind of body and subjectivity which the militarised immune system figures as 'normal' and 'strong', prior to infection or pathology. Following Canguilhem's propositions about the conceptual relationship between the normal and the pathological, I argue that the 'normal' immune system has been reconstituted to some extent in relation to the emergence and conceptualisation of AIDS. Current representations of the immune system can thus be regarded as historical responses to what HIV infection is understood to *be*.[5] This reconfiguration then reciprocally conditions the representation of HIV infection. This reciprocity will be discussed in relation to the ways that it helps set up binaries of sexual difference in association with contagion and abjection.

THE IMMUNE SYSTEM AND SELF/OTHER RELATIONS

It was argued in the previous chapter that the political power of biomedical knowledge derives to a large extent from its capacity to figure its conceptual products, to anatomise its ideas. A central strategy of this figurative process is biomedicine's self-proclaimed capacity to visualise the microscopic activity of the body's interior, and to propose a 'causal' relationship between this activity and the body's morphology. The concept of an organism in biology is one where cellular sub-units are organised to form a higher unit of individuality. Canguilhem notes that the very concept of the 'cell' implies the existence of a greater whole into which it is subsumed. Consequently, specific kinds of cellular relationships and functional distinctions are understood to contribute to or determine the morphology of the organism.

> The cell is both an anatomical and a functional notion, referring both to a fundamental building block and to an individual labour subsumed by, and contributing to, a larger process... social values of cooperation and association lurk more or less discreetly in the background of... cell theory.
>
> (Canguilhem 1994: 162)

The basis of organism coherence has shifted down to a smaller level of scale with the ascendancy of genetics, because genes are posited on a molecular, rather than a cellular, scale. Cellular cooperation is still essential, however, in the posing of organism coherence, because the cells are understood to be instructed by genetic codes and to do their bidding.[6] Biomedicine's power to make pronouncements about the 'real' determinations of bodily difference resides then in its deployment of its various visualising technologies: microscopes which can 'see' cells, and other kinds of processes like the autoradiograph, used to infer molecular structures.

But as my earlier discussion of the biomedical gaze argued, this power of visualisation is always mediated by analogy and inflected through pre-existing concepts of the phenomena under consideration. Furthermore it is always subject to the technological constraints involved in rendering the phenomena observable and describable. Activity inside the body is in general inaccessible to direct observation, and biomedicine's propositions are based for the most part on laboratory practices, and its panoply of magnifying and trace-detecting technologies, on *in vitro* rather than *in vivo* study. Laboratory practices have their own protocols which mediate any immediate sense of visibility; the necessity to prepare cell tissue for the laboratory, the purification and staining of samples before they can be 'seen', and so on. The medical gaze can never, even in the most apparently neutral and transparent forms of visual access like that enabled by the microscope, be considered free of inference or connotation. Nor can it avoid the kinds of semiotic translational procedures involved in rendering the visual data field of a technology into a usable biomedical concept or diagram. As a growing number of laboratory ethnographies have demonstrated, the data produced through various visualising practices always demand active and speculative interpretation to make them meaningful.[7] The production and interpretation of visual evidence is thus a central process of the biomedical imagination, and its conclusions can be reinterpreted in that light.

Consequently biomedicine's pronouncements about the givenness of relations between the body's microscopic interior and social exterior are open to a suspicion of teleological rationalisation. While it understands the relationship to be one where the interior structure of the body works outwards to determine morphology, the direction of inference could be tracked back the other way. Biomedicine could be considered to read the body's social significance back into its interior. Diprose and Vasseleu make this suggestion in relation to the genetic determination of bodily differences.

> Biomedical science has . . . developed a model of the body as a structure – a simplistic text the form of which is derived from the message, the genetic code. . . .Genetic instructions are 'copied' by the duplication of DNA; 'transcribed' into the alphabet of the unstable messenger RNA; and translated by stable forms of RNA from four-letter codes into twenty-letter codings of proteins. These proteins are responsible for cell structure, and the relations between cells give us the morphology of the whole. . . .[But] is this not yet another aspect of establishing and maintaining borders, referring yet again to an elsewhere of identity, difference and motivation? For genetic 'differences' are first identified on the surface of the body – as differences in sex, colour, shape, etc. – and traced back to this original code in order to establish 'cause'.
>
> (Diprose and Vasseleu 1991: 150–1)

Hence bodily differences, including sexual differences and differences between normal healthy bodies and diseased bodies, are rendered as 'effects' of a cause which biomedicine alone can claim to envision with its various clinical and laboratory technologies. In the field of AIDS the immune system is a crucial device for the posing of a similar cause–effect relationship. In this instance cause is attributed to the functioning of the immune system proper, a circulating network of specialised cells (lymphocytes and macrophages) and their antibody and peptide products. The effect is generally understood by biomedicine to be the determination of the body's margins, the threshold where the body's inside meets what is outside. Haraway (1991), in her survey of immunological iconographies, concludes that the job of the discourses of immunology is, in general, the construction of an organism's boundaries.

In immunology's self-understanding the immune system constitutes the organism's integrity in the face of other organisms, the aspect of cellular specialisation which determines distinctions and relations between self and other. For the most part this relationship is conceptualised as intrinsically hostile, a microscopic struggle between species for predominance. The simple existence of other organisms is taken to present the constant possibility of colonisation or fusion. Most immunological textbooks begin with a statement something like the following:

> The human organism, from the time of conception, must maintain its integrity in the face of a changing and often threatening environment. Our bodies have many physiological mechanisms that permit us to adjust to basic variables such as temperature, supply of food and water, and physical injury. In addition, we must defend ourselves against invasion and colonisation by foreign organisms. This defence ability is called *immunity*.
>
> (Sell 1987: 3)

The habitual use of biomilitary analogy in figuring the immune system both flows from and contributes to this Darwinian concept of hostile organism relations. It contributes to the figuring of a particular kind of self/other boundary, organised through the dynamics of attack and defence. Before I go on to elaborate on this figuration, however, it is important to point out that such analogies do not colonise the entire field. Haraway's (1991) survey of immunological iconography indicates that biomilitary analogy is one metaphor among others, whose ascendancy is more evident in the explanation of certain diseases, particularly AIDS and cancers, than in others. Different immuno-iconographies are located in and help produce quite varying conceptualisations of health and illness, of bodies and bodily relations.

Haraway proposes that in the late twentieth century, the 'immune system' is a flexible iconic device which can stand for various kinds of bodily coherence and incoherence, and various delineations of self/other relations. She refers to it as a 'potent and polymorphous object of belief, knowledge and practice', and states:

> The immune system is an elaborate icon for principal systems of symbolic and material 'difference' in late capitalism. Pre-eminently a twentieth-century object, the immune system is a map drawn to guide recognition and misrecognition of self and other in the dialectics of western biopolitics. That is, the immune system is a plan for meaningful action to construct and maintain the boundaries for what may count as self and other in the crucial realms of the normal and the pathological.
>
> (Haraway 1991: 204)

The value of her analysis for this discussion is its sensitivity to immuno-logical iconography which does *not* rely on the rigidity and aggression which characterises bio-military concepts of boundary, and which in some cases is critical of the notion of organism boundary and organism individuality per se. She describes for example the transformations in the immunologist Richard Gershon's illustrations of the operation of the immune system, which utilise an orchestral rather than a military model. These begin in 1968 with diagrams of a well-organised and hierarchical/cooperative 'immunological orchestra', in-cluding a commanding conductor and clearly defined 'parts' for the lympho-cytes (immune system cells) to play, and end in 1982 in orchestral disarray, with several conductors, two conflicting prompters and some wayward musicians. Haraway remarks:

> The joke of single masterly control of organismic harmony in the symphonic system responsible for the integrity of 'self' has become a kind of postmodern pastiche of multiple centres and peripheries....All the actors which used to be on the stage set for the unambiguous and coherent biopolitical subject are still present, but their harmonies are definitely a bit problematic.
>
> (Haraway 1991: 207)

More suggestive still are Haraway's descriptions of the proposals of Neils Jerne and Leo Buss, whose work subverts in different ways the commitment to the policing of body boundaries found in other kinds of immunology. Jerne describes the immune system as an interpretive network, whose capacity to internally recognise an antigen (a potentially dangerous substance) depends upon the organism's continuity with its environment, rather than its defence against it, and upon a modular flexibility and absence of hierarchy in its organisation. Buss presents the immune system as a concatenation of hetero-geneous cell lineages, whose functions only coincide in specific ways and under specific conditions. Organism coherence, the 'individuality' of beings, is here somewhat accidental, if not chimerical.

In these cases immunologically determined organisms function through their porousness, their openness to their environment. Self/other distinctions in these image systems are always provisional and partial, rather than oppositional and absolute, and can be reorganised to meet specific circum-stances. Martin (1994), in her ethnographic study of immunological discourse, found similar kinds of non-military conceptualisations circulating among practising immunologists, instances where communicativeness and continuity with environment was stressed over organism separateness, mobilisation and war. She cites a conversation with one immunologist who declared himself to be a 'pacifist'.

> Stating 'I'm very pacifistic, I won't have a military,' he proceeded to develop an account of the immune system that was phrased entirely in

terms of a communication system: elements in the system 'orchestrate,' 'recognise,' 'present,' 'activate,' and 'turn on or off'.

(Martin 1994: 99)

So there is substantial evidence for the availability of alternative immuno-iconographies, with their different propositions about organism boundary, or their problematisation of 'organism' and 'boundary'. However, as I observed above, other non-military metaphors of organisation and action can be readily accommodated into the biomilitary model, subordinated to its narrative as military communication, and so on. Martin's study suggests that the determination of which metaphor predominates depends on what health or disease situation is under consideration. In this way immunology can manipulate the meaning of boundary in relation to different circumstances.

The immunological literature I used for this research consisted for the most part of technical and popular accounts, written either as direct explanations about AIDS (for example, the AIDS chapters in medical texts) or as more general accounts of the immune system which explicitly take the advent of AIDS into account. As we shall see, this literature generally evokes the most rigid and hierarchical militarised image systems available to immunology, subordinating the other available metaphors to this end. The reason for this militarisation in this site, as opposed to some of the more decentralised or 'chaotic' forms of immunology described by Haraway and Martin, is, I suggest, indicative of the sensitivity of biomedicine to social relations. The ascendancy of a remilitarised immune system in the 1980s constituted biomedicine's response to the crisis of sexual difference and sexual politics precipitated by the appearance of a new, fatal and sexually transmitted disease. The militarisation of the immune system in the face of AIDS is I suspect a symptom of panic in the face of infectious threat. It is an exemplary case where biomedicine translates broader cultural concerns and anxieties into its own technical narratives. In what follows I will examine in some detail the ways that this translation occurred, both at the level of the immune system itself and at the level of the relational, bodily morphology, the kind of self/other configuration, that the immune system describes.

THE IMMUNOLOGICAL NATION-STATE

I have suggested that certain ways of understanding relationships between immune system cells also entail certain biomedical propositions about body boundaries, between self and other, and also between the body's inside and its outside. Such boundary configurations are important considerations in conceptualising the ways that biomedicine deploys sexual identity as 'explanation' for HIV transmission, because as I argued in the previous chapter, body boundaries are caught up in the figuration of both sexual difference and contagious process.

In order to understand the ways these boundaries are both projected and naturalised, this section will investigate the ways that relationships between immune system cells are imagined in biomilitary immunology. How does recourse to military analogy in understanding the immune system condition the ways that the cells and peptides of the immune system are thought to interact with each other? What kind of functional divisions and hierarchies does it produce, and what kind of bodily boundaries does it assume and propose?

If, as I have suggested, bodies are habitually figured as social microcosms in biomedical discourse, the immune system is heavily implicated in contemporary forms of this figuration. In biomilitary immunology the immune system cells regularly appear as the armed defenders of the vulnerable nation-state body, where degrees of health are equated with degrees of mobilisation. This way of figuring the significance of the immune system in the body partakes of biomedicine's tendency, noted by Canguilhem, to resort to political philosophy when thinking about the relationship between cellular organisation and organism morphology. Canguilhem writes:

> In 1899, Ernst Heinrich Haeckel wrote 'The cells are truly independent citizens, billions of which compose our body, the cellular state.' Perhaps images such as the 'assembly of independent citizens' constituting a 'state' were more than just metaphors. Political philosophy seems to dominate biological theory. What man [sic] could say that he was a republican because he believed in cell theory or a believer in cell theory because he was a republican?
>
> (Canguilhem 1994: 171)

Biology and political philosophy share the conceptual problems associated with thinking through relationships between parts and the whole. Both discourses ask questions like: what organisation forms the most efficient kinds of hierarchy; to what degree should individuality be subsumed in the social or biological organism; what kinds of relationships between parts lend themselves to 'optimum' functioning? In biomedical discourse cells often stand in for populations in political discourse, to such an extent that cells are routinely referred to as 'populations', or 'dedicated populations' in medical texts.

Casting the immune system as the body's defence force can be considered as a way of solving some of these problems along particular lines. Jerne's immunology, for example, solves these problems along decentralised, cooperative lines, a kind of anarchic system in the classic sense of the term, where the immune system cells work through bilateral, reciprocal feedback and flexible antigen recognition capacities, without recourse to an overall command structure. This kind of immunology assumes neither internal structural stability nor boundary stability, but rather understands both cell relations and organism coherence as subject to flux and productive perturbation. In this sense it is subversive of 'statist', closed system tendencies in immunology.

If on the other hand the immune system is cast as a militarised hierarchy within the nation-state of the body, it solves problems of cell/organism relations along rigidly vertical lines, where cellular 'means' are devoted to whatever arc deemed to be organism 'ends'. The functions of the biomilitary immune system tend for this reason to be projected out of certain assumptions about the organism's or body's 'interests'.

As a *military* hierarchy the immune system also lends itself to two levels of scale for the figuring of sexual difference and its relationship to HIV transmission. First it provides an already gendered narrative at the level of the immune system cells, where masculine cellular heroics can be pitted against the feminising and perverting influences of disease. Second it proposes a rigid, unnegotiable boundary between the body's inside and outside, and between self and other, a strictly closed system. This boundary is thrown up by what are taken to be the organism's preoccupations with 'self' defence against contagion, and other possible incursions from 'otherness'. This model of health is also, as we shall see, implicitly gendered.

These two representational capacities of the biomilitary immune system are of crucial importance for my argument because they provide the narrative infrastructure for the figuring of sexual difference. As Canguilhem suggests, the normal and the pathological are relational terms, and in the case of AIDS their relationship cannot be extricated from those other relational binaries, those of masculine/feminine and particularly of male heterosexual/homosexual. This is so because, *from the outset, biomedicine's specification of AIDS pathology proceeded through its prior understandings of male homosexuality on the one hand and the immune system on the other.*

The highly heterogenous collection of symptoms[8] which were to be later dubbed the Acquired Immunodeficiency Syndrome were only first perceptible as *symptoms*, as indications of a deeper, underlying and unified pathology, because they could be delimited at the intersection of a social group, 'male homosexuals', and the failure of a bodily system, the immune system. Epidemiological accounts of the emergence of AIDS will in general simply state that the virus was first identified among 'young, homosexual men'. The very first scientific publication about what was to become AIDS identified its subjects as 'all active homosexuals' (Gottlieb 1981). The following is a fairly representative excerpt from an epidemiological account of AIDS' first appearance.

Although the first case of the disease syndrome was reported in 1978, it was not until 1981 that a cluster of several cases emerged indicating a possible problem. Several outbreaks of *Pneumocystis carinii* pneumonia and Kaposi's sarcoma, a rare form of cancer, were reported to the Centres for Disease Control (CDC)....Examination of the cluster of diseases disclosed that the problem appeared to be confined to previously healthy, young, homosexual males. These differing diseases

all showed the common phenomena of the evidence of immunosuppression, depleting the ability of patients to regulate and overcome
infection.

(Chavigny *et al.* 1989: 62)

As this excerpt indicates, in the attempt to organise this series of disparate
symptoms into a coherent entity and to assign it a cause, the notion of immune
deficiency served the first purpose and that of homosexuality the second. The
earliest hypotheses about the origins of immunosuppression attempted to pose
what were considered 'homosexual' practices as direct 'causes' of the syndrome. Some possible 'causes' proposed were the incompatibility of male
bodies with 'foreign' sperm, attendance at bathhouses, numbers of sexual
partners, the use of injectable drugs and exposure to faeces during sex
(Oppenheimer 1992).

Hence the status of male homosexuality as aetiology is inscribed at the very
beginning of the organisation of AIDS as a disease, and as *one important
condition of its emergence as a single disease*. As Patton (1990) speculates, the
disease AIDS might simply not have been organisable into a coherent nosology
at an earlier historical moment. She points out that in the absence of a concept
of the immune system developed during the 1960s and 1970s, as opposed to the
earlier and simpler concept of immunity, the disease 'AIDS' would have been
difficult to conceptualise. Similarly 'gay men' could only be regarded as a
population in the epidemiological sense as a result of the gay activism of the
preceding decade. She suggests that if some disease similar to HIV had
appeared before the 1960s it would have remained unlocatable and hence
undiagnosable, a random scattering of symptoms across a random cross-
section of the population. This historical specificity means that biomedicine's
concepts of male homosexuality cannot be completely disengaged from its
overall concepts of HIV pathology, and thus from the negative representation
against which a concept of immunological health is generated.

This inscription is narrated at the level of the immune system cells involved
in HIV infection, particularly as we shall see, in the drama of the T cell and its
'perversion' by HIV infection. I want to now discuss this narrative in detail,
focusing first on how the microscopic activity of the healthy immune system is
understood and then on the implosion of this system in the face of HIV
infection. I will then take the discussion up one level of scale to address the
relationship between this microscopic activity and the 'clean and proper' body
boundary it assumes and projects.

T CELLS AND SEXUAL DIFFERENCE

It is probably important to provide a description of the key players in the
militarised immune system. The immune system is understood to consist of
two kinds of immunity, innate and acquired, which operate through the two

most important lines of cells and many acellular compounds. Innate immunity, which involves reactions in a general way (inflammation, fever) to any kind of incursion, works through the phagocyte line of cells. Phagocyte cells are so named because they are said to 'kill' micro-organisms by 'eating' them, through engulfment and the breaking down of the organism. Most important of the phagocyte cells in relation to HIV infection are the macrophages. These are large cells which move around the body and in addition to engulfing micro-organisms also present 'antigen', that is 'foreign' molecules which provoke a specific immune response, to the other major line of cells, the lymphocytes.

The lymphocytes include the various kinds of T cells and B cells which are involved in acquired immunity. Acquired immunity refers to the immune system's capacity to react in a specific way to specific forms of infection. Acquired immunity is said to be more evolutionarily 'advanced' than innate immunity, because it is more 'strategic', dovetailing its reaction to infection so that it addresses the specific 'adversarial' features of the micro-organism. The lymphocytes produce specific kinds of antibody, which is a molecule specific to the antigen involved in the infection.

Among the various components which make up the immune system, it is the representation of the T cell and its relationships to the immune system as a whole which are most important for my argument. The T cells, named after their points of generation in the thymus, are divided into several subsets, the helper, killer and suppressor T cells, which include some further subsets. The T cells are my focus here because, first, they are the cells which the HIV initially 'invades'. Viruses live and reproduce through taking over the replicative capacities of other organism's cells, and the HIV 'targets' cells in the human body which have a particular molecule, the CD4 molecule, on their exterior cell wall. The virus is thought to bind itself to the cell surface via this molecule. There are several kinds of CD4 cells which the virus is thought to colonise, but its occupation of the T4 lymphocytes is considered to have the greatest consequences for the rest of the immune system (Tersmette and Miedema 1990).

The second reason for focusing on the T cells is that current conceptualisation of their healthy function and important position in the immune system has come about as a direct response to the emergence of AIDS. Shilts (1987) in his history of the 'discovery' of AIDS notes that in 1981, when the first symptoms of HIV infection began to appear in the United States, the T cell subsets had only recently been identified. Scientists were not sure of their function, nor what constituted 'normal' levels of T cell presence and activity. Since that time the immense research effort directed at the understanding of AIDS has involved the elevation of the T cells, particularly the T4 'helper' cells, to the highest position in the hierarchically conceptualised immune system.

In other words, current understandings of the healthy T cell subset's structures and functions, and of their positions in the immune system hierarchy, have been arrived at in a very strong negative relation to what

HIV is understood to do in the immune system. I have already observed that biomedical understandings of AIDS are marked through its association with marginal sexual identities, particularly gay masculinity. As a consequence the trace of this marking can be seen in the representation of the normal T cells, which are attributed with a 'normal' sexual identity. As I shall demonstrate, the distinction between the healthy T cell and T cell pathologies associated with HIV infection mark out a male heterosexual/homosexual distinction.

The T4 cell is habitually described as the director or commander of the immune system. As Martin (1994) points out, understanding the immune system as a 'system', as a set of complex interactive feedbacks, has particular implications for the ways that normalcy and pathology are figured. When the immune system is conceptualised as a tight hierarchy, rather than a more decentralised and uncertain system, conditions at the top of the hierarchy precipitate profound effects throughout the system, and can lead to its complete collapse or implosion.

HIV infection and subsequent pathology are understood to involve exactly this kind of systemic failure. Because HIV occupies the T4 'helper' cells as its most important point of infection, the T4 cells have thus been allocated their position at the top of the immune system hierarchy. As this textbook account of HIV infection puts it, impairment of the T4 cell function leads to impairment of the whole immune system.

> The relationship between the depletion of T4 lymphocytes and profound immunosuppression is clear. Since the T4 lymphocyte subset is responsible for the induction and/or regulation of virtually the entire immune system, the selective defect in this subset results in global impairment of components of immunity that depend, at least in part, on inductive signals from the T4 cell. These include defects in natural killer cells, virus-specific cytotoxic T cells, B cells, and monocytes.
>
> (Fauci and Lane 1991: 1404)

The importance of the T4 cell derives from its power to communicate unilaterally to the rest of the immune system cells. These cells issue other cells with 'instructions' in case of an 'attack' by antigen. This is one of the capacities which HIV infection impairs.

> HIV mainly attacks a white blood cell at the top of the [immune system] hierarchy, the T helper lymphocyte. The role of the T helper cell in the immune system is to switch on and control the activity of other cells in response to a stimulus such as infection.
>
> (Sattentau 1988: 49)

Biomilitary annexation of the communicative metaphor is evident in this more colloquial description of this process from a popular immunology text. The T4 cells are the 'generals', designed to sound the immunological alarm when the body's integrity is breached . . . .[They] have the special property of alerting other cells and bringing them into the attack. When they sense the presence of the enemy, they can release a chemical they have stored in their cytoplasm called an interleukin, a hormone-like substance that takes messages from one white blood cell or leucocyte to another.

(Dwyer 1988: 35)

These chemical 'orders' stimulate the immune activity of the other T cells, the B cells and the macrophages. It should be noted that representing these communications as 'orders' involves a repression of the reliance of the T cells on signals from the rest of the system, that is on the bilateral nature of communication. While it is readily acknowledged in most immunological texts that T cells depend on the antigen-presenting capacities of the macrophages before antigen can be recognised and 'orders' issued to the other T and B cells, this does not seem to disturb the assertion that the T4 cells exercise 'command' over the system.

What are the capacities which place the T4 cell, and the T cells more generally, at the top of the immunological hierarchy? T cells have the ultimate responsibility in the body for the determination of self/non-self distinctions, because they are equipped in various ways to 'see' the difference between 'self' antigen and 'foreign antigen'. This recognition capacity prevents the immune system attacking 'self' cells, and ensures that its activity is directed against 'foreign' organisms.

[The T4 cells] instruct both the T8 cytotoxic cells and the macrophages to proliferate in relation to a specific antigen, while the T suppressor cells prevent excessive damage to host tissue.

(Wilson 1990: 101)

It is around these self/non-self distinctions and the ability of T cells to determine them that the body is most readily figured as a nation-state, defended by its militarised population of immune system cells. Distinctions between 'self' cells and 'invader' cells are habitually expressed in what might be called 'statist' terms, as for example when we are told,

HIV can also infect macrophages – mobile cells which have the function of 'policing' the body's tissues, engulfing and destroying any foreign . . . microorganisms.

(Sattentau 1988: 52)

This figuration of the body as nation-state readily takes on nationalistic and implicitly racial overtones, where the T cell recognition capacity endows them with the function of state surveillance, particularly in popular immunology texts. T cells are thought to recognise 'self' through the display on the body's cells of class 1 MHC molecules, which are considered to be specific to the individual. Dwyer refers to these molecules as a 'vivid identification tag which can be "seen" ' by the T cells.

> [The] T cells are first taught how to recognise self. To enable self to be recognised, a collection of almost unique proteins is displayed by every cell in our own unique body. This display of 'self' provides the cells of the immune system with a biological mirror into which they can look to simultaneously compare 'self' with foreignness. From the very first development of the immune system, nothing is more important than making sure that we do not attack our own tissues.
>
> (Dwyer 1988: 33)

The T cell's capacity to 'read' the body's proliferating signature, its cellular identity, makes them responsible for the maintenance of the purity of what Dwyer describes as 'our biological nationality'. Biological nationality is repeatedly set against 'foreign invader' as the primary axis of self/other relations in immunology texts. One textbook compares the process of foreign antigen recognition with spotting one Chinese in a huge crowd of Anglo-Saxons (Roitt 1991). Nilsson's popular text *The Body Victorious* describes the same process as follows:

> [Each cell has] 'proof of identity' . . . these constitute the cell's identity papers protecting it against the body's own police force, the immune system . . . . The human body's police force is programmed to distinguish between *bona fide* residents and illegal aliens.
>
> (cited in Martin 1994: 54)

So on a hierarchical model of self/non-self distinction, the body appears as a highly mobilised and racially pure nation-state, one in which all difference is identified and destroyed by the T cells and their 'troops'. Again, this kind of absolute distinction depends on selectivity, because under other representational conditions immunology acknowledges the importance of 'benign' yet foreign micro-organisms that help in the regulation of the body's interior environment – in the gut, the mouth and so on.

What capacities are the T cells considered to have which secure their privileged position in this drama of self and other? The T cells are attributed with a kind of higher order of subjectivity than the other immune system cells, a subjectivity which corresponds to their more recent development in the 'evolution' of the immune system. This subjectivity comes complete with capacities for intentional action, as this rather breathless popular account indicates.

> Our sophisticated [T cell] system is a result of much experimentation over millions of years. The capacity of lymphocytes to recognise, to 'learn' by experience, retain memory function and have the self-discipline to act

differently and yet appropriately in varying situations make such cells truly wondrous creations of nature.

(Dwyer 1993: 57)

The attribution of subjectivity and intentionality is, Montgomery claims, typical of biomedical discourse. The various entities which constitute the body's cell 'population', and its enemies the viruses and bacteria,

are given the role of grammatical and epistemological subject, endowed with one or more tactical intentionalities. Whenever it acts (penetrates, mobilises, binds or proliferates) it does so only in accordance with certain strategies of purpose....Each agent performs a kind of pointillistic subjectivity, an embattled 'self', whose interaction with other such 'selves' defines the level of biological activity at this level of scale.

(Montgomery 1991: 370)

This attribution of subjectivity to the cells seems to me to be biomedicine's way of conceptualising the body's capacity for self-organisation and activity autonomous from the person's consciousness. Each cell is instead attributed with a kind of consciousness, but, as we shall see, assumptions about the consciousness and desires of the cell are also easily confused with those of the person in the biomedical imagination, treated as though they were simply a subdivision of personal consciousness.

The particular status which accrues to T cell subjects, particularly the T4 cells, derives from their 'intellectual' capacity for strategy in relation to the micro-organisms that they are set against. T cells are considered to be 'educated' cells, an education which takes place in the 'boot camp' of the thymus. This endows them with superior capacities for recognition, memory of previously present antigen, and with a strategic capacity to outmanoeuvre the 'adversarial strategies' of micro-organisms, as this immunology text puts it.

We are engaged in constant warfare with the microbes which surround us and the processes of mutation and evolution have tried to select micro-organisms which have evolved means of evading our defence mechanisms... [through] varied, often ingenious, adversarial strategies.

(Roitt 1991: 203)

In addition to education and specialisation, the subjectivity attributed to T cells is decidedly masculine. The hierarchy within the immune system is, as Martin (1994) also notes, organised along lines of sexual difference. The masculinity of the T cells is implied through the use of biomilitary analogy per se, and through the particular combination of intellectual and technical weapon capacity attributed to them. The T cells are the heroes of the immune system, and take part in manoeuvres which could be drawn from the pages of any war novel. In the following excerpt from a popular immunology text, the T4 cells are the strategists, while the killer (cytotoxic) T8 cells are represented as armed or technically augmented 'commandos' who 'kill' invading viruses 'concealed' inside the body's cells.

> The T cells that first detect antigens, known as helper T's, carry no weapons. Rather they send urgent chemical signals to a small squadron of allies in my body – the killer T cells....Like all T cells, killer T's are trained to recognise one specific enemy. When alerted by the helper T's, the squadron reproduces into an army. The killer T's are lethal. They can trigger a chemical process that punctures the cell membranes of bacteria or destroys infected cells before viruses inside have time to multiply.
>
> (Jaret 1986: 716)

Martin (1994) cites the text of an advertisement for a popular immunology book which says of the T cell 'You owe your life to this little guy, the Rambo of the body's immune system', and Dwyer (1988) regularly refers to lymphocytes as 'he'. By contrast Martin (1994) conjectures that the macrophage cells, which are figured as non-specialist and 'primitive' in evolutionary terms, are often feminised. They are represented as the 'housekeepers' of the immune system, which clean up after the real T cell action. The important consistency in this attribution of sexual identity to cells is that, while macrophages and the B cells change sex from text to text (macrophages appear as the circulating 'police' of the immune system in an earlier quote, for example), T cells are, as far as I can tell, *always heroically masculine.*

While sexual difference is used in this way to figure hierarchies of command, metaphors of masculinity are also used to indicate *immunocompetence*, the vigour and efficacy of the immune system. Femininity, effeminacy and emasculation are on the other hand used as analogues for kinds of *immuno-compromise*, the term used to designate pathological deficit in immune system function. One textbook states, for example, 'The spleen is a very effective blood filter, removing *effete* red and white blood cells' (Roitt 1991: 110; emphasis mine). Further on in this text we find an analogy made between the process of anergy, where B cells can recognise and bind antigen but remain inactivated, with the impotence of an 'aging roué'.

> These anergic cells could bind antigen to their surface receptors but could not be activated. Like the aging roué wistfully drinking in the visual attractions of some young belle, these tolerised lymphocytes could 'see' the antigen but lack the ability to do anything about it.
>
> (Roitt 1991: 186)

As this citation implies, relations between cells are habitually figured as kinds of sexual relations, particularly relations between micro-organisms, or their antigen markers, and the T cells. Interestingly it would seem that 'normal' healthy relations between lymphocyte and virus, where the lymphocyte has the upper hand, are sometimes represented as heterosexual, conjugal relationships. So, for example, one textbook explains antigen in the following way.

A man cannot be a husband without a wife and a molecule cannot be an antigen without a corresponding antiserum or antibody – or a T-cell receptor.

(Roitt 1991: 65)

While the sex of the T cell is somewhat ambiguous in this analogy, Martin cites a passage from a popular immunology text which leaves no doubt as to both the masculinity and husbandly heterosexuality of the T cell.

In order to slip inside a cell, a virus has to remove its protein coat, which it leaves outside on the cell membrane. The viral coat hanging outside signals the passing T cell that viral hanky panky is going on inside. Like the jealous husband who spots a strange jacket in the hall closet and *knows* what's going on in the upstairs bedroom, the T cell takes swift action. It bumps against the body cell with the virus inside and perforates it.

(cited in Martin 1994: 59)

This summarises what seem to me to be the most important features of the representation of the healthy immune system and the T cells since the advent of AIDS. The elevation of the T cells to the top of a hierarchised and militarised immune system has been accomplished in part through their attribution with a specific kind of command masculinity. The T cells, particularly the T4 cells, are said to have a capacity for rationality, vigilance and strategy, and their heterosexuality is understood as a mode of relationship to infection.

I do not claim that the masculinity of the lymphocytes or the figuring of the body as threatened nation-state is exclusive to post-AIDS immunological discourse. It is evident from Brandt's (1987) twentieth-century history of syphilis that a nationalism and a masculine sex is attributed to the cells involved in immunity throughout this century. I suggested in the first chapter that analogies are readily made in biomedicine between bodies and social systems, and the contemporary figuring of the immunologically healthy body as military nation-state recapitulates a long history of such figurations, which seem to emerge in times of social 'emergency'.[9]

Nevertheless, AIDS-induced immunology mobilises these existing image systems in a particular way, and gives them certain new inflections. The elevation of the T cell to a command position in the immune system is crucial here, because of the kinds of functions and subjectivity attributed to this cell. In functional terms this elevation has the effect of reorganising the system into a steep hierarchy, one where the stakes are raised around the distinction between self and non-self. This distinction became all important in the wake of AIDS because, as I will demonstrate, HIV infection is imagined to work through the confusion between self and non-self. In terms of the subjectivity of the T cell, a clear equation is made between its (his?) heroic heterosexual masculinity and immunocompetence, the intact and vigorous immune system.

67

These attributes are crucial because HIV infection and pathology are understood to involve the simultaneous 'emasculation' of the T cells and the subsequent erosion of self/other distinctions. HIV infection of the T4 cell is represented as the perversion of the cell's heroic heterosexuality, a perversion which leads to the loss of all its other 'intellectual' attributes, those of surveillance and recognition.

This initial emasculation takes various forms. I have already commented that lymphocyte relations with invading micro-organisms are sometimes represented as conjugal. In the case of HIV infection these relations are habitually represented as forms of perverse sexuality, where the T cell is actually described as being 'compromised' by HIV infection (Sattentau 1988). If conjugal cell relations are ones in which the T cell has the upper hand, HIV infection inverts this power relationship. In the following account the virus appears as a *femme fatale*, a feminised sexual killer, whose victim is the T cell.

> When HIV bumps into the surface membrane of a CD4 cell, an intricate interlocking occurs that will lead to the death of the cell after it has served the virus's purpose. It all reminds one of that terrifying piece of micro-nature where the female praying mantis needs the male to copulate with her so that she can reproduce, but has worked out a way of feeding at the same time. Before the sex act is completed she bites off the head of her mate.
>
> (Dwyer 1993: 152)

On the other hand the virus is often endowed with the power to seduce the T cell into a consensual but perverse union, a power which is regarded as part of its strategy. In the words of one text,

> A critical structural feature of HIV appears to be the outer envelope. It has been well documented that the glycoprotein portion, gp120, interacts *avidly and specifically* with the CD4 molecule, which is expressed predominantly on the T4 cells and acts as a *high-affinity receptor* for HIV.
>
> (Hamburg *et al.* 1990: 1047; emphasis mine)

I have stressed certain terms which recur whenever immunological texts talk about the power of HIV to bind with the T cell CD4 receptor, terms which point towards the understanding of infection in erotic terms. While the 'perversity' of this sexual desire between T cell and virus is usually only implied, it appears as specifically 'gay' sex in this text.

> The CD4 molecule has a binding *avidity* for the gp110 envelope glycoprotein of HIV-1, and this appears to be a major determinant of cellular *susceptibility* to natural infection with HIV-1. Evidence that the CD4 molecule functions as a *receptor* for the virus is fourfold . . . when human cell lines that ordinarily do not express the CD4 molecule . . . are

rendered *CD4 positive* by transfection with the human CD4 gene, virus binds, and the cells are *permissive* for viral replication.

(McDougal *et al.* 1989: 22; emphasis mine)

Here we can see the use of a number of terms which are commonly used in explanations for the relationship between gay masculinity and HIV infection. Infected T cells are promiscuous, susceptible, receptive and most startlingly of all CD4-positive, a formulation which mimics that of the common term 'HIV-positive'. In other words HIV infection involves the transformation of the heroic, heterosexual T cells into gay male T cells that collaborate with the virus in various ways.

This 'feminisation' or 'homosexualisation' of the T cell transforms the T cell into a kind of viral *representative*, precipitating a series of catastrophic events in the immune system. The virus's self-replicative strategy works through the harnessing of the intentionality of the immune system cells to its own purposes. This colonisation takes place at the level of the T cell's genetic identity, where the virus inserts its own 'instructions' for viral replication.

When the virus enters its host cell, a viral enzyme called reverse transcriptase exploits the viral RNA as a template to assemble a corresponding molecule of DNA. The DNA travels to the cell nucleus and inserts itself among the host's chromosomes, where it provides the basis for viral replication.

(Gallo 1987: 39)

This exploitation of the T cell's genetic material represents a perversion of the body's primary instructions for identity maintenance in the biomedical imagination. Because it infiltrates the T cell's genetic code, the HIV is understood to be able to 'reprogramme' the T cell's capacities to recognise differences between self and other. Viral infection is conceptualised as a perversion of the immune system's scopic economy, so that the T cells are both rendered selectively blind and induced to 'turn a blind eye' to HIV infection.

This failure to see is partly due to the protean and duplicitous 'appearance' of the virus itself, which has a range of disguising and mimicking strategies. Once in the body it may for example 'mimic certain molecules normally found on cells of uninfected individuals'. The virus itself displays a high degree of biological variability, so that it can for example alter its viral envelope (Tersmette and Miedema 1990), or, more simply, change its disguise. HIV may also induce the immune system's misrecognition of self, causing it to 'see' its own host tissue as hostile and hence attack it. Initially the immune system is thought to 'see' the virus, but its repertoire of mutability ensures that the immune system response is ineffectual in finding all of the viral material. The net effect of long-term HIV infection is a 'blind' immune system, unable to 'see' any form of invader at all.

The consequence of this capitulation of the T cells to the virus is in other words the eventual complete collapse of self/other distinction as it is figured in immunology. The body loses its biological national boundaries and is overtaken by 'foreign' organisms because its standing army has been successfully infiltrated, perverted and demobilised. Its dehierarchisation is equated with debilitating chaos and dissolution, death by a kind of infectious entropy where the closed system is thrown open to its dangerous outside.

IMMUNOLOGY AND BODY BOUNDARY

So it seems that the immune system provides biomedicine with a kind of corporeal nanotheatre,[10] or perhaps a nanocinema, where the sexual relations and sexual identities understood to participate at the social level in HIV infection can be rendered into scenarios and played out at a microscopic level. HIV infection involves a kind of 'homosexualisation' or feminisation of the T cell and hence the whole immune system, the perversion of a highly organised system of heterosexual, masculine 'self-protection' which is equated with both the stability of a closed system and the interests of a mobilised nation-state. I will say a great deal more about this equation in the next chapter.

This personification of the cells is not, as Montgomery (1991) implies, restricted to the immune system. The attribution of sexual identity to cells can be seen in other biomedical explanations for bodily processes, conception for example, that involve sexual relations and the social relations said to derive from them. Martin (1992) describes this kind of personification in representations of sperm and ova at the point of conception, where sperm appear as eager, competitive little masculine homunculi, which fight to penetrate the membrane of the large passive ova.

As a consequence of this habit of personification, concepts of sexual identity can be readily imported into biomedical explanations for HIV at the microscopic level. And because the direction of biomedical explanation works from the microscopic up to the macroscopic, these concepts of sexual identity are magnified outwards, projected onto the bodies that they claim to explain. This seems to me to be a crucial representational strategy through which biomedicine interprets and configures bodies according to its concepts, as I claimed in the first chapter. In this section I want to investigate the relationships between these immunological narratives and the kind of sexed subjectivities and body boundaries they project and work to naturalise.

In the case of the healthy or immunocompetent body, its most telling feature is the equation it makes between self-enclosure, singularity and cleanliness. Immunological health is assumed to consist of perfect internal cleanliness, where the inside of the body is perfectly distinct from and untouched by what is outside. Immunological texts sometimes go to extraordinary representational lengths to keep this distinction intact. As one popular text states in its introduction:

It seems to me logical to begin discussing immunity by explaining from what exactly we need protection. The body's answer appears to be 'everything'. We human beings recognise our bodies as *sacrosanct, and do not allow anything foreign to remain in our micro-environment*. The only exception we make involves certain bacteria and fungi that live on our inner surface – the lining of our intestinal tract. Strictly speaking these organisms are not 'inside' us and indeed they are attacked viciously if they penetrate the delicate mucous membrane, a sort of inner skin, that protects us from mouth to anus.

(Dwyer 1993: 5; emphasis mine)

Here we have a representation of the body which literally turns itself inside out rather than admit the possibility of benign co-habitation between self and micro-organismic other. What is perhaps even more interesting here is that this citation makes explicit the extent to which the self-defending intentionality of the immune system already commented on is assumed to reflect the intentionality of the person. The immune system effectively acts as the delegate of what is assumed to be a self-protecting and self-identical consciousness, which regards its bodily boundaries as 'sacrosanct'. The immune system offers a way for this consciousness to implement itself at a molecular and cellular level in its body, providing military aid, no less, to this desire. Its task is to ensure the internal homogeneity of the body, to secure the body as a place for the proliferation of self-sameness, represented by the body's infinitely multiplying 'unique' signature, its 'self' antigens. Infection, on this immuno-logic, is anything which might introduce an element at variance with this repetition of sameness, anything which might make it exceed its state as a perfect singularity, a one. This singularity acts as an absolute threshold, in that *any* incursion into the body of what does not conform to identity constitutes an *absolute* threat.

The absolute threshold of clean self-sameness also accounts for the curious morphology of the immunocompetent body. It is a fantasy where the body surface forms a seamless armour, whose impermeability protects a vulnerable interior from hostile exterior. The hyperbolic extent of this enclosure is given graphic force in some immunological texts. Haraway describes a diagram of the 'Evolution of Recognition Systems' in an immunological text which begins with amoebas and 'culminates in the evolution of the mammals, represented without comment by a mouse and a *fully suited spaceman*' (Haraway 1991). Dwyer (1993) invites us to understand the body as 'an ultra-important, indeed ultra-secret industrial complex' where the immune system constitutes its security force. In both these cases we can discern a displacement, where the military analogies used to describe cellular immune system activity are read onto the boundaries of the immunocompetent body, so that these boundaries appear as impenetrable armour.

In this way the vigilant, hierarchical, militarised immune system organises a highly individuated body, a body whose singularity cannot be compromised, at least not without a fight. I want to suggest that post AIDS immunology strives to reconfigure bodies along these lines of individuation as a prophylactic measure. Individuation works both as a kind of psychic prophylaxis, in the sense that it guards against the anxieties associated with contagion, and as the basis for social prophylaxis, for determining who should be 'targeted' for public health education to prevent epidemic contagion. I will discuss this second kind of prophylaxis in the next chapter, but here I want to consider the first kind, the subjective significance of the model of health and the threat of contagion proposed by the immunocompetent body.

When I refer to the immunocompetent body as 'individuated' I am referring to a particular, hegemonic way of organising bodily coherence which confers subjectivity through the assertion of rigid body boundaries between inside and outside and between self and other. I speculated in the first chapter that biomedical representations of bodily normalcy may play a part in the construction of subjective 'imaginary anatomies'. It seems to me that this model of immunocompetence could be considered an instance where a biomedical normative morphology colludes with and extends the construction of the 'imaginary anatomy' of that which Kristeva (1982) terms the 'clean and proper body', the docile, social body of individuation and stable identity. I want to discuss her account of this anatomy in some detail here because it articulates a crucial relationship between the subjective adoption of culturally determined body boundaries and the fear of contagion, understood in its broadest sense.

In the previous chapter I argued that the cultural 'nature' of sexed bodies implied that they were always open to kinds of social completion and reconfiguration. Kristeva's account of the production of the 'clean and proper' body traces one very important form of the body's social configuration, the organisation of the discrete, hierarchical, individuated body out of the polymorphous perversity of the infant body. Central to this process, Kristeva argues, is the closing off of the body's possibilities for fragmentation, for confusion with 'other' bodies. The 'I' of individuated identity is produced through a particular mapping of the body. It must be made 'discrete', existing in perfect separation from and exclusion of other bodies. That is, it is brought into existence through the assertion of a strict self/non-self distinction, the same distinction said to be practised by the vigilant immune system.

The 'clean and proper body' is, as Grosz notes, 'a body bound up and constrained within its skin in quite particular ways' (Grosz 1986: 107). The discrete subjectivity implied by individual identity can only be brought into being by making the limits of the 'I' coterminous with the body's outer surface, its skin. Containment within its skin surface is the condition upon which it can count as a singularity. The body ego of individualistic subjectivity relies upon the impermeability of its skin to guard against disturbance from outside itself, from external objects and from 'others'. It is not surprising that the efficacy of the skin in 'protecting' the body from otherness is often mentioned in immunological texts. One text states, for example, 'skin is almost impenetrable and a superb barrier to infection while its integrity is unbreached' (Dwyer 1988: 126). Another immunologist writes:

> The most potent immediate protection against [infection] is an intact and healthy body surface. Only when the skin is broken or cut ... are the conditions favourable for the invasion of our bodies by these foreign enemies.
>
> (cited in Montgomery 1991: 365)

What is significant in these accounts is the way that skin appears as virtually non-organic. It simply functions to seal off the vulnerable interior from contact with the outside, without being itself affected by this 'outside'. Haraway, however, points out that the imaging technology that immunology relies on to shore up such claims can also be used to subvert them.

> Even the most reliable western individuated bodies ... neither stop nor start at the skin, which is itself something of a teeming jungle threatening illicit fusions, especially from the perspective of a scanning electron microscope.
>
> (Haraway 1991: 215)

In other words, the representation of skin as inside/outside boundary involves a degree of selectivity in immunological practice, an emphasis on some functions and images at the expense of others, including the image of our skin alive with microbial lifeforms. Its selectivity here is driven not by organic 'evidence' but by the phantasmic possibility of well-defended internal purity and bodily safety.

The attainment of the 'clean and proper' body also entails the assertion of a rigid inside/outside boundary in the body, as a corollary to the self/other boundary. Biomilitary immunological representations of the relations between bodily surface and interior tend to avoid points of confusion between them, and the attainment of the clean and proper body involves the same kinds of avoidance. This avoidance arises in both cases from anxiety over the 'contagious' possibilities presented by correspondence between inside and outside.

I put 'contagious' in inverted commas here because it has a different although related meaning in the two discourses under discussion. In the case of Kristeva's account, 'contagion' can be used in the most inclusive sense as a term which connotes all the forms of anxiety involved in blurring the self/other distinction. I argued in the previous chapter that, while bodies are open to modes of social completion, their coherence is also unstable and provisional, prone to disintegration at the margins. In Kristeva's account the 'clean and proper' body is unstable in the sense that it must be maintained against the dangers of engulfment, both from the fluid excesses of its own organic interior

73

and from the excessiveness of the other's body. The achievement of a clean inside/outside distinction is, however, always confounded by the impossibility of completely enculturating certain bodily processes, processes which involve the body's fluid products, its uncontrollable secretions. Processes of sexuality, incorporation and excretion cannot be controlling on the model of identity and singularity, as Grosz (1994) points out.

> Body fluids attest to the permeability of the body, its necessary dependence on an outside, its liability to collapse into this outside (that is what death implies), to the perilous divisions between the body's inside and outside. They affront a subject's aspiration towards autonomy and self-identity. They attest to a certain irreducible 'dirt' or disgust, a horror of the unknown or the unspecifiable that permeates, lurks, lingers, and at times leaks out of the body, a testimony of the fraudulence or impossibility of the 'clean' and 'proper'.
>
> (Grosz 1994: 193–4)

Body fluids and their associated processes are problematic for the maintenance of the 'clean and proper' imaginary anatomy because they involve both the ingress of that which belongs 'outside' the body – food, the body parts of the sexual partner, the effluvia of other's bodies – and the egress of that which is internal to the body – urine, faeces, sperm, saliva, vaginal secretions. They are processes which attest to bodies as permeable, as traversed with vulnerable orifices, as processual, as necessarily extending beyond singularity into confused relations which cannot be well designated by number. In this sense they all partake of the horror associated with the contagious, the anxiety provoked by the spectre of uncontrollable proliferation and the body's dissolution back into nature.

The biomedical concept of infectious contagion is in a sense a subset of this abjected contagion, but at the same time the subjective and representational anxieties provoked by infectious contagion do not always observe this distinction. While in strict biomedical terms infectious contagion only pertains to body fluids that convey microbial agents, fears of infection and illness can readily stand in for more general fears of subjective engulfment. To put it more succinctly, fears of otherness are easily translated into fears of infection of various kinds. This translation can be seen, for example, in the ease with which a generalised homophobia abruptly became a fear of 'gay plague' with the appearance of AIDS in the early 1980s.

The significance of the 'clean and proper body' derives then from the impossibility of its attainment, an impossibility which Kristeva says haunts the subject and constantly reanimates his/her drive to bodily mastery, to reinvestment in its boundaries. It seems to me that the seamless, armoured skin of the immunocompetent body gains its representational impetus from this anxiety, in that it works to guard against the engulfment of the subject by the contagious dangers of other bodies, and the reciprocal dangers of subjectivity seeping away from within. AIDS gives this anxiety an adequate referent, as a mortal disease transmitted through bodily confusion, the 'exchange of body fluids' warned against in AIDS education literature. The intensification and reinforcement of body boundary is carried out in the age of AIDS as a means of projecting infectious capacities safely 'outside' the body, as effects of other bodies, and simultaneously guarding against this infection. As Butler puts it, otherness becomes associated with the contagious dangers of the excremental on the logic of the 'clean and proper' body.

> What constitutes through division the 'inner' and 'outer' worlds of the subject is a border and boundary tenuously maintained for the purposes of social regulation and control. The boundary between the inner and outer is confounded by those excremental passages in which the inner effectively becomes outer, and this excreting function becomes, as it were, the model by which other forms of identity-differentiation are accomplished. In effect, this is the mode by which others become shit. For inner and outer worlds to remain utterly distinct, the entire surface of the body would have to achieve an impossible impermeability. This sealing of its surfaces would constitute the seamless boundary of the subject.
>
> (Butler 1990: 133–4)

But there is a profound asymmetry in this process of projection, in relation to which sexual identities become associated with contagion at the level of institutional discourses. In the introduction I marshalled some examples of public health education policy which indicated that women and gay men were the principal 'targets' of HIV transmission control, while heterosexual men were not addressed in the same way. It seems to me that this asymmetry is in part due to immunology's instillation of the 'clean and proper' body as the immunocompetent body. The rigidly bounded, immunocompetent body works to associate both feminine bodies and gay male bodies with the dangers of contagion, because both these bodies are understood to be permeable, orificial bodies which both absorb and transmit contagious body fluids. It simultaneously works to exempt phallic bodies, the imaginary anatomies of heterosexual masculinity, from association with infectious process, because these bodies are understood to conform to the morphology of immunocompetence. They exercise a vigilant body boundary, and hence maintain a clean and stable bodily system.

The marginalisation and pathologisation of feminine bodies through the privileging of individuated forms of subjectivity has been demonstrated by a number of feminist writers in relation to both medical and political discourses (Young 1985; Pateman 1988). They point out that feminine bodies, with their capacity for receptive sexuality, pregnancy and giving birth to other bodies, cannot be made to conform to a singularity, a one, with its simple self/other oppositions. The pregnant body can count neither as singular nor exactly as a double, in that the foetus cannot be completely incorporated, that is mastered by the woman's consciousness, nor can it be autonomous from her. The foetus is neither simply an extension of her body, a part of her self, nor can it stand as completely other to herself. Pregnancy and birth also present problems for simple inside/outside oppositions, and thus for the demarcations of corporeal boundary, as Young points out:

> Pregnancy...challenges the integration of my bodily experience by rendering fluid the boundary between what is within, myself, and what is outside, separate. I experience my insides as the space of another, yet my own body....The integrity of my body is undermined in pregnancy not only by this externality of the inside, but by the fact that the boundaries of my body are in flux. In pregnancy I lose the sense of where my body ends and the world begins.
>
> (Young 1985: 31)

Pregnancy summarises the permeability of the feminine body in that it is regarded as the result of its capacity for receptive sexuality, for ingress of the penis, and as the precursor to birth, when that which is within emerges. But on the model of the immunocompetent body, such permeability can only appear as synonymous with the confusion which is infection.[11] In the case of HIV transmission, which is associated exactly with bodily effluvia, these permeable bodies seem, within the representational framework provided by the valorisation of the 'clean and proper', to be sites for both the leakage and incorporation of body fluids, for the intensification and spread of infection. Lack of proper boundary immediately connotes the contagious dangers of fluidities and continuities and, as Grosz observes, this capacity is associated with the feminine body in a number of cultural discourses.

> An hypothesis: that in the west, in our time, the female body has been constructed not only as a lack or absence, but with more complexity, as a leaking, uncontrollable, seeping fluid, as formless flow, as viscosity, entrapping, secreting, as lacking...self containment....My claim is that women's corporeality is inscribed as a mode of seepage....The metaphorics of uncontrollability...the deep-seated fear of absorption, the association of femininity with contagion and disorder, the undecidability of the limits of the female body...are all common themes in literary and cultural representations of women.
>
> (Grosz 1994: 203)

A similar associative chain links the gay male body to contagion, although in this case the association of otherness with the excremental that Butler articulates finds direct expression. Anal sex is both the genital practice which connotes gay masculinity, and the exemplary 'act of HIV transmission'.[12] Significantly it is the receptive position in anal sex that is nominated in biomedicine as the act associated with contagion. One epidemiological study states, for example,

In all the major cohort studies of prevalent HIV-1 infection, receptive anal intercourse has been the major mode of transmission when other risk factors . . . were controlled.

(Winkelstein *et al.* 1989: 125)

While anal sex requires both an insertive and a receptive partner, it is the position of 'passivity', of the reception of the penis and semen of 'others' which is nominated as the deadly act. It is the permeability of the gay male body, rather than its phallic or penetrative capacities, which place it on the side of contagion.

The rigid boundary of the immunocompetent body helps to naturalise an association between sexually receptive bodies and HIV infection. The establishment of boundary is equated with the successful enculturation of the body, its sealing off from dangerous associations with the natural world. Orificial, permeable bodies are on the other hand bodies which are associated with the encroachment of nature upon culture.

Because the heterosexual male body is figured as always sexually active, the phallic body which penetrates but is never penetrated, it is protected from this association. At the same time the projection of contagious capacities and boundary breaches onto feminine and gay male bodies is a sign of anxiety about the stability of this phallic status. Grosz observes that the repetitive figuration of women's bodies as contagious and engulfing,

may be a function of the projection outwards of their corporealities, the liquidities that men seem to want to cast out of their own self-representations.

(Grosz 1994: 203)

In other words, men are able to secure a self-image as stable, self-enclosed and individuated, untroubled by fragmentation and confusion, only through projection of these fluid and cloacal qualities onto women and, in the context of AIDS, gay men. The association between anality and contagion is, I suspect, particularly important in this projection, because anal eroticism has perhaps the greatest potential to undermine the phallic body's claims to integrity, and hence to the status associated with masculine heterosexuality. The possibilities of anal pleasure, with its connotations of passivity and the abdication of power, are perhaps the possibilities which require the most violent repulsion from the phallic 'imaginary anatomy'.[13] The advent of AIDS has donated extra force to this repulsion, leading to the relentless association found in AIDS discourse between gay masculinity, anal sex and HIV transmission. As Patton notes, in biomedical AIDS research,

Rarely are gay men imagined to do anything *other* than anal sex . . . . Even in current epidemiology, gay men with multiple exposure routes (gay haemophiliacs, gay drug injectors, gay transfusion patients) are counted as 'gay' without regard to their particular sexual practices.

(Patton 1990: 119)

It is my contention that biomedicine assists in the articulation and naturalisation of this projection in the age of AIDS, and doubtless at other times. In the next chapter I will take up this contention in relation to epidemiology and the institutions of public health.

To complete my discussion of the sexuality of the immunocompetent body, I want to return to the AIDS chapter in a particular popular immunology text, *The Body at War* (Dwyer 1993), in order to summarise a number of the themes and relationships already discussed.

THE PRIMAL SCENE OF HIV INFECTION

I have speculated about the extent to which the T cell augmented immune system reciprocates a rigid body boundary, and the kind of implicit homophobia and misogyny involved in setting up this model of singularity. Sections of Dwyer's *The Body at War* help make these relationships between immune system and implicitly sexed boundary explicit.

These relationships are depicted in the scene of HIV transmission which appears in the book's chapter about AIDS. My contention is that this 'scene of transmission', which depicts an episode of anal sex between men, can be interpreted as a kind of primal scene for HIV immunology. It is also a graphic instance of the kind of cinematic quality often evident in the biomedical imagination, its drive to 'picture' processes as scenarios, to engage in *mis en scène*, as it were.

I am using the term 'primal scene' much as it is used in psychoanalysis, to refer to a traumatic sexual scene which is both assumed and forgotten, and which acts to shape discourse without appearing in it. Most immunological discourse about AIDS simply assumes that the scene of sexual infection has already taken place, and articles typically begin with sentences like 'When the virus enters its host cell...' (Gallo 1987). The inclusion of this scene in Dwyer's text has allowed me to verify what might otherwise remain intuitions about immunology's conceptualisations of sexual difference as 'cause' of infection. At the same time I am not suggesting that this 'scene' is anything other than a foundational fantasy, a 'scene' elaborated in the biomedical imagination, whose inclusion helps to expose immunology's assumptions about relationships between gay masculinity and contagion. As Freud (1955) suggested in his analysis of the Wolf Man's dream, the primal scene may be a screen memory, a retrospectively constructed rather than a recollected scenario.

In the section entitled 'The Spread of Infection', Dwyer discusses the 'origin' of the AIDS epidemic as an event located at the confluence of two other events. One event was biological, the evolution of a deadly virus transmitted during sexual activity, and the other event was social, the 'gay revolution' of the 1970s. I have already provided an account of the extent to which the figuring of HIV infection at the cellular level plays out a miniature scenario of perverse, homosexual sex. Dwyer uses a very telling rhetorical strategy which could stand as the moment when gay sex is miniaturised in the biomedical imagination, shrunk down to a microbial scale like the heroes in *The Incredible Journey*. He writes:

> It is important to examine homosexuality as a co-factor in the dissemination of this disease....For this reason scientists have had to draw aside the veil of privacy that usually surrounds people's sexual habits and place the intimate behaviour of gay men under the microscope in the hope that they may learn more of the way that AIDS is spread.
>
> (Dwyer 1993: 175)

When the reader looks through this microscope s/he finds 'James', whose story is related in reverse order. First the microscope pictures James as an 'AIDS case' in hospital, someone for whom the inside and the outside of the body has lost all distinction. The surface of his body is inscribed with the stigmata produced through the cellular activity of the 'foreign' organisms who have made him their creature.

> James, lying pale and obviously exhausted in the bed, was only thirty-two years old but looked twenty years older. He had recently lost his eye-sight as a virus infected and destroyed his retina....Standing out from his pallor were numerous round purplish discolourations, some rising from the skin in discrete lumps....Cancerous cells developed in the blood vessels of this man's skin and were now multiplying and migrating out of control: Kaposi's sarcoma.
>
> (Dwyer 1993: 177)

The scene then moves out of the hospital to the site of HIV transmission as it is habitually represented in the conservative imagination, the gay bath house, whose 'steamy atmosphere' connotes both illicit pleasure and infectious miasma. The reader, with the aid of the very useful microscope (which here doubles as the keyhole exploited in a hundred pornographic scenarios), is then treated to the following eye-witness account of James, caught in the act.

> His first lover that day was an old friend with whom he had experienced sex on many occasions and they moved into the privacy of one of the dressing rooms for their encounter...in this first sexual session James not only kissed his lover on the mouth, but took his lover's penis and semen into his mouth, and then he kissed with his tongue his lover's anus...one of his lovers, to increase further the pleasure he was experiencing, twisted and pushed his fist into James' well-lubricated anus...he willingly accepted the pain because his sexual pleasure far

outweighed the physical discomfort involved. By the end of the day five different men had discharged their sexual fluid into his rectum and he had returned the favour for three of them.

(Dwyer 1993: 179)

If according to immunologic the functioning immune system is taken to constitute an hermetically sealed body protected by an armoured boundary, the transgression of this boundary leads conversely to a dysfunctional immune system. By permitting the breaching of his boundaries in anal sex, James is represented as precipitating a series of breaches throughout his body, creating a conduit for the HIV to travel straight from his anus into his T cells.

[James] may have taken infected sexual fluid from a man with AIDS into his mouth or rectum and then flushed open his blood vessels [with orgasm and amyl nitrate] facilitating the ease with which a virus or some other deadly micro-organisms might enter his body. When you realise that the surfaces of his mucous membranes were already breached by his genital sores and the traumatic nature of his lovemaking, it appears that James was actually inviting the deadly guest to come inside.

(Dwyer 1993: 180)

This conduit finally terminates in the victorious breaching of the cell wall of the lymphocytes and the 'occupation' of the body. The HIV virus can 'open a window in the membrane of the T4 cell and march right in'.

There are two aspects of this 'primal scene' which seem particularly pertinent for my argument. The first is the way the narrative draws upon all of the panoptic strategies of biomedicine, for which the microscope stands synecdochally. It first miniaturises the social scene it wishes to examine, and so maps itself onto the interpretive strategies of the laboratory, which read cultural practices into the behaviour of microbial life. It then moves in quick succession through the clinical gaze, which concerns itself with the relationship between the patient's symptoms and their invisible bodily interior, to the epidemiological gaze, which pictures the 'act of transmission' for biomedicine, and which in this case demonstrates a certain debt to a pornographic gaze. Finally it returns to the level of the cells, picturing a direct relationship between breach of bodily boundary and breach of the T cell's integrity. In moving so effortlessly through these different optic registers and levels of scale it provides a succinct map of biomedicine's claims to visualise the entire social field of bodily activity, from the molecular to the national, from the external and publicly visible to the most recessive and private. The significance of this claim is taken up in detail in the next two chapters.

The second theme that it summarises and makes explicit is the relationship I have suggested between immune system activity, body boundary and sexed subjectivity. The gay male body is here represented as the negation of the immunocompetent body, a body whose sovereign consciousness is fatally unconcerned with the protection of its integrity. This lapse of vigilance in the policing of bodily boundary translates directly to a lapse of vigilance in the immune system. So just as James consciously permits and even desires 'others' to penetrate his body, so too his immune system allows or even welcomes the penetration of his 'self' cells with the deadly foreignness of the HIV virus. Not only does the HIV-infected immune system fail to detect otherness in the virus's presence, it gradually loses all ability to distinguish self from other, as infection gradually develops into full AIDS. The AIDS-afflicted body indiscriminately invites all 'deadly guests' across its threshold like so many vampires.

This absence of self-defending consciousness and boundary enforcement is thus understood as a conscious capitulation to the virus, a collusion with its self-propagating interests. In the next chapter this assumption of gay male collusion with the virus is taken up in relation to the figuration of gay sexuality in epidemiological discourse.

CONCLUSION

This chapter has investigated the micro-anatomy of AIDS, the biomedical representation of infection and its consequences at the level of the body's immune system. I argued that the immune system is an important conceptual device for the biomedical imagination, enabling it to propose relationships between the body's microscopic interior and its social surface. In the case of AIDS, and doubtless other diseases, the biomilitary analogies which help figure the immune system also lend themselves to the inscription of a 'causal' relationship between infection and sexual difference, both in the interior and at the boundaries of the body.

The steep hierarchy and strict boundary typical of the AIDS immune system works to produce a model of the immunocompetent subject, an individuated subject who shares his (sic) T cells' concern with self-defence and the maintenance of identity. It is evident here that claims to stable identity work as a kind of masculine prophylaxis, a means of pre-empting the contagious dangers of both viral infection and passive eroticism. Subjects who fail to share these preoccupations appear on this model to effectively align themselves with viral interests and the infectious destructiveness of epidemic. Gay men in particular are held to be guilty of this kind of collusion, made to appear as a viral representative in the body politic, as we shall see in the next chapter.

Furthermore, the narrative of the T cells and their tragic seduction by the virus clearly constitutes an instance where the biomedical imagination re-orders particular developments in the history of sexuality through its own technical optic. AIDS immunology inflects its understandings of sexual difference through its concepts of the normal and the pathological, narrating this understanding both at the scale of the cells and the body boundaries they are held to describe. The immune system provides AIDS biomedicine with particularly productive representational resources through which to think relations between sexual difference and social order, because its dynamics are already sexed and already conceived as a hierarchical social microcosm. At the same time the representation of the immune system is able to be transformed in relation to historical developments. The biomedical imagination is not static but able to assimilate social changes into its own terms, to translate historical moments into organic order.

It is evident from the analysis presented in this chapter that one of the chief means through which biomedicine anatomises cultural events is through *homology*, where similar propositions about and models of relations and processes are moved through different levels of scale. It narrates similar understandings about social order at the molecular, the cellular and the organismic level, and, as I shall discuss in the next chapter, the macro-anatomical level, where the social order is imagined as itself a body.

Here we can see a *homologic* which presides over the scientific imagination more generally. The micro and the macro are effectively the scales specific to the scientific imagination and its imaging technologies, technologies which allow it to 'see' and thus narrate natural scenarios whose logic can only be found at the molecular and sub-atomic scale on the one hand, and the global or universal scale on the other. It is this homologic which helps create the pleasing symmetries that science 'discovers' in nature, between the behaviour of atomic particles and the behaviour of planets, for example. Similarly, biomedicine's imagination works, at least in part, through the repetition of cause–effect paradigms, whether they are 'seen' with a microscope among the cells, or 'seen' in the national population using the various surveillance technologies deployed by epidemiology. This macro-anatomy of AIDS is the subject of the next chapter.

4

EPIDEMIOLOGY AND THE BODY POLITIC

The previous chapter investigated the micro-anatomy of AIDS, biomedicine's representation of the microscopic activity of the virus and the immune system. The immune system provides biomedicine with a way to conceptualise relationships between the body's cellular and molecular organisation and its boundaries. In AIDS immunology these relationships readily take on associations with sexual identity, and I demonstrated the extent to which every aspect of the micro-anatomy of AIDS is intertwined with, and indeed dependent on, concepts of sexual identity and sexual difference. Concepts of sexual identity are caught up in AIDS immunology's specifications of normalcy, and of pathological departure from this normalcy, both at the level of the cells and of the boundaries they are understood to create. Hence the immunocompetent body is figured as a phallic body, taken to be heterosexual and masculine, while immunocompromise is attributed to various kinds of passive, erotically receptive or 'excessive' bodies, which can be made to stand for feminine or gay masculine identity.

This chapter is concerned with the macro-anatomy of AIDS, the representation of infection in the social body. It will be addressed to the discourse of AIDS epidemiology, the biomedical sub-discipline which concerns itself with the incidence and distribution of AIDS in the population. If immunology specifies the relationship between the body's interior and its boundary, epidemiology is concerned to regulate relationships between its boundary and social space. In this sense epidemiology effectively takes the models of immunocompetence and immunocompromise up one more level of scale, using them as the basis for distinctions between degrees of infectious risk associated with different sexual identities, considered as homogeneous 'sub-populations'.

In this way epidemiology utilises immunology's models of the normal and the pathological to determine the optimum regulation of sexed bodies considered as a population. This regulation is undertaken to protect the 'public health', the health of the social body or body politic. I argued in the first chapter that biomedicine habitually figures bodies as social microcosms, and in this chapter I will pursue the analogy in the other direction. If particular bodies can be modelled as social orders, so can social orders be imagined as bodies. This reciprocity is intrinsic to analogy, because if A can be likened to B, so too can B be likened to A. This reciprocity extends biomedicine's social power, allowing it to make authoritative pronouncements not only about particular bodies but also about the proper biopolitical ordering of large numbers of bodies, in so far as they are conceptualised as the component parts of the 'public health'.

In either case the crucial feminist question is 'whose body stands as the model of social order, and whose social order is anatomised as a normal body?' In the previous chapter I demonstrated the extent to which the immunocompetent body, as it is specified in the age of AIDS, anatomises an idealised or schematised heterosexual masculine subjectivity. In this chapter I will investigate ways that AIDS epidemiology protects the health of this body, through an implicit equation between its health and the health of the body politic as a whole. Heterosexual male bodies in this way come to be the bodies that the resources of public health institutions are dedicated to protect through the disciplining of other kinds of bodies.

In what follows I will first marshal my evidence for the operation of an implicit equation in AIDS epidemiological discourse between the 'public health' and the health of heterosexual men. I will then investigate the concept of the health of the body politic in detail, developing this concept as a way to consider the positioning of sexed bodies in epidemiology's hierarchies of risk.

THE SEX OF THE 'GENERAL POPULATION'

AIDS epidemiology's equation between heterosexual masculinity and the 'public health' can be seen if we consider some of the permutations in the central binary that has historically organised AIDS rhetoric, that of the 'general population'/'risk group' division.[1] Epidemiology states its task to be the protection of the 'public health', a term which implies the greatest health for the greatest number of members of the social body. One epidemiological textbook, for example, defines the purpose of the discipline to be 'the prevention, surveillance and control of health disorders in populations' (Susser 1973: 3), while another states, 'Its main [purpose is] to provide information to achieve the goals of public health' (Chavigny et al. 1989: 59). In AIDS epidemiology the term 'general population' is habitually used as a synonym for the 'public health', as the entity which its knowledge is dedicated to protect. In this manifestation the 'general population' would seem to offer maximum inclusion, while 'risk groups' are a residual category. This kind of usage can be seen in the following excerpt from an AIDS epidemiology text.

> Owing to the longevity and fatality of HIV infection, the public requires protection against a protracted, virulent, and, often, sequestered hazard. But AIDS is also a social disease; its major risk groups are associated

with lifestyle behaviours such as homosexuality and illegal intravenous drug use, about which the larger society has moral and ethical preconceptions. Public policy, therefore, has to weigh civil liberties against the healthy survival of society.

(Chavigny *et al.* 1989: 60)

'Risk group' members in this kind of usage are clearly a residual and exceptional part of the population. Here epidemiology understands its task to be the identification of the conspicuous and singular 'risk group' member on behalf of what is assumed to be a uniformly clean and undifferentiated 'public' majority.

However, it is evident in other usages that the boundaries between 'general population' and 'risk groups' are very malleable, and not as mutually exclusive or exhaustive as they seem. The term 'risk group' was first used in relation to AIDS in 1983 by the Centres for Disease Control (CDC) in the United States to designate those groups thought to be the sub-populations vulnerable to both contracting and transmitting AIDS (Oppenheimer 1992). In the USA these groups were initially the 'three Hs' – homosexuals, haemophiliacs and Haitians – and intravenous (IV) drug users. Australia adopted the 'risk group' terminology initially to designate homosexuals, haemophiliacs and IV drug users.

While 'risk group' was the formal term to describe epidemiological surveillance categories for AIDS, it is important when considering the constituency represented by the 'general population' to realise that other groups have from time to time been nominated as 'at risk' for AIDS to varying degrees, without being formally designated as 'risk groups'. To designate a group as 'at risk' indicates that they require some kind of special education and surveillance, and that they thus stand in an ambiguous relationship to the 'general population'/'risk group' division, neither quite one nor the other. This practice can be seen, for example, in the Australian federal government's green paper on national management of AIDS, where we find the following list of 'priority groups' to be targeted for education and prevention measures: homosexual and bisexual men; needle-sharing drug users; Aboriginal and Islander people; people in prison; people in other closed institutions; adolescents; women; people who work as prostitutes; and blood product recipients (Commonwealth Department of Community Services and Health 1988: iv).

This list clearly includes a large number of people, and is so comprehensive as to make the category 'general population' seem residual. Who is left after this series of exclusions? The idea of the 'general population' implied by this list can be designated by the negative of each of the groups nominated. The 'general population', the group designated not to require 'special education', would in this case include non-indigenous people rather than Aboriginals, adults rather than adolescents, people who have not received blood products, and so on. On this logic, the groups designated as 'priority groups' on the grounds of sex or sexuality mark the relevant blind spot in its taxonomy. They imply a 'general population' which includes men but not women, and hetero-sexual men, but not gay and bisexual men.

So here the term 'general population' is one which functions to exclude rather than include, a movement which Grover bluntly argues is typical of its use in relation to AIDS. 'The "general population" ', she writes, 'is the repository of everything you wish to claim for yourself and deny to others' (Grover 1988: 24). In the use described here it works to exclude everybody with the single exception of heterosexual men, a regression which the term performs very readily.[2]

This ultimate reservation of the category of 'general population' for heterosexual men is not consistently visible in AIDS discourse, but its most reliable symptom is the difficult and ambivalent relationship that women maintain to this category. While gay men are easily excluded from the 'general population' as the exemplary 'risk group', and as a minority easily subtracted from the public health majority, women constitute half of the population and cannot be so readily dispatched. They tend rather to be simultaneously included and excluded, acting as markers of the tension between the 'general population's' inclusive claims and its excluding and regressive movement. In other words, women are positioned at the threshold of the 'general population' rather than securely within it. They may be included as married or at least monogamous women or as virgins, that is to the extent that they conform to the notional borders of the family as safe haven from AIDS.[3] They may also be included to the extent that they act as the guardians of the purity of the 'general population', the enforcers of safe sex practice.[4]

On the other hand, women are vulnerable to exclusion in the sense of becoming the subjects of special education and epidemiological surveillance, as 'sex workers' or simply sexually active, as pregnant, as the partners of bisexual or IV drug-using men or even as passive and unable to negotiate safe sex.[5] Their ambivalent position is further evident in the tendency for bio-medical literature to use statistics about HIV prevalence in women not as significant in themselves but as displaced indicators of potential infection in other sectors of the 'general population'. Pregnant women are routinely the subjects of epidemiological prevalence surveys, where they are anonymously tested for HIV antibodies, because they are understood to pose a contagious threat to both their partners and those other denizens of the 'general popula-tion', foetuses and infants. As one prevalence study put it:

> More than three fourths of women diagnosed with AIDS are of reproductive age, and transmission of [HIV] from mothers to infants accounts for over 80% of AIDS in children...the median duration of HIV infection preceding the development of AIDS is approximately 10 years; during this interval, asymptomatic women are capable of transmitting the infection to their sex partners and offspring.
>
> (Gwinn *et al.* 1991: 1704)

Treichler points out in her survey of the AIDS literature that women's infection rates are sometimes subsumed under the category 'paediatric AIDS' (Treichler 1992: 32).

More transparently, epidemiological discussions of AIDS and heterosexuals often measure risk as risk to heterosexual men. Epidemiological studies of women's rate of HIV infection are often presented as indexes to the pool of infection in the heterosexual population, rather than as simply significant in themselves.[6] A number of commentators have noted the weighting of epidemiological and social science research towards HIV infection in prostitutes and the corresponding absence of research regarding clients.[7] In other words, it is the risk posed by prostitutes to their clients which is of concern, and not vice versa. One article on the subject of HIV among heterosexuals begins its discussion of transmission with the observation that 'the reality of female-to-male transmission of the virus is now almost universally accepted' and then offers the following explanation to account for the lower rates of infection in heterosexual, as compared to homosexual, men.

> The cumulative incidence of AIDS has been greater in the homosexual male population than in the heterosexual female population, particularly in epicentres of the disease on the coasts of the United States ....Therefore, for each random, anonymous sexual encounter, a homosexual male is more likely to contact an infected male partner than is a heterosexual male to encounter an infected female partner.
>
> (Haverkos and Edelman 1989: 144–5)

So in an article nominally addressed to the risks of HIV transmission for heterosexuals, it is men who appear as the endangered, the ones for whom epidemiology determines risk of transmission, while women figure only as potential source of infection. Certainly not all epidemiological discussions of HIV and heterosexuality display such transparent bias, and some epidemiological studies make the rate of infection in women their primary concern.[8] However, as I shall demonstrate in greater detail later in this chapter, there are certain tendencies in the epidemiological imagination, the way that it images the direction of infection in the body politic, which make the heterosexual masculine body appear as *threatened rather than threatening*.

Once the equivocal position of women as a category is taken into account, the term 'general population' can be seen to regress very readily to the point where it is only heterosexual men and their progeny who it reliably denominates, although it still acts *as if* it denominates the 'public health' in its most general sense. This is not just a rhetorical assimilation but is determining of the allocation of resources, the shape of policy, the designation of some bodies as valuable, and others as dangerous, and hence in need of education and responsibilisation. How is this assimilation effected and naturalised in AIDS epidemiology discourse?

This question can be answered through a consideration of biomedicine's

87

deployment of another singular model of implicitly sexed health, that of the 'public health'. In order to open out the concept of the 'public health' I will discuss it in relation to the concept of the body politic as it has been articulated in some feminist and health literature. The body politic is a representation of biopolitical relations within a nation, and it can be attributed with both a health and a sex. I will argue that the discourse of AIDS epidemiology acts as a site for the elaboration and reconciliation of these two attributes under conditions of sexual epidemic. Furthermore, AIDS epidemiology uses the micro-anatomies provided by AIDS immunology as a way to bring the health and the sex of the body politic into alignment.

THE BODY POLITIC

What do I mean by the term 'body politic'? In popular usage it is a term used to designate the unity of the polity or some other form of social organisation. Recent theoretical interest in the body as the privileged site of political forces has precipitated a more literal regard for the bodily aspect of the 'body politic', raising questions about the relationships between the organisation of power and the representation of bodily order implied in the term. This literature cannot however provide a definitional answer to my question, because the theoretical status of the body is itself subject to considerable contestation.[9] My development of the question here must thus be regarded as context bound and provisional, a treatment limited to the purposes of this argument.

At its most straightforward the body politic is a term which implies imagining the nation or some other governmental unit, a city for example, along anthropomorphic or organic lines. As Anderson (1991) suggests, all national formations, all 'societies' must imagine their conditions of unity, their boundaries, internal structures and the relationship between parts, in much the same way that, as I have already suggested, subjects must imagine their body's conditions of unity. In both cases the process of imagining unity clearly depends on circulating ideas and images about bodies available in the culture, rather than on the use of a 'natural' body to serve a basis.

A considerable amount of historical and anthropological literature indicates that images of human bodies readily act as models for kinds of social unity and coordination in a number of different societies. Kantorowicz (1957), for example, identifies the image of the king's two bodies, one mortal and the other divine, presiding over the social order of absolutist monarchy. The king represents the intersection of a private, human body and a political divine body. Hence, as Foucault (1979) points out, the reservation of the worst of tortures for the regicide, who simultaneously commits murder and treason.

Douglas's anthropological work on the use of bodily images to designate social boundaries suggests that the significance of the body politic extends beyond that of an heuristic device, a convenient and eventually discardable way of thinking social unity. It rather carries serious and continuing repercussions for the particular bodies of the society's members, repercussions which depend upon the way that the idea of the body politic rationalises or naturalises social order based on bodily differences. She posits a reciprocity between images of particular bodies and bodily images of social order, where ideas of the body work as double-edged signifiers. She writes:

> The body is a model which can stand for any bounded system. Its boundaries can represent any boundaries which are threatened or precarious. The body is a complex structure. The functions of its different parts and their relation afford a source of symbols for other complex structures. We cannot possibly interpret rituals concerning excreta, breast milk, saliva and the rest unless we are prepared to see in the body a symbol of society, and to see the powers and dangers credited to social structure reproduced in small on the human body.
>
> (Douglas 1984: 115)

If images of the body act as diagrams of social order, so do particular bodies live out ideas of social order in their flesh. A shared set of corporeal metaphors are drawn upon to imagine the conditions of unity and integrity for both the social field and the particular body, and in the process to reconcile the one to the other. Douglas's work suggests that the idea of the body politic involves a cultural capacity to move certain bodily iconographies through different levels of scale, and thus to set up normalising relationships between particular bodies and forms of social organisation through analogy. It is this flexible power to create analogies in different social sites which makes the body politic a force of social order.

Following Foucault (1980a) and Haraway (1991), I would argue that the form taken by the body politic in our own social formation is that of the 'population'. This 'population' is not simply an amassing of individual citizens but has its own form of organisation, its own dynamics, symptoms and economies. Foucault implies that the population is imagined as itself a composite body,

> with its specific phenomena and its peculiar variables: birth and death rates, life expectancy, fertility, state of health, frequency of illnesses, patterns of diet and habitation.
>
> (Foucault 1980a: 25)

The management of the health of this population, Foucault suggests, is a primary commitment and source of legitimacy for modern forms of governmentality, concerned to maximise a healthy and thus productive and reproductive citizenry. Commenting on the historical transition from a monarchical body politic to that of the social contract, he writes:

> It's the body of society which becomes the new principle [of the political system] in the nineteenth century. It is this social body which needs to be

protected, in a quasi-medical sense. In place of the rituals that served to restore the corporeal integrity of the monarch, remedies and therapeutic devices are employed such as the segregation of the sick, the monitoring of contagions, the exclusion of delinquents.

(Foucault 1980b: 55)

This commitment to the protection and promotion of the health of the population involves the elaboration of knowledges adequate to the task of analysing relationships between the health of particular bodies and the health of the composite body of the population. The biomedical science of epidemiology is an exemplary instance of such knowledges, which would also include demography, actuarial statistics and nutrition, for example. The practice of epidemiology consists precisely in the amassing of a series of discrete clinical 'cases', medical knowledges of particular bodies, and considering their implications as mass phenomena at the level of the population.

As Foucault's words imply, the population, as a composite, can itself be imagined as an entity, a singular organism which itself has a health and is liable to disease. This implication of the notion of the population is evoked whenever the term 'the public health' is used, designating as it does a unified and singular state. This notion historically has lent itself to arguments about social policies which are not necessarily defined by literal medical health. Kendell and Wickham note the flexibility of the idea of 'health' in relation to government intervention.

In addition to strategies which are aimed at the medical health of populations, other governmental strategies aim at making target populations more economically healthy, more mentally healthy or more educationally healthy.

(Kendell and Wickham 1991: 1)

The appeal of the notion of the population as an entity with a health resides, I suggest, in its usefulness as a metaphor for social cohesion and for the forging of consensus about what counts as an appropriate social strategy. It provides a set of well-disseminated metaphors for imagining a variety of social processes and problems in terms of health and illness, so that social problems can be represented as 'cancers' or 'infections', for example, and their control equated with cure or recovery.

The notion of the population as composite body with a singular state of health has, as Douglas's formulation suggests, implications for the particular bodies that comprise it. If certain historically specific ideas of health work upwards as ways to organise the 'public health', they also work downwards to organise the health of individual bodies. This is not simply a matter of a uniform replication of healthy discipline upon each body in simple repetition, but also the ways that bodies are ordered in relation to each other, the ways they are organised. A threat to 'the health of society' implies that all or some bodies need to be reordered and reinscribed in ways deemed appropriate to remedy the threat.

Importantly for my argument, threats to social order from 'undesirable' groups have historically been represented as *infectious threats*. Gatens notes the use of the rhetoric of 'invasion, corruption or infection' to rationalise the exclusion of women from political participation during the eighteenth century (Gatens 1988: 65). Lefort, in a more contemporary example, describes the paranoiac image of the social body produced in totalitarian regimes.

> The [unity of the people] requires the incessant production of ene-
> mies....The campaigns of exclusion, persecution and for quite a while
> terror reveal a new image of the social body. The enemy of the people is
> regarded as a parasite or a waste product to be eliminated....The
> pursuit of the enemies of the people is carried out in the name of an ideal
> of social prophylaxis....What is always at stake is the integrity of the
> body. It is as if the body had to assure itself of its own identity by expelling
> its waste matter, or as if it had to close in upon itself by withdrawing from
> the outside, by averting the threat of an intrusion by alien ele-
> ments....The campaign against the enemy is feverish; fever is good, it
> is a signal, within society, that there is some evil to combat.
>
> (Lefort 1986: 298)

If socio-political threat can be readily assimilated to infectious threat, so too can the spectre of literal infection, of infectious disease proper, be assimilated to socio-political threat. Brandt's (1987) history of syphilis in North America, for example, demonstrates a profound confusion, during both world wars, between the threat of enemy invasion and of syphilitic infection. Significantly for this argument, this confusion had profoundly different implications for the social groups directly involved in the war effort or the syphilis epidemic, implications imagined through the use of the then newly-elaborated notions of germ theory and the body's 'immunity'. On the one hand the military were conceptualised as the nation's 'antibodies'. Brandt relates the extensive measures undertaken by the War Department to ensure a healthy soldiery free from syphilitic infection, able to form a 'clean fighting organism' to do battle with enemy invaders and defend the boundaries of the nation. The health of each soldier's body was required to both contribute to and also represent the health of the threatened nation-body, to fight off sexual infection in order to be able to fight off the enemy's threat to the nation's well being.

On the other hand prostitutes, the putative bearers of syphilitic infection, were habitually cast as allies of the enemy, dedicated to the subversion of the US war effort through the infection of soldier-bodies. As part of a civilian national campaign against syphilis during the First World War ('no citizen is exempt from service in the war against disease'), over 20,000 alleged prostitutes were quarantined in the United States, often behind barbed wire, as a measure to stem a declared syphilis epidemic.

These cases where political and infectious threat are made synonymous through the imagining of the nation as a body indicate that the idea of the body politic can function to create steep political hierarchies within its population. Furthermore, Brandt's work suggests the specific usefulness of the conceptual repertoire of militarised immunological discourse in the creation of these sexed hierarchies. The militarised idea of immunity and its more contemporary form, the immune system, provide a ready made corporeal schema for this process, organised as they are through internal hierarchy, mobilisation and degrees of external or internal infectious threat. As we shall see, immunological and epidemiological discourse about AIDS share a similar imagination about infectious process and the 'war on AIDS', drawing on each other's figurations at a number of points.[10]

This hierarchical capacity of the body politic is largely absent from Foucault's (1980a and b) proposals about the health of the population. His formulations seem to assume that governmental pursuit of a healthy population always involves the optimisation of each person's health, particularly their sexual health, in a fairly even-handed fashion. Foucault singles out the sexual processes of population because he argues that sex came to be seen as the densest point of connection between individual bodies and the abilities of the population to guarantee the processes of reproduction and heredity. Hence sex itself is the object of numerous and dense institutional strategies designed to ensure its optimal healthy deployment and guard against its dangers. However, for Foucault, each person's sex is equally implicated in the articulation of the normal and the pathological. So while his work indicates the kind of crisis that sexual epidemic poses for the composite body of the population, it offers little in terms of conceptualising the implications of such a crisis for sexually differentiated bodies and their position in the body politic.

I think this blind spot in Foucault's work derives from his conviction that the body politic is primarily constituted with reference to its health, and that the significance of sexual difference is secondary to or subsumed within this attribute of health. The body politic itself, the body of the population is conceived in his work to be neutral with respect to gender, a sexless organism. I would argue that, while the discourse of the public health is one of the legitimate sites for the articulation of the nature of the body politic, it does not encompass all aspects of its morphology. The body politic, like all bodies, also has a sex.

In making this claim I am following some of the proposals of Moira Gatens, who has addressed the question of the sex of the body politic in a series of articles (1988, 1991a, 1991b). She has addressed it not to medical discourse, however, but to classical and contemporary political discourse, where an explicit or implicit idea of the body politic has been articulated. In reading some of the classical texts of liberal political philosophy, Gatens points out that the body politic created by the social contract is a sexed body, an implicitly masculine body presented as a sex-neutral, ideal body. Hobbes's 'artificial man' articulated in *Leviathan* is precisely that, a social body whose parts and functions are ordered to correspond to the bodies of its male members.

The purpose of the social contract is to represent its members, but the implicit masculinity of the body politic introduces a series of systematic displacements into this process of representation. Gatens argues that the device of the body politic functions to blur a distinction between two meanings of the term 'representation'. 'Representation' may refer first of all to the process of production of an image. The body politic can be said to represent the body in the sense that it takes a human body as its analogy, it constructs itself in the image of this body. The second meaning refers to the conventional understanding of political 'representation', where one person stands for many, to represent their interests and secure them a place in the polity. Of this second meaning Gatens writes:

> [This] sense of 'representation' surfaces when considering *whose* body it is that is entitled to be represented by this political corporation. This involves understanding 'representation' in the sense where one body or agent is taken to stand for a group of diverse bodies. Here we are considering the metonymical representation of a complex body by a privileged part of that body.
>
> (Gatens 1991a: 79)

This double operation of representation facilitated by the device of the body politic ensures that the masculine bodily analogy through which it imagines itself has political consequences for its embodied subjects. The image of the body that it employs as principle of unity and order works also to determine whose bodies incarnate this order and are deemed compatible with its interests, whose interests can be fully represented without threatening its order. Gatens argues that the social contract only creates 'political representation' for those whose bodies are 'represented' as the image of the body politic, its masculine citizens. The body politic functions to exclude from political privilege 'those whose corporeal specificity marks them as inappropriate analogues to the body politic' (Gatens 1991a: 82).

Hence the body politic is a means of naturalising women's exclusion from public participation, but, more importantly for this argument, it is a means of effecting a slippage between masculine bodily interests and an idea of general social interests. In so far as the body politic is an implicitly masculine body which presents itself as a sex-neutral 'human' body, then masculine bodies can claim to 'represent' the interests of all other bodies. Male bodies can thus claim to literally incorporate other bodily interests within their own, including the interests of health, because they are the bodies which are seen to incarnate the desirable social order. Hence the health of the heterosexual male body can be made to stand for the health of body politic in its entirety. Conversely, a threat to the health of this body can seem like a comprehensive threat to the public health.

So if the body politic can be said to have both a health and a masculine sex, what is the relationship between these two attributes? This I suggest is a historical question in the sense that their relationship is contingent and mutable. Gatens's work and that of some other feminist theorists, notably Pateman (1988), demonstrate that the sex of the body politic can be articulated without reference to its health. In turn many aspects of the protection of the 'public health' have little or no relationship to sexual difference, for example the measures taken to control influenza. Under these circumstances the constellation of discourses which articulate the 'public health', those of epidemiology, health promotion, screening and so on, are neutral with regard to the sexuality of those they administer.

It seems possible to argue, however, that the conditions of sexual epidemic like those presented by AIDS constitute the kind of crisis in the body politic where the protection of its health and its sex are made isomorphic. I have suggested that public health discourse is one of the constitutive discourses of the body politic, facilitating the articulation of political order in biomedical terms. In the rest of this chapter I will examine some of these modes of articulation as they are practised in AIDS epidemiology, ways that this technical discourse helps to organise the masculinist bodily interests enshrined in the body politic by translating them into terms of health and infection control. This translation is enabled through epidemiology's use of the ana- tomies of the normal and the pathological elaborated in AIDS immunology, wherein the capacity of a body to infect is conceptualised according to its departure from phallic integrity.

EPIDEMIOLOGICAL SURVEILLANCE

Epidemiology as a knowledge and a technology occupies a central place in the imagining of a national body politic. It is the biomedical sub-discipline specifically concerned with the monitoring and maintenance of 'the public health', the study of disease not in the individual body as in clinical medicine, but of its incidence and distribution in the composite body of the population. The following is a description of epidemiology from its own literature.

> Epidemiology is logical thinking applied to health problems that threaten the public. A more generally accepted definition of epidemio- logy is the study of patterns of disease and their precursors in communities....Its main purposes are to provide information to achieve the goals of public health; to prevent and control sickness as well as disease precursors in communities, and to promote community health.
>
> (Chavigny *et al.* 1989: 59)

All first world governments employ extensive and permanent epidemio- logical programmes to monitor disease in their populations. The activity of these programmes, like that of clinical medicine, is understood in scopic terms, as an extension of the medical gaze over the nation. Epidemiological activity is self-designated as surveillance, a 'single gaze [that sees] everything constantly' (Foucault 1979: 173). This is an epidemiological description of such surveillance.

> Disease surveillance involves the ongoing, centralised, comprehensive collection of case reports, along with a minimal demographic description of each case, and the collation, analysis and timely dissemination of the information collected. The main objectives of surveillance are to evaluate the extent of disease in the population, and to indicate crudely which groups are most affected.
>
> (Commonwealth AIDS Research Grants Epidemiology Advisory
> Committee 1990: 1)

The techniques of epidemiological surveillance, those of notification, sentinel testing, contact tracing, and seroprevalence surveys, are thus a means of visualising the presence and location of disease in the population from a central, comprehensive vantage point. It is this central vantage point which distinguishes the status of epidemiology from that of clinical medicine. While the latter can see disease in the individual body, it can have no means of judging the possible repetition or distribution of disease in a way that is meaningful for 'the public health'. For this reason the clinician is obliged to bring particular instances of disease to the attention of epidemiological institutions.

> The insularity of the clinician may inhibit definition of a common disease problem occurring among a group of people and thus delay or inhibit the institution of appropriate control and prevention measures. Multiple cases of a single disease entity may appear simultaneously in a population who have had a common exposure to the aetiological agent. If the individual cases diagnosed by different physicians are not reported, no association among the cases can be made.
>
> (Brachman 1990a: 147–8)

So the singular state 'the public health' requires a single, nationally comprehensive point of view from which to be judged. In other words, epidemiology seeks to do in the social body what the immune system does in the healthy body and clinical medicine does in the diseased body. It provides the conditions for its maintenance as, or restoration to, a singular, clean, and unified organic system. Epidemiology undertakes hierarchical observation of the social body's internal milieu, monitors for infection and provides a means of co-ordinated action against pathological phenomena. Just as the immune system is endowed with the capacity to distinguish between clean and infected cells and to prevent the spread of infection through the healthy cells of the body, so epidemiology has the capacity to distinguish between the infected and the uninfected and to protect the latter from the former. In the case of AIDS, epidemiological vision seeks to compensate for the 'blindness' of the HIV afflicted immune system. While the HIV infected immune system cannot properly detect infection in the body, clinical medicine can 'see' infection in the particular body and epidemiology can 'see' infection in the population through the device of the HIV test. This coupling of the clinical medical claim to see the inside of the body down to molecular levels of process with the epidemiological claim to see disease in the population forms the basis of biomedicine's panoptic dream, the control of health and illness through the envisioning of its most elusive manifestations.

To say that epidemiology 'sees' disease in the population however is to take its panoptic claims too literally. While it characterises its activities as 'surveillance', it cannot 'see' a thing called the health of the population. Population health is not an entity which can be discovered but is rather a series of disparate developments in scattered locations which must be analysed and assembled into an entity. Epidemiology is a knowledge dedicated to 'imaging' and hence to 'imagining' the entity 'population health', extrapolating its morphology and dynamics from an extensive data collection infrastructure. It solves the 'problem of invisibility' in a fashion similar to that of clinical medicine, through the procedure of diagnosis. Clinical medicine must generate its images of the body's interior through inferential and interpretive strategies which take as their evidence certain effects produced *in vitro*, or certain visible symptoms on the body's surface. It is only by amassing a number of indicative traces – in the case of the HIV positive body, for example, diagnosis might involve the evidence produced by the ELISA test, the Western Blot test, T cell counts, and antigen testing – that the clinical situation can be determined, and hence translated into an account of occurrences in the body's interior.

Similarly, judgements about the health of the population are derived from the gathering of morbidity and mortality data, from sentinel-physician reporting, from case investigations, epidemic investigation, laboratory and clinical notification, and so on. Large amounts of such data are collected in a standardised fashion and relayed to a central bureau for analysis. It is only at the end of extensive collation, statistical analysis and the organisation and simplification of data into tables and columns, that an entity called 'the health of the population' can be envisaged.

Thus the knowledge practices of epidemiology allow the state of a large numbers of bodies to be presented to the eye in a synoptic form. I would argue, following Latour (1990), that the social power of epidemiology, or at least its amenability to use for biopolitical ends, derives from these features of compression and centralisation. Latour (1990), in his treatment of the political power of scientific inscription, points out the uses made of compressed informational formats in the bureaucratic wielding of power. The point of distilled and abstracted information which is the end result of data collection practices like epidemiology, Latour argues, is precisely the increased power such formats provide their interpreters in summarising an extensive domain. Epidemiological knowledge commands a repertoire of statistical practices to summarise disease processes and the number of bodies implicated in them. Furthermore, the representational practices of epidemiology facilitate connection with those of clinical medicine, allowing biomedically valid relationships to be set up between ostensibly rather heterogeneous domains. In the case of AIDS we have on the one hand a concern about T and B cells, lymph, tissues and glycoproteins, and on the other patterns of sexual practice and alliance. These diverse phenomena can be made to coalesce precisely through their transformation into a shared technical imaginary which is characterised by a maximum of schematisation. Wherever possible, pathological processes in both bodies and the population are quantified and mathematicised, rendered into units which can be graphed, plotted, counted. Such mathematicisation places the divergent spheres of clinical and epidemiological medicine into modular and compatible relations with one another, allowing a relationship to be expressed between each of the phenomena so rendered. An example of this process can be found in the following piece of advice found in an AIDS immunology text.

> There are clear differences in the amount of HIV-1 replication and the rate of cell death between so called resting CD4+ cells and CD4+ cells that are proliferating or have been activated by mitogens of lymphokines. Although activated and non-activated CD4+ cells bind HIV-1 equivalently, HIV-1 penetration, replication and cell death occur much more slowly and less efficiently in non-activated CD4+ cells....This phenomenon may have implications in risk-groups whose life-style results in repeated antigenic stimulation of T cells.
>
> (McDougal, Mawle and Nicholson 1989: 23)

This is, I suggest, a characteristic itinerary of an AIDS biomedicine concept. The authoritative account of differential cell susceptibility to the virus, an account which is generated out of *in vitro* observations of serum culture over a two-week period, is translated with no intermediary steps into advice about 'risk-group' lifestyle, through the quantification of cell activity.

Another example is epidemiology's formula to determine AIDS epidemic, known as the Case Reproductive Rate or R_o. Epidemic is said to occur when the case reproduction rate exceeds 1, that is when each case of HIV infection produces more than one other infection. Its calculation is determined by a multiplication of a formula to express viral activity in the body, by the virulence of particular sex acts, by rates of partner change (May *et al.* 1990). In this way formulae like the case reproduction rate allow the compression of complex, numerous, far flung and heterogeneous processes into a simple numerical expression, so that, as Latour says, the masters of such formulae can 'consider millions as if they were in the palm of their hands' (Latour 1990: 55).

Two pertinent effects are achieved through these highly schematised informational formats. First of all it allows the spheres of clinical and epidemiological medicine to set up a seamless reciprocity between what might otherwise remain two rather different spheres of knowledge, the first a knowledge of individual symptoms and prophylaxis, the second – in the case of AIDS epidemiology – a knowledge of the social complexities of sexual relationships, drug usage and sexual identification. The mathematicisation of both fields means that a discovery in one can be translated easily into the knowledge of the other without distortion or 'noise'. It allows fewer concepts greater latitude, so that similar explanations can be used to bind different fields together analogically. Biomedicine elaborates a version of events – of the nature of the virus, of the dynamics of infection, of the meaning of the HIV test – and shifts them through various levels of scale and numbers of instances so that they accumulate explanatory power. A small number of concepts work to create a similitude between sites which might otherwise appear incommensurate, expediting biomedical explanations into all corners of the social field.

Such similitude can be seen, for example, in the analogy between notions of cell susceptibility to HIV infection in immunology and the idea of 'risk group' susceptibility to HIV infection in epidemiology documented in the previous chapter. In both instances the distribution of infection is taken to be indicative of a certain complicit and eroticised susceptibility, a biological compatibility or desire between the virus on the one hand and the cell and/or body on the other. A similar notion of sexual infectious process presides over both cells and bodies, and only a shift in scale distinguishes them.

The second effect of such compressed informational formats is their usefulness in providing 'facts' in a polemical situation. Latour writes:

> 'You doubt what I say? I'll show you.' And without moving more than a few inches, I unfold in front of your eyes figures, diagrams, plates, texts, silhouettes, and then and there present things that are far away and with which some sort of two way connection has been established.
>
> (Latour 1990: 36)

And this I would argue is precisely the function epidemiology serves for various institutional and governmental interests. It provides forms of expert knowledge in formats which draw together far flung processes of health and illness in a central location, which summarise large numbers of bodies in simple formulae and standardise terms, and which does so in ways which translate the technical discourse of medical research into terms that are legible and useful to bureaucracies. Certainly this knowledge is often used for benign ends, acting as the basis of policies intended to transform the everyday life practices of sectors of the population to enhance longevity, prevent heart attack, encourage infant nutrition, and so on. Under conditions of sexual epidemic, however, such knowledge becomes contentious, bound up in the defence of particular orders of expertise and privileged sexualities. In these circumstances epidemiology must martial its claims to superior knowledge of the field and hence its right to set out the measures appropriate to its control. As one epidemiologist puts it in her explanation of the uses of epidemiology, its data allow 'convincing arguments' about forms of intervention to be mounted.

> Policymakers require facts to understand the risk of HIV infections, to ascertain the spread of the epidemic and to assign resources. Basic scientific information is required to make convincing arguments for change which can be justified as objective, unprejudiced, and realistic. Epidemiology provides a comprehensive resource of scientific information about group problems for the use of administrators and legislators.
>
> (Chavigny *et al.* 1989: 60–1)

The demand among policymakers for the epidemiological databank and the convincing arguments that it underwrites relates to the *dirigiste* nature of public health measures to control epidemic and maintain the 'public health'. In epidemiology's own terms its extensive surveillance infrastructure enables the even application of the medical gaze to all corners of the population, so that the image it provides to policymakers is a transparent and disinterested one, an empirically accurate photograph of the state of the population's health. On the basis of this accurate topography public health under conditions of epidemic has historically exercised extensive kinds of control over sexual liaison, domestic arrangements, the location of groups and individuals, and the arrangement of urban space, to mention but a few of its domains. This interventionism is nowhere more visible than in the field of AIDS, and forms the basis for its intense politicisation.

However, I have suggested that the entity 'the public health' is not a neutrally descriptive concept but necessarily draws upon particular medicalised and implicitly sexed bodily morphologies to imagine and to organise itself. These morphologies in turn have different implications for the bodies that comprise them, implications which correspond to the extent to which bodies conform with the overall corporeal schema considered appropriate to the 'public health'. In other words, the power of epidemiology to conceptualise the entire social domain is also its power to reorder bodies in a systematic and legitimated fashion across that domain.

It seems to me that AIDS epidemiology effects this reordering through its ability to represent the social topography of HIV distribution. It can graphically depict the current location and direction of infection and provide authoritative speculation as to its future direction. This mapping procedure is performed through the assimilation of certain groups of person to categories generated by its explanatory schemata, that is with reference to 'risk groups' or the more contemporary 'transmission categories'. In the next section I will examine in detail AIDS epidemiology's reliance on sexed categories and the way this organises hierarchies of infection between different groups.

THE TOPOGRAPHY OF INFECTION

Epidemiology is the science of the *repetition* of disease in the population, but in the analysis of such repetitions it also seeks to generate a higher order system of explanation than that of clinical medicine. As one epidemiologist notes, epidemiology seeks not only to register the incidence of disease but also to analyse its distribution and organise this into a 'coherent narrative' which organises the determinants of disease into their proper temporal, spatial and social relationships.

> The epidemiological investigation provides the opportunity of collating information from cases temporally related into a coherent narrative, examination of which should describe the cause, transmission, and host factors that may suggest an intervention point leading to control and prevention.
>
> (Brachman 1990a: 148)

Epidemiology attempts to establish reasons for the concentration of particular diseases within particular sub-populations in order to provide a map for clinical and public health intervention and prevention. The envisioning of patterns of disease distribution is the first step towards establishing these relations, as this excerpt describes.

> [Epidemiological surveillance] can . . . be used to suggest determinants of disease. Once surveillance has established the pattern of disease, more detailed epidemiological surveys may be required to identify the determinants of disease. For economic reasons, [epidemiological] surveys cannot usually be carried out on all people in the population, and must also focus on a limited number of hypothesised determinants. . . . The identification of disease determinants should lead to the establishment of prevention programs, designed to limit the occurrence of disease by eliminating or reducing exposure to these determinants.
>
> (National Centre in HIV Epidemiology and Clinical Research 1990: 1)

As this quote indicates, the distribution of disease, its uneven spread within a population, is held to be the first indication of a pattern of causality, of a probability of association between the disease, conceived as the effect, and some causes.

Epidemiology differs from clinical medicine in its subscription to the notion of multiple determinants of disease. Clinical medicine tends to locate causal power in the 'aetiological agent', the specific organism which has a one-to-one relationship with a specific disease. Epidemiology as social medicine is committed to the consideration of disease as overdetermined, as emerging out of a field of multiple causalities, a nexus of interactions between 'specific agent' (virus) and 'host'. It seeks to tip the balance of medical attention away from 'germ theory' and towards what it refers to as 'host factors' (Susser 1973). In the words of one epidemiologist:

> Endemic diseases, where the communication or transmission factors are a constant, require an explanation more sophisticated than the presence of the microorganism, the means of its transmission and the opportunity for communication. A receptive host is necessary and a collection of conditions that make for receptiveness in the host.
>
> (Richmond 1980: 87)

Hence epidemiology brings to bear its more intensive forms of study on these 'host–agent interactions'. Detailed surveys are mounted in order to discover what characteristics of the 'host' population interact with the causative agent to intensify disease in that group compared to the rest of the population. This conceptualisation of disease aetiology means that epidemiological science can only proceed through the specification and classification of sub-populations. If the social topography of disease is taken to indicate a pattern of disease aetiology constituted at least in part through host factors, then hosts must be categorised according to these factors. They must be designated as a group because of the factors which place them at higher risk of infection, compared to other groups who are relatively free of infection. The epidemiologists Chavigny and colleagues succinctly state that the function of epidemiology is the provision 'of objective data that allow comparisons between communities for decision making' (Chavigny *et al.* 1989: 61).

In the field of AIDS this comparative method led, at the beginning of the epidemic in the industrialised democracies, to the designation of the 'general population'/'risk group' binary as the principle of surveillance. Most notable of the risk groups were homosexual and bisexual men and intravenous drug users, whose sexual and/or drug use practices were identified as behaviours which spread the HIV virus, in comparison to the benign sexual practices and non-drug use of the notional 'general population'. While women have never been formally nominated as a 'risk group' by epidemiology, they have, as I indicated earlier, been nevertheless denied a secure position within the 'general population' and subjected to surveillance and disciplinary intervention of various kinds. In what follows I will examine what epidemiology considers that gay and bisexual men and heterosexual women have in common.

THE SEXUALITY OF RISK

Gay men are considered by epidemiology as natural loci for HIV for two reasons. First, they are understood to already harbour other infectious agents prior to HIV infection. Here is an excerpt from another epidemiological account of the emergence of AIDS.

In a number of major cities such as New York, Los Angeles and San

Francisco [after World War Two] large geographic concentrations of homosexual men developed. By the late 1960s and early 1970s, sexual promiscuity became a prominent feature of these communities. Along with these changes in life style, sexually transmitted diseases such as syphilis, gonorrhoea, and hepatitis B became hyperendemic. Parasitic infections of the colon, known collectively as 'gay bowel syndrome', were widespread. These communities were clearly vulnerable to the introduction of other sexually transmitted diseases.

(Winkelstein *et al.* 1989: 117)

In epidemiological terms, homosexual men act as an infectious *reservoir*, a central concept in its repertoire of terms. 'The reservoir is the location in which the organism is normally found, that is, where it becomes established, metabolises, and multiplies' (Brachman 1990b: 156). The term reservoir may refer equally to a part of the population or a part of the environment. In the case of HIV the virus cannot live outside the human body, so that infected bodies form the only reservoirs. The representation of male homosexual enclaves as extant reservoirs of infection was influential in the initial proposals of AIDS as a condition caused by a virus. The earliest viral proposals came from those epidemiologists and research scientists who had studied the distribution of hepatitis B among gay men in San Francisco and Los Angeles during the late 1970s (Shilts 1987).

Second, homosexuality is an habitual reservoir because it forms a naturalised locus of the determinants of viral transmission. In epidemiology's imagination, sexual practices which are said to be the exclusive domain of homosexuality are taken to be *both the behaviours which generate and spread HIV and the acts which delimit gay identity.* This equation is evident in the following quotation from a clinical text.

Certain sexual behaviours that are especially common among homosexual men, especially those involving direct or indirect contact with faeces, specifically increase the risk of sexual transmission of enteric infections. Similarly, behaviours that may result in mucosal trauma are more common among homosexual men than heterosexuals, probably contributing to an elevated risk of hepatitis B. Some homosexual men regularly have multiple sex partners, which increases STD risk. The risk is further enhanced by the anonymity of partners, a former common feature of homosexual behaviour. Such anonymity makes it nearly impossible to interrupt disease transmission through contact tracing and epidemiological treatment.

(Rompalo and Handsfield 1989: 4)

The sexual practice most closely associated with both viral transmission and gay identity in epidemiology is that of anal intercourse. In the previous chapter I argued that the 'scene of HIV transmission' in the biomedical imagination was a scene of anal sex between men. Unlike immunology, epidemiology does not assume this 'primal scene' as an event outside its own frame of representation. Rather AIDS epidemiology is dedicated to the imaging and analysing of this primal scene, to its explicit elaboration. Extensive survey research, cohort studies and cross-sectional studies have been mounted in first world countries among gay populations to gather quantifiable information about gay male sex practices.

In these analyses of the 'scene of transmission' a great deal of attention is paid to the active/passive distinction as an analytic principle. This distinction in anal intercourse is conceptualised by epidemiology to form a self-enclosed infectious circuit within gay populations, where active penetration is understood to 'give' infection and receptivity to 'take' infection. For this reason HIV infection among homosexual men is generally imagined by epidemiology as endogenous, wherein the nature of the risk group is established through its putative capacity to generate and intensify infection within its own borders. This concentration of infection is further enhanced by the repetition of sex, the tendency to 'increased numbers of sex partners' which epidemiology attributes to gay sexuality (Chamberland and Curran 1990).[11] Epidemiology is a statistical practice, concerned with the quantification of disease as a repetition and distribution of singular cases. Consequently the repetition of sex becomes almost synonymous with the processes of epidemic in the epidemiological imagination.

In the case of women, AIDS epidemiology considers the danger they pose as exogamous, the carrying of infection across specified borders. As this excerpt states, it is the feminine capacity to act as a transmission point between high and low risk males, and between high risk male and foetus, that epidemiology considers problematic.

> Because women have the possibility of sexual contact with groups at high risk of HIV infection, such as bisexual males, they are viewed as the interface between homosexual/bisexual groups and the heterosexual population, where seepage of the infection to non-high-risk groups may take place. Following the progress of the epidemic through analysis of the frequency of cases in women may be a method of categorising the spread of the infection into the heterosexual population....It is also obvious that infected women are the source of the transplacental transmission that takes place from mother to infant, increasing the threat of AIDS to the unborn.
>
> (Chavigny *et al.* 1989: 66–7)

Epidemiological surveys of bisexual men also form part of this chain of anxiety, where women's bodies are modelled as the threshold to the 'heterosexual population'. In an article entitled 'A potential source for the transmission of the human immunodeficiency virus into the heterosexual population: bisexual men who frequent "beats" ', we find the following conclusion.

If we cautiously assume that 25% of these female partners [of the bisexual male sample] show half the frequency of different sexual partners of their regular male partners, the potential for the rapid diffusion of HIV infection into the heterosexual population is obvious.

(Bennett, Chapman and Bray 1989: 316)

This conceptualisation of women's bodies as mediums of boundary transgression is evident too in the tendency described at the beginning of this chapter to regard infectious prevalence in women as primarily indicators of infection elsewhere, rather than as indicative of the state of health of women as such. Guinan and Hardy (1987), for example, state blandly that the rate of HIV infection in women is 'of special interest' to epidemiological surveillance because they are the 'major source of infection of infants with AIDS' and because the rate may act as a 'surrogate for monitoring heterosexual transmission of infection'.

In some accounts of feminine transmission, the fact of the woman's infection is omitted altogether and transmission is represented as though it has occurred directly between two other groups. One medical text states, for example, in a passage which also exemplifies the ease with which women can be excluded from the 'general population':

The majority of cases [of AIDS] so far have occurred in male homosexuals with other groups at risk including intravenous drug users, haemophiliacs . . . and infants of sexually promiscuous or drug addicted mothers. None the less, the number of infected heterosexuals is steadily increasing.

(Roitt 1991)

Here the infection of the 'sexually promiscuous or drug addicted mothers' is made redundant to that of her infant, whose infection is the actual case under discussion.

I stated earlier that the term 'risk group' designates some homogeneous group predisposition to both contracting and transmitting infection. The coupling of 'women' with 'gay men' as AIDS sexual risk groups indicates that in the epidemiological imagination these two sexual identities share some predisposition. So what do they have in common, from the point of view of epidemiological notions of causality? In both cases, I would argue, gay men and women are again conceptualised as lacking proper boundaries. We can see here that epidemiology implicitly relies upon the immunocompetent model of bodily health to create its hierarchies of risk. However, this common lack of boundary has different implications for the way that the two groups are positioned in the epidemiological topography of infection. In the case of gay men, a lack of boundary renders them sites of viral replication, *reservoirs* which both harbour and intensify infection. The endogenous nature of gay sexuality, its assortive rather than disassortive character in epidemiological terms, tends to intensify this reservoir image, a channelling of infectious flow within particular social borders. For women, a lack of boundary renders them as *carriers*, whose epidemiological significance relates to their ability to transmit infection between other bodies.

In both cases, too, this lack of boundary is imagined not as a general formlessness but as a capacity for sexual receptivity, for the accommodation of phallic breach of their body boundaries. Receptivity is the practice which all members of the two groups 'gay men' and 'heterosexual women' are thought to hold in common, the practice which allows them to constitute a group in epidemiological terms. Hence the importance attached to receptive anal intercourse in gay sexuality and the coy reference in the quote stating that 'women have the possibility of sexual contact' with both high and low risk men. In both cases this is immediately equated with a capacity for receptive accommodation of a series of such bodies, with 'anonymous multiple partners' among gay men, and with a mixture of high and low risk men, or men and foetus in the case of women. Their bodily capacities for repeated, receptive sex are considered by epidemiology to implicate such bodies in the circulation of viral infection.

THE CONTROL OF INFECTIOUS FLOW

In the previous chapter, I demonstrated that sexual receptivity was imagined in AIDS immunology to constitute a breach of immunological boundary. This breach in turn facilitated the spread of the HIV through the body's internal milieu. The virus itself is imagined as a self-propagating primordial force, seeking maximum self-aggrandisement. Only an intact and armoured body surface can thwart its replicative bid.

Thus epidemiology allocates risk of viral spread to certain groups because they are composites of bodies which are held to lack proper boundaries. Just as these bodies are considered to individually facilitate the spread of virus within themselves, so too do they facilitate its circulation throughout the social milieu. And just as the virus seeks to colonise the body it has entered, so too does it seek to colonise the entire social field, through its propagation in the maximum number of bodies. The bodies of 'risk group' members are the means of the virus moving both from cell to cell and from body to body. And as 'causes' of infection they are conceptualised as themselves untouched by infection. Infection in less valuable bodies does not count as infection, except in so far as they threaten to infect more valuable bodies. It should be noted that this implicit economy of value also underpins the idea of the spread of infection within the immune system, as is evident in the following excerpt.

Several [research] groups have demonstrated that, in general, HIV is not cytopathic for monocytes/macrophages and replicates to low, often undetectable, levels in *in vitro* cultures. However, infected monocytes readily *transmit* infectious virus to *susceptible* CD4 cells. Thus, tropism for and cytopathic effect on CD4 lymphocytes and *replication and sequestration* in intracytoplasmic vacuoles in macrophages, which serve as *reservoirs* of infectious virus, are properties of HIV that could account for the progressive *loss* of helper T cells and resulting immunodeficiency. *Latent* infection of monocyte/macrophages by HIV might also provide an ideal mechanism for spread of infection to the central nervous system.

(Fultz 1989: 7; emphasis mine)

I have italicised a number of words which convey the nexus between lesser value and 'cause' of infection. The monocyte/macrophage line of cells, which here appear as 'transmitters' and 'reservoirs' of virus, are also understood to be more 'primitive' and less specialised lymphocytes than the T and B cells. While they contain infectious virus they are understood as themselves unaffected by its presence or, as the citation puts it, HIV is not cytopathic for macrophages. Their significance in the HIV-infected immune system lies in their ability to carry invisible infection between the valuable T cells.

The following excerpt from an epidemiological essay provides a highly schematic hydraulic model for characterising the bodies of those groups implicated in infectious transmission.

The transmission of an infective agent requires a reservoir that harbours the infective source; a route of transmission or vehicle for spreading the organism; a susceptible host; a portal of exit from the infected reservoir; and a portal of entry into the susceptible host.

(Chavigny *et al.* 1989: 67)

For AIDS epidemiology the bodies of gay and bisexual men and women furnish the virus with precisely this kind of fluid pathway, *conduits* which carry the virus throughout the corporeal matrix of the 'public health'. It is precisely this capacity for flow and circulation between bodies that AIDS epidemiology is committed to control, as the quote goes on to state.

The greater the knowledge about transmission of infectious disease, the more likely that methods of prevention and control will be effective. Administrative and legislative initiatives utilise epidemiological information to break the chain of transmission.

(Chavigny *et al.* 1989: 67)

So it is the putative capacity for forming fluid relations of contagion specific to the sexually receptive body that epidemiology is committed to control. Why, however, is this capacity considered specific to sexually receptive bodies? It should be stated here that in seeking what gay men and women have in common, I have somewhat overstated the absence of phallic sexual implication in transmission among gay males in epidemiology's understanding. Receptive sexuality is considered the means of contracting the virus among gay men, while phallic sexuality is considered its means of transmission. There is no analogue when considering women's capacity for contraction and transmission, however. Both are considered to occur as a function of sexual receptivity.

In answer to my question of epidemiology, however, the equation made between sexual receptivity and lack of proper boundary is crucial, because this renders the position of sexual receptivity as one in which singularity is dissipated and confused. It was argued in the previous chapter that immunology equates singularity with health and internal cleanliness, and contagion with a confusion of this singularity, a merging of one with another, of self with other. It was further argued that the equation between this improper lack of boundary and feminine and gay masculine subjectivity could be considered an effect of masculine projection, a way for a phallocentric culture to protect heterosexual masculine bodies from the political implications and psychic costs of abjection and intersubjectivity.

This projection is not simply an intra-psychic matter, I would argue, but one which is shored up and guaranteed by a number of institutional practices and discourses, of which the epidemiology of sexual epidemic is a paramount example. It may be possible to claim that the securing of this projection, its stabilisation in various orders of knowledge, is one of the most important effects of the masculine imago of the body politic.

AIDS epidemiology betrays precisely the same kind of projective logic in its organisation of infection into cause and effect, an indication of the extent to which it shares or more precisely constitutes the point of view of a strictly phallic body, a body conceptualised as bounded, non-receptive and endowed with a phallic genital sexuality. This parity can be seen in its anxieties about the capacities of the feminine body in the following ways.

First, if epidemiology poses women's bodies as cause or source of infection it does so by adopting a phallic point of view. Bodies which are understood as strictly receptive, that is women's bodies, can only pose an infectious threat to a strictly phallic body. For women, it is of course phallic bodies which are the 'source' of infectious threat, but epidemiology only recognises this when the phallic body is not strictly phallic, that is when it is also receptive, a bisexual male body. Considerable public health attention has been recently dedicated to the task of alerting women to the possibility that their husband or partner might be bisexual. If epidemiology were to be elaborated from a feminine point of view, however, this distinction would be redundant.

Second, an implicit economy of bodily value underpins the epidemiologic of cause and effect and its representation of women's bodies. Women are considered important in AIDS epidemiology not because they are themselves infected, but because they are infecting. They have the status of vectors or carriers in AIDS epidemiology. The first is an animal which carries virus from one group of humans to another, the second is a person who is infected and may transmit infection but remains themselves unaffected by illness (Brachman 1990b). In both cases they are simply the medium of infection, its means of getting from somewhere important to somewhere else important, as are the macrophages in the representation of infection in the immune system that was cited above.

Women's bodies are relay points rather than the end point of infection. The point of infectious origin is provided by the gay male *reservoir*, where infection is siphoned off by bisexual men and transferred to heterosexual women. They in turn carry it to its end point, which is always imagined as either a phallic body or its progeny, a foetus or infant. It is this status which explains the logic of women's conditions of inclusion in and exclusion from the 'general population' that I described in the introduction. Women who are married, monogamous or virginal and not pregnant can be included in the 'general population' because they do not act as a transmission point between one male body and another, they keep the borders of the 'general population'/'risk group' division intact. This logic also, I suspect, helps to explain the absence of lesbian identity from AIDS epidemiology's transmission categories. Lesbian sexual practice has no connection with or implications for male bodies.

Third, the epidemiological anxiety about 'promiscuity' is, as Bersani points out, an implicitly phallic anxiety, one which is directed against the at least potential ability of receptive bodies to repeat sex, an ability which strictly phallic bodies so plainly lack.

> Promiscuity is the social correlative of a sexuality physiologically grounded in the menacing phenomenon of the nonclimactic climax. Prostitutes publicise (indeed, sell) the inherent aptitude of women for uninterrupted sex. Conversely, the similarities between representations of female prostitutes and male homosexuals should help us to specify the exact form of sexual behaviour being targeted, in representations of AIDS, as the criminal, fatal and irresistibly repeated act. This is of course anal sex and we must . . . take into account the widespread confusion in heterosexual *and* homosexual men between fantasies of anal and vaginal sex. The realities of syphilis in the nineteenth century and of AIDS today legitimate a fantasy of female sexuality as intrinsically diseased; and promiscuity in this fantasy, far from merely increasing the risk of infection, is the *sign of infection*. Women and gay men spread their legs with an unquenchable appetite for destruction.
>
> (Bersani 1988: 211)

In AIDS epidemiology sexually receptive bodies act as *conduits* in an *a priori* fashion, but they are also the bodies which can, in the phallic imagination, repeat sex indefinitely with an uncountable number of phallic bodies. The promiscuous capacities of sexually receptive bodies hence intensify their contagious dangers, both in the sense that they multiply the number of phallic bodies they come into contact with, and in that each previous contact increases their virulence for each subsequent man.[12] It is for this reason that the prostitute's body is such an object of concern for AIDS epidemiology. As a site for the meeting of many male bodies the prostitute is doubly dangerous, because she generates a kind of homosocial erotic fascination *for the same reason* that she represents an infectious threat.

So what I am suggesting here is that within AIDS epidemiology the heterosexual male body is not assigned a causal status. Rather it is reserved the membership of the 'general population' because AIDS epidemiology is a knowledge which generally replicates or constitutes the point of view of that body. The heterosexual male body fails to appear as an object in AIDS epidemiology precisely because it occupies the position of subject of that discourse's enunciation. Heterosexual male bodies are not implicated in the circulation of the virus within the social matrix, because they are not transmission points, they are rather the ultimate end point of infection.

It is the arrival of infection at this end point which epidemiology equates with the absolute decline of the 'public health', and which the interventions of public health institutions are designed to avert. Heterosexual male bodies are threatened by the virus, but only in so far as the contagious circulation of other bodies is not controlled. The control of circulation, of sexual alliance particularly between high and low risk groups, of 'promiscuity', of 'vertical transmission' between woman and foetus, is precisely what epidemiology and public health education set out to do in the field of AIDS. Because hetero-sexual male bodies are not conceptualised as being implicated in this flow they form the privileged 'general population' which is not subject to surveillance or educative intervention and which is implicitly protected by the control or responsiblisation of other bodies. Heterosexual men remain the masters of contagious circulation because they are not implicated in that circulation.

CONCLUSION

This chapter has attempted to read AIDS epidemiology as a political, or more specifically a biopolitical discourse. I have demonstrated that the implicit valuation of bodies which informs its logic indicates that AIDS epidemiology habitually represents the epidemic from the point of view of heterosexual masculine bodily interests. It does this partly through the use of the figure of the immunocompetent body which I investigated in the previous chapter as the basis for its distinction between the normal and the pathological or, in epidemiological terms, the distinction between the 'general population' and 'risk groups'. This implicit hierarchy of value assigned to bodies on the basis of sexual identity is not self-evident, however, because the rhetoric of AIDS epidemiology creates an identification between the health of heterosexual male bodies and a general idea of 'the public health'.

In considering this process of metonymic displacement, where the health of a particular part of the social body is taken to stand for the health of the entire body, I have utilised a particular idea of the body politic as an explanatory framework. The body politic is, I have argued, a means of determining whose bodily interests can be represented in the polity and whose bodily interests are inimical to the social order it enshrines. The admissibility of interest is determined by resemblance, by the degree of analogy which can be established between particular bodies and the morphology of the body politic itself. Biomedicine is a central discourse in the articulation of this resemblance, because it deploys similar regulatory images of the body at both levels of scale. It both analogises particular bodies to the social order and analogises the social order to bodily order, through the use of its 'imaginary anatomies' of health and illness as its basis for intervention and prescription.

The notion of the 'public health' as an entity, the singular state of health of a single composite body of the population, is I have argued one of the most important discourses in the articulation of the body politic. On the one hand casting the 'public health' as a singularity renders it a powerful metaphor of social cohesion and proper order, and furthermore of a vital, productive order explicitly concerned with the well being of its population. On the other hand it naturalises power relationships within the body politic as relationships of the normal and the pathological, where the latter is specified according to degrees of departure from the particular idea of 'health' incorporated in the 'public health'. Hence the idea of the 'public health' can serve the crucial political ends of imagining social unity and naturalising power relationships.

Epidemiological knowledge is concerned, in the case of AIDS, to control the flow of infection within the social body, to localise and prevent infection in the interests of the preservation of the public health. The figure of the immunocompetent body is utilised to imagine the biopolitical order proper to the control of sexual contagion. The immunocompetent body's normalisation of individuated, impenetrable bodies and pathologisation of receptive, multiple bodies provide epidemiology with a means of mapping the direction of threat along the lines of sexual difference.

The bodies of gay and bisexual men and women are considered to be implicated in the spread of infection because of their inherent permeability. They are imagined to form fluid, infectious circuits and ambiguous relationships with other bodies, either sexual or uterine. Just as bodily permeability is the means for the virus to gain access to the fluid matrix of the particular body, to move through its blood stream and lymph system, so too does bodily permeability provide the fluid conduit from body to body which allows the virus to move through the body politic, threatening the public health. Impermeable bodies, heterosexual male bodies, are not implicated in this causal flow but are nevertheless the bodies which are understood to be threatened by it, they are the potential end points of infection. The distinction between *conduit* bodies, through which infection flows, and bodies which serve as the terminus for infection, is inseparable from a notion of the value of these bodies. *Conduit* bodies are significant in the calculation of the public health first as transmission points, through which infection moves. They are considered important in the first instance not because they are themselves infect*ed*, but because they are infect*ing*.

Hence the point of view which functions in AIDS epidemiology, while claiming to be panoptic, a neutral, centralised and evenly distributed gaze, can be seen to be a phallocentric one. Like all knowledges which claim panoptic neutrality, epidemiology is irretrievably perspectival, and its representation of the AIDS epidemic is assembled from the point of view of phallic bodily interests and their protection. The bodies that are less valuable in AIDS epidemiology are either specifically non-phallic, women's bodies, or not exclusively phallic, gay male bodies. Furthermore in the case of women's bodies the capacity for receptivity and multiplicity which aligns them with infectious flow is also the capacity which renders them objects of phallic and paternal desire. AIDS epidemiology can be seen to enact phallocentric bodily interests when it promotes HIV testing of pregnant women and addresses safe sex exhortations not to heterosexual men but to women. Women must be made responsible for safe sex practice because it is the cleanliness of their bodies which is at issue, not that of heterosexual men. Women must be the guardians of safe sex because they are more implicated in infectious flow. Women who comply with this task are rewarded with a provisional inclusion in the 'general population'.

In summary then, heterosexual male bodily interests are made to coincide with the interests of the 'public health', as it is conceived in the age of AIDS, through their resemblance to an ideal bodily order which remains outside the circuits of AIDS contagion. They are the bodies which are held within biomedicine to enact within their morphology the protocols of individuation which Foucault tells us are the strategies undertaken by public health institutions to control infectious spread.[13] They are bodies which are considered to be *already* controlled, to *already* conform to an order proper to the public health.

This public health, the health of the body politic, is however lethally threatened by bodies with unstable boundaries and fluid tendencies, bodies which seep beyond the borders dictated by individuation. These bodies are considered to form contagious circuits within the body politic, to act as weak points in its corporeal matrix which enables the propagation of the virus. Epidemiology imagines its task to be the control of infectious flow, but in making flow an effect of departure from phallic singularity it addresses its strategies to the disciplining of feminine and gay sexualities in order to protect the true denizens of the 'general population', heterosexual men. The bodies of heterosexual men remain on the side of the 'public health', exempted from infectious process except as the valuable bodies upon which viral threat converges.

TECHNOLOGIES OF THE BODY POLITIC

The HIV antibody test

protean, polymorphic, polyvocal,...invisible, soulless, transient, super-humanly mobile, infectious, murderous, suicidal, and a threat to wife, children, home and the phallus.[1]

The previous chapters investigated the conceptual practices through which the biomedical imagination makes explanatory linkages between events in the body's cells and events in the health of national populations. These linkages I have claimed are forged through the deployment of a simple concept of infectious process which is applied at every level of processual scale, with only minor modifications to allow for differences between the microscopic and the macroscopic. HIV infection is understood to move in a similar fashion between cell and cell, body and body and category and category. In all cases its movement is motivated by the self-propagating, anti-human aggrandisement and deceitfulness of the virus, aided first by the perverse desire of the T cell for its own occupation and death, then by the colonisation of the HIV-infected person, rendered into a viral agent through their sexual practice. Finally the virus's interests are aided by the disorderly movement of the virus across mutually exclusive categories of sexuality: from the gay male enclave to the bisexual male, to the 'promiscuous' or pregnant woman and finally to the 'heterosexual population', the heterosexual man, his progeny and, under certain conditions, his wife.

In this chapter I want to investigate more closely the technology which allows the tracking of the virus's progress through these various media, the HIV antibody test. When I refer to this as a technology I mean to evoke a double sense of the word. The HIV test is first of all a technology in the sense that biomedical science understands the term: a series of procedures performed under specified conditions with particular kinds of instrumentation, which produces results held to have a standard and universal significance. Within these terms the HIV test is a specific serological practice whereby a standardised and licensed biochemical reaction, the enzyme-linked immuno-sorbent assay (ELISA) is performed under strict laboratory conditions upon a sample of blood from a particular person. This assay detects antibodies to

HIV proteins, and is usually combined with a second confirmatory test, the Western blot. Two positive ELISA tests and a positive Western blot test are required to determine a person's seropositivity, that is to determine their status as HIV infected. Because HIV infection is generally devoid of symptoms, often for ten or more years after contraction, the HIV test carries a particularly heavy diagnostic weight, producing the only evidence that infection has taken place.

The HIV test is also a technology in the sense developed in Foucault's writing, a technology of sex.[2] 'Technology' here refers to a constellation of administrative and discursive techniques whereby subjects are classified and socially ordered through the securing of a confession as to the 'truth' of their sexuality. The HIV test is not simply a diagnostic laboratory practice but describes an entire bio-administrative regime, taking place over several days or weeks. It involves the voluntary or compelled presentation of a person for testing to a clinic or hospital, the taking of a blood sample, preliminary counselling, the biochemical analysis of the sample, and the return of the person for the report of results. If the laboratory test is positive the next stage of the test begins, the confessional test for transmission 'identity'. Each seropositive subject is asked to provide a history of their sexuality, to review sexual practices for the probable 'mode of transmission', so that they can be positioned in the classificatory schemas of AIDS epidemiology as a case of homosexual, (male) bisexual or heterosexual transmission, and so on. A positive test also marks the beginning of an intricate process of medical surveillance, referral and management which generally continues for the rest of the person's life.

In its double sense as a technology then, the HIV test works to both position the virus in the particular body, to detect the signs of its presence, and to mark the positively tested subject not just with the sign of seropositivity but also with the sign of 'transmission category', of a sexual category which the logic of the administrative form dictates must be exhaustive and mutually exclusive. In this way the HIV test is the central technology in the biomedical mapping of the virus's presence in the body politic. The procedures of the laboratory tests render the concealed infection visible in the particular body, while the designation of each subject's infection according to the classificatory logic of sexual identity renders them visible and *meaningful* to the scopic technologies of epidemiology and various other bureaucratic surveillance practices. This classification is the necessary corollary of their being positioned within epidemiology's hierarchical mapping of risk.

Furthermore the HIV test works as a 'technology of the self'. It is a crucial inscriptive technology through which the recent forms of pathologised sexual identity, those that have emerged out of the biopolitical field of AIDS, are introjected into the identity processes of sexed subjectivity. The HIV test is a technology not just of subjection but of subjectification, a technology which not only compels subjects in certain ways but which also induces the internalisation of new norms of identity and self-management, above all the management of one's health and one's sexual practices, in the interests of minimising illness and HIV transmission.

The HIV test thus acts simultaneously as a diagnostic technology for clinical medicine, a surveillance technology for epidemiology, and a disciplinary technology for the medico/social management of the infected. For these reasons HIV testing is a key technology in Australian HIV policy and the policies of other first world countries. The test is widely available to those who volunteer, and compulsory in certain contexts.[3]

Part of the general AIDS education strategy in Australia and other first world nations has involved asking that every citizen assess their own risk and decide accordingly whether or not to be tested. Of course the implications of this request differ according to the 'transmission category' that each subject identifies as their own. The demand for risk assessment is far more rigorous for certain groups than it is for others, depending on what position their self-identified categories occupy in the hierarchy of infectiousness determined by epidemiology. As the Commonwealth white paper puts it, 'Voluntary testing will be encouraged. People whose activities places [sic] them at greater risk will be strongly encouraged, and indeed have a duty, to be tested' (Commonwealth Department of Community Services and Health 1989: 38). This category position will further determine the extent to which they are actively medicalised, sought out, or 'targeted' by programmes designed to encourage testing.

For gay identified men, as Patton notes, this amounts to a strong sense of obligation to be tested. Gay male identity has become, in a sense, incomplete without the further qualifier of HIV positive or HIV negative. Gay men, she writes,

> [are] under pressure to identify themselves as and organise their life around the idea of being a 'positive' or a 'negative' ... serostatus has become part of the identity of gay men involved in urban gay communities.
>
> (Patton 1990: 39)

A similar sense of obligation circulates among pregnant women, engendered through the various general medical strategies of responsiblisation of the pregnant body, and also through more specific policy-defined requests that women presenting for the first ante-natal visit be 'offered' an HIV test, an offer which is unlikely to be refused (MacDonald et al. 1992).

Predictably enough the category least obliged to be tested are 'heterosexuals' (not including pregnant women) and this dispensation from obligation is lived out in demonstrable ways. Heterosexual men, for example, evince a general conviction that they themselves are 'clean' without resort to testing as proof (Waldby et al. 1993b) and are far less likely to present for testing compared to men who identify as gay or as bisexual (Waddell 1993). A survey conducted in the emergency department of a major Sydney hospital found that only 7 per cent of self-identified 'heterosexuals' had been tested for HIV antibodies, while a similar survey in another Sydney hospital found 11 per cent.[4]

So the category 'heterosexual' can be seen to escape problematisation, although there are differences within the category in this regard, along similar lines to those discussed in the previous chapter. The most salient exception to heterosexual privilege here is the case of pregnant women and sex workers, both of whom are subject to high amounts of HIV testing. But more important than the implications of this category's dispensation for assessments of personal risk is the way that the interpretation of test results and the organisation of 'transmission categories' themselves work to protect the cleanliness of the *category*, as opposed to the cleanliness of any particular subject who might identify with it. This protective drive is evident, I will argue, in the ways that the uncertainties of the laboratory test results and the ambiguities in classifications of sexual behaviour into 'transmission categories' are adjudicated.

I have sketched out two interlinking arguments about the political operation of the HIV test. First of all I have characterised the test as a biomedical scopic technology and a technology of sex, which classifies viral presence in the body according to the sexual/transmission identity of that body, and inserts it into various medical and self-management regimes. Second I have claimed that in doing so the HIV test systematically privileges and protects the category of heterosexuality through its rendering into the most residual category of infectivity. This chapter will expand upon these two propositions in turn.

PART I – THE HIV TEST AS A TECHNOLOGY OF SEX

The HIV test is used in two different ways to measure the incidence of infection in a population. It may be used in sentinel or unlinked testing, where blood samples taken for other purposes are additionally tested for the presence of HIV in an anonymous fashion. These test results are not attributed to particular persons but are taken to indicate infectious levels within particular populations. The test is also used diagnostically, as a test for infection in particular persons. It is this second use I will discuss here, in relation to the idea of 'screening' populations for disease.

Screening is a medical strategy which uses a diagnostic procedure to identify pathology in the absence of symptoms. Screening programmes are the primary strategy of what has become known in public health terminology as secondary prevention, a strategy which involves an intensification of medicine's temporal and spatial interventionist tendencies. What I mean by this is that screening partakes of the medical drive to envision the ever more minute, the ever more remote and concealed parts of the body, and to push the temporality of aetiology back further and further, so that the causes of illness can be detected at ever earlier stages of the organism's life. This drive is well represented by the current search for genetic origins of illness, which have the advantage of both working at a molecular level of scale and being locatable not only in the foetus but in the genetic line of parents and grandparents.

Screening is the application of this drive to the problem of the public health, where concealed signs of disease are systematically sought in the bodies of a large part of the population deemed to be at potential risk of later disease. Its necessary correlate is the existence of a medical 'test' of some kind, a simple, inexpensive, relatively rapid technique that can be used repeatedly upon apparently well bodies to discern which conceal incipient pathology. Tests include visualising techniques like X-rays and procedures that require the analysis of samples in pathology laboratories, like pap smears, and so on. Such tests form the threshold, for those who are positively diagnosed, of entry into regimes of either cure, where such a possibility exists, or medical management of some kind where cure is not possible or where it fails.

Screening then occupies a hinge position between clinical and public health. Testing provides two kinds of medical knowledge. First it produces vital signs for the purposes of monitoring the state of the public health with regard to particular diseases. In this way increases in the incidence of, for example, cervical cancer and pre-cancerous neoplasias can be measured and analysed, causes for the increase can be sought, education campaigns designed and so on. Second, testing works as the first component in an individual diagnosis for the person screened. It either provides reassurance that no hidden pathology exists, or it brings them into the ambit of clinical medical attention and demands a reordering of everyday life around a new status as ill or, as Sontag (1989) puts it, 'future ill'.

The HIV test was first developed to facilitate the screening of blood donations, and then modified to be used in individual diagnostic screening in the sense described. Much of the initial impetus to 'discover' the putative virus which caused AIDS was derived from the desire to design such a test (Shilts 1987). Prior to the existence of the test the only way in which an AIDS diagnosis could be reached was through the interpretation of an heterogeneous and idiosyncratic array of symptoms. While the possibility of an asymptomatic latency period of infection was suspected, it was not able to be verified. The existence of an antibody test allowed AIDS science to make its first step away from reliance on the interpretation of visible symptoms and into the interior of the AIDS body (Ariss 1992).

The gradually standardised HIV tests then became research technologies, used by epidemiologists to determine the possibilities and extent of asymptomatic infection. By 1986 it was generally thought in AIDS biomedical circles that asymptomatic infection with HIV could have a very long period of latency, a perception which increased the significance and centrality of the HIV test in the medical strategies for the control of AIDS. Long latency implied that large numbers of the infected could act for years as unwitting viral agents, doing the virus's bidding with every sexual encounter. The

116

confirmation of long asymptomatic latency motivated demands on the part of sectors of both US and Australian medical establishments for compulsory testing of 'high risk' groups, or at minimum for the use of the HIV test as the centrepiece of prevention and education strategies (Ballard 1992; Patton 1990).

The strong favour found among biomedical interests for the widespread use of the HIV test derives, as I suggested above, from its simultaneous efficacy as a scopic/identificatory technology and a disciplining technology. I have grouped the scopic and identificatory functions together here because it seems to me that they present a biomedical solution to the general problem of the invisibility of HIV infection. The invisibility of disease is always a problem for biomedicine, hence the emphasis it places on the importance of the diagnostic gaze and the array of scopic technologies dedicated to overcoming the body's opacity. However, HIV infection is particularly elusive to the biomedical gaze, compounding a number of problems of invisibility within a single disease. These problems are posed by certain qualities particular to the HIV virus. HIV demonstrates a unique ability to 'pass', to imitate normalcy, both at the level of the cells inside the body and the level of the 'carrier', the viral agent in the social body.

Viral passing

Within gay/queer subculture, 'passing' is the term for the practice of mimicking the straight world successfully, of adopting the appearance of the 'normal' and the heterosexual. When I say that the virus can 'pass' in the body, I mean that the biomedical representation of the virus constantly attributes it with a repertoire of mimicry, deceitfulness and false identity. The itinerary of the virus within the body's cellular matrix is narrated as a drama of concealment, disguise, misrecognition and protean transformation.

One of the major reasons that the virus is thought to be so successful in its occupation of the body is because it can conceal its true nature from the surveillance of the immune system. It gains access to the body through its concealment in blood and semen, a method which one popular immunology text likens to the Trojan horse.

> Like Greeks hidden inside the Trojan horse, the AIDS virus enters the body concealed inside a helper T cell from an infected host....Once inside an inactive T cell, the virus may lie dormant for months, even years.
>
> (Jaret 1986: 723)

Once inside the body the virus is thought to use a range of disguising and mimicking strategies, which both protect it from immune system attack and induce the immune system to attack healthy cells. The virus can, for example, conceal itself within certain cells. Cells of monocytic/macrophage origin are

117

particularly effective in this regard. Unlike the infected T4 cells, there is no sign visible to biomedicine's visualising technologies of the virus's presence in the monocyte/macrophage cells.

> In an individual subject, many infected cells seem to harbour proviruses but not express them as virus. . . .At least some monocyte and neural cell lines infected with HIV do not express viral RNA or proteins in large amounts, apparently because of transcriptional inactivity of the pro-virus. . . .These results are consistent with the emerging notion that latently infected cells of the macrophage/monocyte lineage are impor-tant reservoirs of virus *in vivo*.
>
> (Coffin 1990: S3)

The virus does not express on the cell surface, it leaves no trace of its occupation of the cell, but it nevertheless makes use of the cell as its proxy. The infected macrophage can circulate unhindered in the body because it cannot be distinguished by the rest of the immune system from other uninfected macrophages, and so can spread infection to other cells without interference. In other words the infected macrophage presents the same problem for the immune system as the infected person presents to epidemiology and public health strategies. In the absence of visible signs of infection both infected cell and infected person can spread infection unhindered.

The HIV is also a 'master of disguise'. It is said to display a high degree of biological variability, along a number of parameters. Gallo observes that 'Unlike many viruses, which have only a few [genetic] strains, HTLV-III[5] comprises a great many variants that form a continuum of related strains' (Gallo 1987: 47). It is this multiplicity of genetic identities under a single viral name which makes the development of vaccines difficult, because the vaccine must be able to alert the T cells to the spectrum of genetic variations.

These variants may themselves mutate rapidly within the body, outpacing the immune system's capacity to deal with viral presence. Ironically it is through an accumulation of replicative 'error, the making of bad copies of its own RNA genetic code with each replicative cycle, that certain core proteins and the protein coat of the virus rapidly alter' (Brown 1992).

The virus can also reconfigure its outer surface, described as the variability of its viral envelope (Tersmette and Miedema 1990), or it may 'mimic certain molecules normally found on cells of uninfected individuals' so that it does not appear 'foreign' to the immune system (Sattentau 1988). On the other hand the virus may be able to mimic a particular group of human proteins, the MHC molecules, with the net effect of inducing the immune system to 'see' its own host tissue as hostile and hence attack it (Brown 1992).

So the efficacy of the HIV, its 'strategic' status as a kind of metavirus within biomedicine, derives from a lack of proper, singular viral identity. It is protean, chimerical, but its transformations are purposive in the logic of biomedicine. It seeks to 'pass' within the body, to dissemble its identity as virus and to take on the appearance of either a benign entity or to render itself invisible through its concealment inside host cells. It is a secret agent sent from the inhuman world, as Treichler (1988a) is led to observe, a 007 of viruses.

The immune system, however, is not completely misled by these protean strategies, and the ability of the HIV test to detect viral presence depends upon the limited and partial forms of recognition that the immune system extends to HIV infection. The HIV test tests not for the existence of virus but for antibodies to certain of the virus's proteins, that is it tests for the products of the body's immune system generated in a protective response to infection. The HIV test will only produce a proper result after what is termed 'seroconversion', that is after the immune system produces antibodies to HIV infection. These antibodies are thought to not confer a fully protective effect against HIV infection because they fail to react across the broad range of variability of HIV strains and their mutations (Hamburg *et al.* 1990). The HIV test is designed to test antibodies produced to what are considered more stable core proteins, and the test procedures effectively amplify and render visible this antibody response.

In this sense the HIV test is a test organised around the virus's failures to 'pass' within the immune system. However, the partial and somewhat idiosyncratic nature of the antibody response to viral presence lends a degree of uncertainty and ambiguity to the operation of the test technology. Viral presence or absence cannot always be determined in the absolute sense implied by the either/or logic of the positive or negative test result. While this binary logic of the HIV test implies that biomedical technology can exceed the limitations of the body's own interpretive and scopic 'technologies' with regard to the HIV, it is nevertheless dependent upon the ambiguous and partial antibody recognition that it is designed to overcome.

This problem of the ambiguous identification of the virus is not simply a technical but also a political problem for the status of the HIV antibody test. Its status as a dependable technology of public health rests upon its claim to be able to make clear determinations of infectious status, to sort the infected from the uninfected in a straightforward fashion. Consequently the test must use some method to limit the possible range of error in its results. As we shall see these limits are set through the categorisation of the infected person into a transmission 'identity', which carries with it a preordained probability of infection. This dynamic is crucial for my consideration of the HIV test's implication in the process of representing infection. However, before I discuss this more fully I will turn to the second problem of invisibility posed by the virus, the problem of the carrier's invisibility, and the way that the technology of the test helps to solve this problem.

Carrier passing

If the HIV test is a test for a virus which can mimic the body's normal cellular identity, it is also a test for the infected who, in the absence of visible symptoms, can pass as uninfected. The HIV seropositive person may 'pass' irrespective of their own knowledge of their infection, because the virus's ability to 'pass' within the immune system for a number of years renders them asymptomatic. The symptom is the phenomenal mark of illness, perceptible to the sick person and to the casual or professional observer. In the case of HIV infection, there are generally no signs that mark the person off as infected, either to themselves or to others, until the development of AIDS symptoms, which may emerge up to fifteen years after the moment of infection.[6]

At various times there have been calls among conservatives for the marking of the HIV seropositive in a fashion which is clearly discernible to all, through tattooing, the compulsory carrying of cards, and so on. The point of this demand is that it would make the mimicking of 'normalcy' impossible, but these demands have been treated as unreasonable in the industrialised democracies.[7] So while the HIV test is not associated with such crude identificatory strategies it nevertheless compels a less literal and more acceptable form of identification, more acceptable because it is a form of identification general to first world political culture.

What I mean here is that the HIV test compels the 'truth' of transmission identity against the dissimulation of carrier passing. The HIV test is, as Patton (1990) observes, a 'coercive technology of confession'. In Foucault's elaboration of the concept of technologies of sex, the eliciting of sexual confession is the crucial moment in the working of such technologies, enabling the forcible establishment of sexual identity. Through the technologies of confession to authorities, technologies which include official interviews, medical examinations, questionnaires and so on, subjects are both obliged to know themselves as sexual identities and to make themselves available for sexual identification and administration. In this sense confession can be understood as the opposite practice to that of 'passing'. Both practices work off an equation between truth and identity, but while confession poses itself as an expression of this truth, 'passing' involves a lie, a dissimulation of the truth of the self. Foucault writes of this social imperative to know the truth of one's sexuality, and to offer up this truth for scientific/rational administration.

> One had to speak of sex: one had to speak publicly and in a manner that was not determined by the division between the licit and the illicit . . . one had to speak of it as a thing to be not simply condemned or tolerated but managed, inserted into systems of utility, regulated for the greater good of all . . . . Sex was not something one simply judged; it was a thing to be administered.
>
> (Foucault 1980a: 24)

The form and consequences of the HIV test are exemplary instances of such confessional imperatives. Through linking together a confession of 'transmission identity' with such consequential classificatory procedures, the HIV test effects permanent, although not literally or generally visible, forms of identification upon the seropositive. The test marks its subjects in the following ways. First, by assigning them a 'transmission category' it allocates them a position within its gallery of 'types', reductive personifications of the HIV carrier. This typification works at a general level as a kind of diffuse public identification, a pale ghost of the tattoo strategy. Second it renders them visible to certain technologies of socio-medical surveillance. Third it marks or seeks to mark them with an introjected guilt and sense of responsibility, the internalisation of 'transmission category' as dangerous self-identity. I will discuss these marking strategies in turn.

Transmission category as personification

In counterposing the process of 'passing' with that of identification I have tried to set up a resemblance between the classificatory logic of the HIV test and the general social drive to identify the 'homosexual'. This drive is made more urgent, Edelman observes, precisely because the 'homosexual' man or woman is difficult to distinguish from the 'normal' man or woman, and so the image of the homosexual 'type' must be elaborated to act as a guide to identification (Edelman 1992). This elaboration of putatively identifiable 'transmission types' is part of the task of the HIV test. Allocation to an 'exposure category' literally personifies the virus, giving a generally recognisable persona to an otherwise anonymous disease process. The following paragraph from an AIDS epidemiology text comes very close to acknowledging this personification effect.

> Surveillance of infection . . . requires the systematic collection of serum and epidemiological information on population groups. The results are collated and analysed according to various epidemiological classifications of risk. Ideally, regular collection of samples from such groups . . . *should yield information that is valuable for informing the public on their chance of contacting an infected individual.*
>
> (Francis and Kaslow 1989: 255; emphasis mine)

Here the 'chance of contacting an infected individual' refers not to a random chance spread across the population described here as 'the public', but rather to a kind of index of virulence of members of the various 'exposure categories'. The HIV test and the transmission 'type' stand in a mutually connotative relationship here, where the HIV test 'diagnoses' the type of person who is seropositive, while the 'type' also points towards an imaginary probability of infectiousness. This personification process engenders general social effects which extend beyond and don't necessarily single out the HIV seropositive person. Rather anyone who might be identified with the category is vulnerable to possible characterisation as HIV seropositive.[8]

In relation to picturing the HIV positive person, this typification process occurs not only in relation to the 'homosexual transmission' category but also to some of the other categories for which reductive images are readily available in the culture, particularly that of 'injecting drug user'. Recently there have been attempts within both professional and media AIDS discourse to invent a similar persona for the bisexual man, the category which, not incidentally, is one of the current foci of epidemiological anxiety.

Given the general circulation of these authoritative personifications of the virus, the idea that it is possible to 'tell' from appearance if someone is HIV seropositive is, not surprisingly, a commonly held belief. Kitzinger's study (1991), for example, found a tendency among a very diverse range of people to rely on ideas about the 'look' of an HIV-infected person, ideas which combined images of dirt and disease with images of 'risk group' membership.

> Participants accepted that you could 'carry AIDS' without looking ill, but rejected the idea that there were no visual clues at all to help you identify someone who might have the virus. Different groups, including doctors, male prostitutes, . . . social workers and prisoners, were all able to describe 'safe-looking' versus 'unsafe-looking' patients, clients, punters or lovers.
>
> (Kitzinger 1991: 158)

The assumption here reproduces the identificatory logic of the HIV test, although there is a significant difference. While both everyday identification and the test combine signs of illness with signs of sexuality, the first applies itself to the social surface of the body, the 'look' of the person, while the superior technology of the test applies itself to the person's interior, the combination of their antibodies and their confession, their sexual history. Here again the biomedical imagination takes the body's surface meaning, its social interpretation, and reads its back into the microscopic interior.

The HIV test as a technology of institutional visibility

The HIV test also marks the seropositive by acting as a threshold to various regimes of medical management, and to changes in legal status precipitated by a positive test result. A positive test result ushers the tested into a state of permanent institutional visibility.

In Australia and some states in the USA a positive HIV test is a notifiable disease, meaning that a specified, centralised monitoring body is informed of the result. In some states in Australia notification involves linking a positive result with the name of the person, while in others notification is anonymous. In the latter case the person's name must nevertheless be retained by the doctor requesting the test, and this information can be demanded by a court order (Patterson 1992).

Hence a positive HIV test ushers the person tested, and also their sexual partners in some cases,[9] into a state of at least potential visibility to centralised public health surveillance. The test result also inserts them into a 'medical management' regime, a nexus of medical and paramedical services and institutions designed to address their seropositivity in particular ways. These services include 'in-patient and out-patient hospital services, a variety of medical specialists, community services, home support services and self-help groups' (Tindall *et al.* 1992: 211). The asymptomatic HIV seropositive person will be referred to dietitians and to counsellors, invited to volunteer for clinical trials and epidemiological cohort studies. For the asymptomatic a three monthly medical monitoring regime is recommended, involving,

> [performance of] baseline tests [T cell counts], monitoring immune-function and encouraging the person to self-monitor...early and aggressive treatment of treatable infections...[and] routine vaccination against infections such as hepatitis B.
>
> (Tindall *et al.* 1992: 216)

In other words by virtue of a positive HIV test the tested is at least partially removed from the world of normalcy and symptomless health and delivered over as a subject of various institutional regimens. These regimens act as hinge technologies for a two-way visibility. They place the microscopic developments of HIV infection within the person under a regular form of inspection, and they place the person's practices under a regular form of surveillance.

They also work to create a particular kind of circumscribed social location for the HIV seropositive, organised around institutional recognition of seropositivity. While HIV status is not generally available knowledge it is nevertheless a known status within a particular set of medical and paramedical institutions, and forms the basis for referral to others. Within certain institutional contexts, particularly hospitals, the HIV seropositive are often marked in a generally visible fashion, at least for staff, through the marking of accessible files or patient's rooms with 'bio-hazard' stickers and other such distinguishing practices (New South Wales Anti-Discrimination Board 1992). This limited circulation of identification of course always threatens to spill over into more general circulation through lack of staff discretion, blackmail, inappropriate referral and so on.

Furthermore under certain conditions tests for HIV seropositivity can be legally requested by police and public health officials, and can form the basis for detention and prosecution. Under some Australian state legislation an HIV seropositive person is legally required to inform potential sexual partners of the fact, and to reveal the names and addresses of sexual contacts (Patterson 1992). Doctors in some states may make immediate detention orders for HIV seropositive persons who 'persistently behave in such a way as to place other persons at risk of infection' (Commonwealth Department of Community Services and Health 1989: 41) which in practice refers to the practice of 'unprotected' sex with different people.[10] Similar legislation operates in most of the US states (Patton 1990).

Hence the HIV seropositive are marked through their assimilation into the economies of such institutions, which seek to make the invisible developments of their infection visible in a regular and measurable way, that can be communicated between institutions. In short the HIV seropositive are *identified* as such within these contexts, identification which also seeks to mark the seropositive with this status as an *identity*. This is the third inscriptive practice that I have attributed to the HIV test. It attempts to induce the internalisation of a sense of self as dangerous, as infected, and hence to precipitate a new ethics of sexual practice and institutional deportment for the seropositive person. If the infected person is understood in biomedicine as a proxy for the virus, this inducement of a sense of responsibility is a means of pre-empting the person's cooperation with viral interests, through propagation of infection in other bodies.

Ideally the seropositive person undertakes two obligations. They are placed under a continuing obligation to confess their positivity to appropriate authorities, and an obligation to adopt a disciplined and prudent sexual practice oriented towards the protection of others.

The knowledge of seropositivity gained through the inaugural test confession places the person under obligation to repeated confession of seropositivity. They are obliged to inform doctors and medical staff, for example, to signal the need for various kinds of prophylaxis and precautionary measures (the use of 'universal precautions' or 'barrier nursing') and to ensure that this status is taken into account in medical procedures. They are encouraged, and ultimately obliged, to inform current and former partners so that they too can have their serostatus checked.

They are also encouraged to volunteer for one or more of the many clinical trials and epidemiological cohort studies which are in train at any given time, studies which in general rest upon extended sexual confession. As Patton points out, current levels of scientific knowledge about AIDS owe an enormous debt to the confession of the infected.

> In the first few years of the epidemic . . . science needed the speech of people with AIDS and their friends in order to unlock the 'mystery' of AIDS – a Nobel-prize winning task. Many men (and some women) willingly gave evidence of their illness and their lives, describing symptoms and answering long epidemiological questionnaires about the intimate details of rich and complex sex lives.
>
> (Patton 1990: 130)

The medical management of seropositivity also involves the inducement of a permanent state of self-examination and confessional imperative about

124

sexual practice. Social demands for transformations in sexual practice are not, of course, limited to those directly identified as infected. As Singer observes, the conditions of sexual epidemic create a climate in which everybody's sexual practices are subject to some degree of scrutiny.

> Because the prospect of contagion raises the social stakes attached to individual behavioural choices, and because in an epidemic situation such latitude carries the signification of threat and risk, epidemic conditions can and in fact are being represented as occasions necessitating organised efforts to co-ordinate the behaviour of individuals through the generation of new forms of sexual discipline and management.
>
> (Singer 1993: 62–3)

This imperative has motivated both 'general population' and specific group education efforts in order to inculcate new norms of sexual practice throughout the population. For the HIV seropositive, however, the adoption of such norms is made obligatory rather than desirable, through intensive counselling and support group pressure, and through ultimate recourse to the criminalisation of unprotected sex on the part of an HIV seropositive person.

So the HIV test works as the most important technology through which the virus is personified, that is made coterminous with the person infected, who is in turn rendered into an identity category. Because the spread of the virus within the body cannot be controlled by medical prophylaxis, the scale of control moves up to the level of the person infected. The strategies associated with the HIV test both confirm the person's status as a viral representative and seek to prevent the person's furthering of viral interests, through their systematic responsibilisation as the potential 'causes' of infection in the social body.

It is important to note that this responsibilisation of the infected has been and continues to be contested among the infected themselves and among the 'risk groups' associated with AIDS, particularly among gay male communities. Contestation takes a number of forms, including resistance to pressures to be tested, on the grounds of a refusal of medicalisation (Ariss 1992). The development of new non-transmitting erotic practices under the rubric of 'safe sex' have constituted another effective subversion of this responsibilisation. 'Safe sex' offers, at least potentially, the possibility of each person rechoreographing their sexual practice according to the new dangers posed by HIV infection. If 'safe sex' is adopted as a general practice, rather than a practice limited to the infected, it effectively makes the distinction between infected and uninfected redundant. Ideally safe sex involves everybody acting *as if* they were infected, so that nobody need declare themselves as such.[11] In this sense it represents an effective counter to the imperative to identification represented by the HIV test, and an ethical alternative to the logic which holds that the infected are inherently culpable and the uninfected inherently innocent.

PART II – INTERPRETATION OF THE HIV TEST

The HIV test is thus the AIDS technology which carries the most severe implications for particular subjects. The HIV seropositive are made to bear the heaviest weight of responsibility for the ways that the virus and infectious process have been conceptualised. Having examined how this responsibilisation is facilitated by the test, I want now to turn to the question of how the test procedure classifies the tested, and how this classificatory logic works within the broader sexual politics of AIDS. I want particularly to investigate how the test classifies sexualities into hierarchies of infectiousness within its exposure categories. I will demonstrate that the interpretation and classification of test results works to make the heterosexual category the most residual, the least likely to be nominated as a 'source' of infection. This classificatory logic works both at the level of the 'technical' interpretation of test results, and at the level of statistical/classificatory procedures, which I shall discuss in turn.

Adjudications of ambiguity in test results

The HIV test acts *as if* it is a simple indicator of the presence or absence of virus, but as I tried to suggest in the introduction to this chapter the binary logic that this claim depends upon, the logic of either positivity or negativity, can be read as the simplification of an ambiguous field in the interests of a notion of the public health. The HIV test can be problematised as both more constitutive of the 'fact' of HIV infection that it ostensibly tests in an objective fashion, and more subject to uncertainty, and hence to interpretation, than the rhetoric of the test result suggests.

Fleck (1979) in his analysis of the development of the Wassermann test for syphilis demonstrates that serological tests can only function *as tests*, as simple, rapid determinations of presence or absence of an infection or condition, within very limited interpretive constraints. The test can only function as such when the definition of the disease to be tested has been simplified as far as possible into an A/not A formula, on a strong principle of exclusion. The disease must be defined in a way which allows a simple distinction to be made between either its presence or its absence. It is only after this definition is brought into line with the limited capacities of the test that a test becomes a standardised reaction, and hence useful in a large number of cases. In other words the test and the disease tested must become implicated in each other's definitions before a test can identify disease in a regular and repeatable way. Fleck writes:

> The perfection of the Wassermann reaction can be seen ... as the solution to the following problem: How does one define syphilis and set up a blood test, so that after some experience almost any research

worker will be able to demonstrate a relation between them to a degree that is adequate in practice?

(Fleck 1979: 98)

In other words the creation of a serological test has the effect of actively redefining the conceptualisation of a disease entity, refining it and orienting it in a certain direction based on the limitations of the test. The creation of a standardised and hence usable test depends upon a reciprocal standardisation of the concept of the disease. The disease becomes that condition which can be tested by the test.

This reciprocal redefinition is evident in the history of the relationship between the HIV test and AIDS. The earliest HIV tests developed were implicated in the 'confirmation' of AIDS as a single disease and this confirmatory action also worked in the reverse direction, so that the already proposed coherence of AIDS symptoms confirmed the efficacy of the early HIV tests. As I argued earlier, one principle of coherence initially used to link together the heterogeneous range of symptoms that were provisionally classified together as Acquired Immunodeficiency Syndrome was the homosexuality of the sufferers of symptoms. Before the term AIDS was coined these symptoms were classified together as Gay Related Immune Deficiency (GRID). It was only when evidence of a similar constellation of symptoms began to appear among other populations in the USA (haemophiliacs and intravenous drug users) that some medical specialists began to propose a viral 'common cause' as the principle of the symptoms' coherence (Shilts 1987).

When the virus(es) termed HTLV-III and/or LAV[12] were proposed as the aetiological agent of AIDS in 1984, antibody tests to the virus(es) were used to 'prove' the coherence of AIDS symptoms as manifestations of a single disease entity, because a characteristic antibody reaction could be demonstrated in the sera of patients with such constellations of symptoms (Oppenheimer 1988). At the same time the communality of symptoms among those administered a positive antibody test could be taken to 'prove' the efficacy of the test. The HIV test is in this sense inextricable from the definition of what AIDS is. Nor can it be extricated from the definition of the asymptomatic presence of the virus. Patton (1990) evokes this mutually constitutive relationship when she states 'HIV does not *exist* outside the test'. It is this mutual implication which belies the test's status in the popular imagination as simply a technical means of identifying an existing pathological condition. Rather the configuration of the test and its 'workability' can be regarded as itself symptomatic of certain ways of defining AIDS.

The crucial point in all this is that the configuration of the test as it is used today, its procedures and interpretations, incorporate the pre-test history of the definition of AIDS symptoms as coherent syndromes through their location in 'high risk' populations. This is one of the important ways that the definition of the disease AIDS has been simplified to enable testing to work in a relatively straightforward fashion. While the test technology overtook this epidemiological principle of coherence with a viral principle, it also assumed it into its interpretative baggage as it were as a necessary 'fixed point' from which to adjudicate the ambiguity of test results. Consequently the process of interpreting test results depends, in the final instance, upon the way that the person tested is classified, to which 'transmission category' they are assigned.

Within serological/epidemiological practice this cross-referencing counts as a way to eliminate uncertainty, a way to narrow down the range of probable error in the interpretation of test results. A fixed idea of sexual identity and 'risk group' membership functions here to pre-empt a Heisenbergian uncertainty in the significance of test results. However, if, as I have argued, sexual identity can only ever be considered a provisional category whose coherence is at best problematic, the HIV antibody test result can also be considered to compound two kinds of ambiguity, those of antibody response and sexual identity.

Nevertheless, within the terms of epidemiologic, transmission identity is treated as stable for purposes of classification and test interpretation. It is the configuration of the two primary tests for HIV, the ELISA and the Western blot, the particular ways that they play off seropositivity against identity, that I will now discuss.

Serological tests are necessarily 'tuned' in certain ways, to control for certain kinds of uncertainty and to admit other kinds. The two primary co-ordinates in the design of a serological test are those of sensitivity and specificity, qualities which tend to work at odds with each other. The sensitivity of a test refers to its reactivity, the limit to which it will detect the presence of the substance for which it is testing. A very sensitive test will detect very small amounts of substance, or substance in very weak solution for example, which may be a desired quality of tests within certain contexts. Highly sensitive tests tend, however, to be volatile and over-reactive. They tend to cross-react, to react to other substances which are similar in some way to the substance being sought, and they are also easily contaminated. The design of an effective serological test always involves a trade-off between this oversensitivity and test specificity, that is the extent to which the test only reacts to the specific substance being sought. Highly specific tests tend to produce false negative results, that is they will fail to detect the substance in a certain percentage of cases, while highly sensitive tests will produce false positives, finding substance where there is none.

The ELISA test historically has been a sensitive test which sacrifices some specificity and produces false positives. This configuration reflects its initial purpose as a screening test for blood donors to secure the blood supply against HIV infection, a function where false positivity is considered safer than false negativity.

False-positive screening tests result in many discarded, even though non-infected, units of blood . . . .Conversely, a relatively high number of false-negative results would result in HIV-1 transmission to transfusion recipients. This outcome is minimised by optimising screening test sensitivity rather than specificity.

(Sloand *et al.* 1991: 2861)

The early configurations of ELISA, which was first licensed for commercial use in 1985, were cross-reactive to malaria antibodies (Patton 1990) and to some immune system changes in pregnancy, among other things (Sloand *et al.* 1991). Later refinements of ELISA continue to produce false positives, estimated to be as high as 70 per cent of the first ELISA performed (Sloand *et al.* 1991). Even after a second test false positives are estimated to stand at two per one thousand uninfected persons (Ascher and Kaslow 1989).

This engineering of the ELISA test as a sensitive blood screening test has led to the use of a second test, the Western blot, as a confirmatory test. An individual diagnosis of positivity requires two positive ELISAs and a positive Western blot. While the interpretation of an ELISA test is regarded as relatively straightforward, and is now performed by computer, Western blot tests are more ambiguous and require particular scientists to have considerable skill and experience in their interpretation (Patton 1990). Western blot tests, more so than ELISAs, depend upon the particular vagaries of the immune system's recognition of the HIV. The WB test separates out various antibody reactions to particular viral core and envelope proteins of the virus into discrete coloured bands, and a certain characteristic pattern of bands is taken to indicate HIV infection.

These tests have certain limitations at the margins of infection. They cannot detect the presence of virus until after what is termed the 'window period', the lag between the virus entry into the body and the formation of an antibody response. They may fail to detect infection in persons with advanced immunodeficiency, because they have lost the ability to produce antibody altogether. But they also have the possibility for ambiguous results and for false positive results, and the interpretation of these results depends upon the way that the person concerned is classified, whether they count as high or low risk.

This is so because false positives are considered to be predictable artefacts of the test technology. Any particular form of the ELISA test will produce a certain regular percentage of tests as false positives. The likelihood of any particular person's test being a false positive is then determined by the overall seroprevalence within the population to which the person is deemed to belong. The following explanation of this interpretative framework is taken from a microbiology text.

For any laboratory test, methodological error, regardless of source, occurs with a relatively fixed frequency; therefore, for each population tested, regardless of risk for HIV-1 infection, the number of false

129

positives per 1000 tests will be approximately the same. However, in a low-risk population (with few true positives) the number of false positives will be a much greater percentage of those called positive than for a high risk population. Therefore, the positive predictive value [the likelihood of the result being correct] of such a screening test in a low-risk population may only be 10%, while it could be as high as 97.3% in a high-risk population.

(Schleupner 1990: 1094)

The standard procedure of performing two ELISA tests and a Western blot test upon any given serum sample to determine serostatus is designed to minimise the production of a false result due to methodological error. A positive result requires all three tests to be positive. In serological terms these tests are considered to have very low levels of error, and there has been considerable refinement in recent years to eliminate contaminates and cross-reactivity.

Nevertheless, interpretations of test results depend ultimately upon the tested person's 'transmission category', the constant against which the variable of seropositivity is measured. Two types of test ambiguity are recognised in the literature. First of all there are indeterminate tests, generally a positive ELISA combined with a WB result which shows some but not all the colour bands said to be typical of HIV infection. In this case the 'transmission category' of the person tested will have a decisive effect on the way that the results are interpreted. Category membership may determine, for example, whether the person is notified as positive or whether further tests are called for.

> Great care must be exercised in the use and interpretation of the Western blot in evaluating [ELISA] positives. Based on current, extremely stringent criteria, a high proportion of early positive samples are categorised as indeterminate. In screening low-risk groups without notification, as in blood banks, where most positives are false positives, the impact of the problem is slight. But in screening high-risk groups, where as many as 96% of the indeterminate blots by current criteria may actually represent positive specimens, the impact of the uncertainty of classifying such specimens is more significant. For the purposes of notification of healthy individuals who meet blood donation criteria, the requirement for antibodies to all three gene products – *gag*, *pol* and *env* – is appropriate, whereas in sick or late-stage individuals, such criteria are clearly inappropriate, and other approaches are required.
>
> (Ascher and Kaslow 1989: 44)

Note here that 'healthy individuals who meet blood donation criteria' refers to the process of self-screening that is required of blood donors, who must be assessed as at 'low risk' for HIV before their donation is accepted. Sloand *et al.* (1991) report that, within the 'blood donor population', a serological shorthand for the low risk 'general population', individuals can show 'persistently indeterminate Western blot patterns' and still be classified as uninfected, despite the fact that the US Federal Drug Administration will not accept their blood donation. Indeterminate WB pattern for a person classified as 'high risk' will be treated quite differently, either as a positive or a provisional positive, subject to further, more lengthy and expensive tests.

The second type of ambiguity relates to how a positive result is interpreted, whether it is simply accepted or suspected of being a false positive. As Patton points out, at the level of counselling protocols,

> positive results among people reporting risk behaviours go unques-
> tioned, even though a number of gay men and injecting drug users are
> among the false positives.

> (Patton 1990: 35)

On the other hand a positive result for someone at 'low risk' is liable to be treated as a false positive and subject to further investigation. As one serological article puts it, 'all individuals whose risk, after epidemiologic and clinical evaluation, is not compatible with a positive test should have another blood specimen tested' (Ascher and Kaslow 1989: 44). In other words, the risk category of the person tested will determine whether and in what direction resources are deployed, either to accept or to seek to disprove seropositivity or seronegativity.

So at the margins of interpretation the determination of serostatus by the HIV test can be seen to be inextricable from the determination of 'risk group' membership. The presentation of epidemiological statistics for seropositivity proceeds as though it consisted of simple arithmetic cross tabulations. In these tables the HIV positive status of the person is added to the sex of the person, which is cross-referenced to their transmission category, to show that say 204 homosexual men were tested positive in May 1993. But in a sense what I have demonstrated here is that the category homosexual male, among other 'high risk' categories, helps to *produce* seropositivity, while the category of low risk heterosexual helps to produce seronegativity, at least at the ambiguous margins of serological interpretation. A range of HIV tests are now available, engineered to different mixes of sensitivity and specificity in order to address the different presumed levels of infection in particular risk populations and so eliminate the interpretive problem presented by the uniformity of methodo-logical error applied to heterogeneous populations. However, here too the absolute dependence of the test on risk classification is still evident, this time operating at the point of test design, prior to interpretation.

Not surprisingly a reciprocal constitutive effect can be discerned in the determination of 'transmission category', the determination I will now examine. If risk category membership helps to produce seropositivity or negativity, so does seropositivity or negativity help to produce risk category membership.

131

The HIV test as a test for identity

As I argued above, the HIV test is a confessional technology, and part of the test procedure involves eliciting the newly-diagnosed positive person's account of the way they contracted infection. This account must then be organised into a single 'exposure category' so that it accords with the logic of the HIV notification form. The form presents a series of 'exposure categories' which are intended to be both exclusive and exhaustive. They are designed to classify and count *as a singularity* the route by which every person tested has become HIV seropositive.

The notification form (Figures 5.1) is the primary technology for the garnering of epidemiological knowledge about the distribution of HIV infection in sub-populations and the population as a whole. Like the design of the HIV test, the classificatory logic of the form is only workable within certain tautological limits. These limits are set by the administrative necessity that each person be allocated one 'exposure category' and that this category in turn counts as a singular administrative unit, a statistical 'one'. In practice this means that while any given person may narrate what amounts to numerous possible 'exposures' to HIV, and more than one category marked by the interviewer, a final determination must be made about which possible exposure is the 'official' one, the one counted in the epidemiological surveillance totals. Exposures are then tabulated according to the categories shown in Figure 5.2 (p.135) – the tables used in the *Australian HIV Surveillance Report*. Such decisions are made on the basis of pre-existing hierarchies of risk, themselves derived from previous epidemiological statistics.

This reliance upon probability as the way to determine transmission identity has, as Bloor and colleagues point out, a tautological effect. Writing about the similar British and Scottish AIDS statistical procedures they observe:

> In order to allocate cases exposed to multiple risks to a single transmission category, the monitoring agency must take informed (but essentially speculative) decisions on which of those several risk practices was the most likely to have been the actual route of transmission of infection....It will be evident that there is an unfortunate tautological element here: multiple risk cases are categorised to the riskiest transmission category and become in turn components in epidemiological analyses which identify the riskiest transmission categories....Not just the monitoring agency, but also the agents providing the case information, are naturally influenced in their ethnostatistical activities by existing statistical data.
>
> (Bloor *et al.* 1991: 134)

CONFIDENTIAL

Form revised: 1 July 1995

National Centre in HIV Epidemiology and Clinical Research

Notification of AIDS

1. NOTIFYING DOCTOR

Name

Address

Hospital/Clinic name
(If appropriate)

2. IDENTIFICATION OF THE PERSON WITH AIDS

Family name (First two letters only)

Given name (First two letters only)

Date of birth ___ / ___ / ___

Sex ☐ Male ☐ Female ☐ Transsexual

3. OTHER CHARACTERISTICS OF THE PERSON WITH AIDS

Country of birth ☐ Australia ☐ Other (Specify)

If **OTHER**, state year of arrival in Australia 19 ___

Aboriginal/Torres Strait Islander ☐ Yes ☐ No

Postcode of current residence

Current status of person

Person is alive ☐

Date of most recent contact ___ / ___ / ___

Person has died ☐

Date of death ___ / ___ / ___

4. DATE OF DIAGNOSIS

Date of AIDS diagnosis¹ in Australia ___ / ___ / ___

Has the person been previously diagnosed with AIDS elsewhere? ☐ Yes ☐ No/Unknown

If **YES** and diagnosis was in another State/Territory, specify

If **YES** and diagnosis was overseas, write country

5. LABORATORY TESTS

Month / year of first diagnosis of HIV infection ___ / ___

CD4+ count at AIDS diagnosis

Date of specimen collection for CD4+ count analysis ___ / ___ / ___

6. ANTIRETROVIRAL THERAPY

If the person has been treated with any of the following antiretroviral agents, specify the month/year when started.

AZT ___ / ___   ddI ___ / ___   ddC ___ / ___

Other (Specify) ___ / ___

7. DISEASES INDICATIVE OF AIDS AT DIAGNOSIS
(At least one must be ticked)

	Definitive	Presumptive
Pneumocystis carinii pneumonia	☐	☐
Oesophageal candidiasis	☐	☐
Kaposi's sarcoma (Site)	☐	☐
Herpes simplex virus of > 1 month duration	☐	
(Site)		
Cryptococcosis (Site)	☐	
Cryptosporidiosis (diarrhoea > 1 month)	☐	
Toxoplasmosis (Site)	☐	☐
Cytomegalovirus (Site)	☐	☐
Mycobacteriosis (Type)	☐	☐
(Site)		
Pulmonary tuberculosis	☐	☐
Lymphoma (Site)	☐	
(Type)		
HIV encephalopathy	☐	
HIV wasting syndrome	☐	
Invasive cervical cancer	☐	
Recurrent pneumonia (2 or more episodes in 1 year)	☐	☐
Other	☐	

OFFICE USE ONLY   State number   National number

Figure 5.1 Australian National Centre in HIV Epidemiology and Clinical Research, Notification of AIDS Form

8. EXPOSURE CATEGORY

Person was interviewed with regard to exposure:

Not at all (Detail) ☐
To a certain extent (Answer questions below) ☐
In depth (Answer questions below) ☐

More than one exposure category may be ticked.
Sexual exposure **must** be answered.

Sexual exposure (At least one must be ticked)

Sexual contact with person of same sex ☐

Sexual contact with both sexes (If FEMALE see **8A**) ☐

Sexual contact **only** with person of opposite sex ☐
(See **8A**)

From specified country[2] ☐

(Specify country) ☐

No sexual contact ☐

Sexual exposure not known ☐

Vertical exposure

Mother with / at risk for HIV infection (See **8B**) ☐

Blood exposure

Injecting drug use ☐
Detail ☐

Recipient of blood, blood products or tissue ☐
Detail ☐

Haemophilia / coagulation disorder ☐
Detail ☐

Other exposure

Exposure other than those above applies ☐
Detail ☐

Exposure could not be established ☐
Detail ☐

8A. SEXUAL CONTACT WITH PERSON OF OPPOSITE SEX

At least one must be answered if MALE reports sexual contact
with person of OPPOSITE sex, or if FEMALE reports sexual
contact with OPPOSITE or BOTH sexes.

Sex with bisexual male (women only) ☐

Sex with injecting drug user ☐

Sex with person from specified country[2] ☐

(Specify country) ☐

Sex with a person who received blood, blood products
or tissue ☐

Sex with person with haemophilia/coagulation disorder ☐

Sex with a person with HIV infection whose exposure is
other than those above ☐
Detail ☐

Sex with a person with HIV infection whose exposure
could not be established ☐

Heterosexual contact not further specified ☐

8B. VERTICAL EXPOSURE CATEGORY

At least one must be answered if parent/guardian
reports vertical exposure only

Mother with/at risk for HIV infection due to:

Sex with bisexual male ☐

Sex with injecting drug user ☐

Sex with person from specified country[2] ☐

(Specify country) ☐

Sex with a person who received blood, blood products
or tissue ☐

Sex with person with haemophilia/coagulation disorder ☐

Sex with person with HIV infection, exposure not specified ☐

Injecting drug use ☐

Recipient of blood, blood products or tissue ☐

Origin in specified country[2] ☐

(Specify country) ☐

Has HIV infection, exposure not specified ☐

Other (Detail) ☐

9. STATE/TERRITORY HEALTH AUTHORITY USE ONLY

State/Territory ☐☐☐

Initials of State/Territory Officer ☐☐

Date notification received at
State/Territory Health Authority ___/___/___

Date forwarded to National Centre ___/___/___

FOOTNOTES

1. **Australian case definition for HIV infection and AIDS**
   ANCA Bulletin 18.

2. **Specified countries**
   Countries in Africa, the Caribbean, South East Asia or India, where
   HIV is transmitted predominantly by heterosexual contact.

Figure 5.1 (continued)

Table 4.2
Number of new diagnoses of HIV infection for which exposure category was reported, by sex and exposure category, cumulative to 31 March 1995 and for two previous yearly intervals.

EXPOSURE CATEGORY	1 Apr 93 – 31 Mar 94		1 Apr 94 – 31 Mar 95		Cumulative to 31 Mar 95			
	Male	Female	Male	Female	Male	Female	Total	%
Male homosexual/bisexual contact	664	-	631	-	9903	-	9903	80.7
Male homosexual/bisexual contact and ID use	34	-	43	-	368	-	368	3.0
ID use	37	9	17	10	446	152	620	5.0
Heterosexual	*16*	*6*	*8*	*5*	*110*	*53*	*166*	
Not further specified	*21*	*3*	*9*	*5*	*336*	*99*	*454*	
Heterosexual contact:	88	50	79	51	548	350	901	7.3
Sex with ID user	*4*	*8*	*1*	*4*	*13*	*24*	*37*	
Sex with bisexual male	*-*	*3*	*-*	*3*	*-*	*22*	*22*	
From specified country	*12*	*3*	*13*	*8*	*42*	*23*	*65*	
Sex with person from specified country	*13*	*6*	*9*	*11*	*45*	*28*	*73*	
Sex with person with medically acquired HIV	*1*	*0*	*1*	*2*	*4*	*6*	*10*	
Sex with HIV–infected person, exposure not specified	*4*	*5*	*5*	*3*	*23*	*22*	*45*	
Not further specified	*54*	*25*	*50*	*20*	*421*	*225*	*649*	
Haemophilia/coagulation disorder	0	0	1	0	191	2	193	1.6
Receipt of blood/tissue	8	0	6	3	107	66	173	1.4
Health care setting[1]	1	2	0	1	2	7	9	0.1
Total Adults/ Adolescents[2]	832	61	777	65	11565	577	12167	99.1

Children (under 13 years at diagnosis of HIV infection)

Mother with/at risk for HIV infection	1	3	6	8	22	20	42	0.3
Haemophilia/coagulation disorder	0	0	0	0	51	0	51	0.4
Receipt of blood/tissue	0	0	0	0	12	5	18	0.2
Total Children	1	3	6	8	85	25	111	0.9
Sub-total	833	64	783	73	11650	602	12278	100.0
Other/undetermined[3]	105	14	76	10	4320	304	6711	
TOTAL	938	78	859	83	15970	906	18989	

Figure 5.2   Australian HIV Surveillance Report (detail)

135

Within the 'Exposure Category' section (section 8, Figure 5.1) of the AIDS notification form, the large category 'Sexual Exposure' can be seen to be organised in descending order of risk practice, at least in so far as risk is measured against a concept of sexual identity. It begins with homosexual contact and moves through (male) bisexual contact, to heterosexual contact with its various sub-divisions (section 8a, Figure 5.1) and then to persons from pattern two countries[13] and the catch-all 'Exposure not known'. The heterosexual subsection is likewise ordered against an idea of risk, this time in terms of 'risky' partners.

Reading from top to bottom of the 'Sexual Exposure' category we find not just a list of 'exposure categories' but a hierarchy of risk, where ambiguous accounts of exposure are adjudicated as far up the page as possible. This means that each successive sexual identity category, moving down the page, is less likely to be nominated than the category before or, to put it another way, categories become more difficult to get into as they go down.

So a sexual history might for example involve a man who has predominantly anal sex with men, interspersed with occasional vaginal sex with women. His allocation to an 'exposure category' is then carried out through a revision of all relationships and practices into the category considered to be most risky. With such a history the seropositive man will be classified as 'Male homosexual/bisexual contact' in the surveillance report tables. Despite the reference to 'bisexual' in this classification its implication is that he contracted HIV infection from another man rather than a woman, on the basis that sex between men is considered a riskier practice (for men) than sex between men and women.

These assumptions about risk are the motivation for the classification of (male) 'bisexuals' with 'homosexuals' on the form, rather than their constituting a classification of their own or a grouping with 'heterosexuals'. The classification 'bisexual' cannot stand alone because it contravenes the demand for the specification of a singular route and a singular source. The term 'bisexual' necessarily carries a doubled and ambiguous status, suggesting that infection could have been contracted either from another man or a woman, either from anal or vaginal penetration, or perhaps from both. Its grouping with 'homosexual' works as a containment of this propensity to exceed both a singular route of infection and a singular sexual identity. If a man says he has sex with both men and women, the grouping 'homosexual/bisexual' implies that his sexual identity *for purposes of establishing HIV transmission* is homosexual.

This insistent classification of the male bisexual with the male homosexual is symptomatic of AIDS biomedicine's drive to protect the status of the heterosexual masculine body, to ensure that the category 'male heterosexual' is not contaminated by the infectious ambiguities of masculine bisexuality. All other possible forms of sexual contact must be eliminated before a man will be classified as HIV seropositive due to 'heterosexual contact'. It is important to note that there is no symmetrical drive to protect 'heterosexual feminine' identity in the same way. Women who report sexual activity with both sexes are automatically classified within the sub-divisions of heterosexual contact (section 8a, Figure 5.1), because sex between women is deemed to have no transmission consequences. For purposes of establishing HIV transmission all women are deemed to be heterosexual, irrespective of their self-identification.

The same descending order of probability organises the internal subdivisions within the 'heterosexual contact' section (8a, Figure 5.1). These subdivisions are designed to map contact between 'high risk' groups and the 'heterosexual population', an innovation introduced into Australian data collection in 1991 to sensitise the form to possible movement of HIV infection into the 'heterosexual population' (Kaldor 1992). Hence the form is subdivided into heterosexual contact with a bisexual male (for women), an injecting drug user, a recipient of blood transfusion and so on, ending with 'heterosexual contact, not further specified'. On this basis the most difficult sexual exposure category to occupy is the unalloyed 'heterosexual contact, not further specified' at the bottom.

In epidemiological terms the various 'specified' forms of heterosexual contact – with a bisexual male, with an injecting drug user, and so on – represent infection moving out of identified 'risk groups' and into the 'heterosexual population'. The last category represents either an incomplete report, implied by the words 'not further specified', or the movement of infection between two persons deemed to be 'low risk', and hence contained purely within the borders of the 'heterosexual population'. While all transmission recorded under this rubric represents 'heterosexual transmission', the organisation of the form in descending order of epidemiologically determined probability demonstrates the tension in the term 'heterosexual population' that was discussed in the previous chapter. I argued that while the term 'general' or 'heterosexual' population appears at first glance to be a majoritarian, maximally inclusive term which only excludes the 'sexual minorities', the borders between 'general population' and 'risk groups' were highly variable, indicating a strong tension between an inclusive and an exclusive, residual usage of the term 'heterosexual population'.

Here this tension is evident in the ambiguous status in the 'heterosexual population' of the majority of persons whose transmission category is determined on the form. Their status is ambiguous because one of the definitions of groups 'at risk' used in targeting groups for education is that of 'partners of risk group members'.[14] While they are classified under 'heterosexual exposure' they are also amenable to being retrospectively characterised as 'at risk' by virtue of being sexual partners of bisexual men, injecting drug users and so on. They are effectively 'high risk' heterosexuals by virtue of their sexual relations with members of 'high risk' groups,[15] which on the excluding tendencies of the term 'heterosexual population' is oxymoronic.

The excluding tendency of the 'heterosexual exposure' category is also evident in the indeterminate position occupied by those who ghost this category, who appear within it yet who are not the subjects of the category. I mean here the 'sources' of infection represented by the categorisation of the sexual contact – the 'bisexual males', 'injecting drug users' and so on – from whom the person tested is said to have contracted infection. I call their position indeterminate because while they are evidently engaged in heterosexual activity they fail to qualify for categorisation as 'heterosexual' by virtue of their 'risk activities' which have priority in determining their categorisation. This failure to qualify as heterosexual also places them in a position of infectious causality to the 'heterosexual population'. Not only do they not belong *within* the 'heterosexual population', they become the source of infection *for* that population.

These multiple exclusions indicate that the excluding tendency of the term 'heterosexual population' still structures the AIDS epidemiological enterprise to a large extent, but it seems to me that at the same time the sheer proliferation of 'high risk' heterosexual categories might indicate an increasing problematisation of this tendency. Even within the discreet logic of epidemiology, HIV infection has become increasingly difficult to identify with particular groups as viral transmission slowly exceeds the borders of the groups with which it was initially associated. The creation of ever more detailed subdivisions of heterosexual exposure categories is indicative both of a desire to protect the cleanliness of the category, that is to sharpen the epidemiological gaze and create more detailed maps of routes of infection into the category, and a tacit admission of an inability to do so.

The formerly clean category has itself become contaminated, so that the maintenance of a last bastion of cleanliness – the subdivision at the very bottom of the category – requires more and more detailed exclusionary defence, and hence more and more detailed acknowledgements of the existence of contamination within the borders of the category itself. In this sense the proliferating subdivisions within the 'heterosexual' category partake of the contradictory movement of what Singer refers to as 'epidemic logic': 'Epidemic logic depends on certain structuring contradictions, proliferating what it seeks to contain, producing what it regulates' (Singer 1993: 29).

CONCLUSION

The HIV test is, in the biomedical imagination, the solution to the problem of the invisibility of the HIV virus in both the body and the body politic. Through the inscription of a 'transmission identity' upon the seropositive, the test renders the virus visible, in the sense that it is personified in the person infected. As Patton (1990) graphically puts it, in the biomedical regime laid out by the test 'the person with AIDS speaks for the virus, becomes the talking virus'. The HIV test prevents the virus from 'passing' in the body politic, by compelling the confession of the infected and marking them with the truth of their infection. The logic of the HIV test, and perhaps the biomedical representation of AIDS more generally, could be summarised as an homology: *the virus stands to the body, as the body stands to the body politic*. Just as the invisible virus is a silent danger to the immune system and the person who does not know they are infected, so too is the invisible HIV seropositive person a danger to the body politic. On the other hand the person who has been diagnosed as seropositive must take on their new identity *as virus* in a way which does not endanger the health of the body politic. They must identify themselves as virus to others.

This demand for identification demonstrates the extent to which, in the biomedical imagination, the containment of infectious spread in the absence of specific prophylaxis is understood to be a function of its visibility to biomedicine's surveillance technologies, supplemented as they are with various disciplinary and policing regimes. If specific viral activity cannot be controlled in particular bodies then the level of control moves upward to the control of the person infected, or at least their responsibilisation. As representatives of the virus, even if unwilling representatives, the HIV seropositives are placed under medical scrutiny and their sexuality is rendered vulnerable to criminalisation. It is this partial removal of the HIV seropositive from 'normal' civil status which has helped to politicise the disease so sharply, and which had led to the formation of PLWA groups as political constituencies to defend the civil status of the infected.

While the HIV test sorts the infected from the uninfected, and constitutes the former as threats to the latter, the interpretation of test results has been demonstrated in this chapter to depend upon an implicit assumption about the probable cleanliness of the heterosexual. I have argued throughout that all determinations of the pathological are necessarily made against an implicit concept of the normal, and the HIV test makes its determinations of infection and transmission category against just such an implicit concept of the heterosexual 'low risk' norm. In this sense the epistemology of the test works to position the infected as threats to the 'heterosexual population', even if this logic demands an ever more excluding and residual definition of that population.

At a more theoretical level the implication of the test's results in the categorisation of the person tested demonstrates the extent to which biomedical knowledge is implicated with its object. It can only secure its status as a stable form of knowledge about a stable pre-existing object if it forcibly constitutes this object in ways that are amenable to its interests. While some branches of the physical sciences, notably theoretical physics, have been able to come to terms with an inherent uncertainty in its subject/object relations, biomedical knowledge seems unwilling to admit this kind of ambiguity and relativity into its knowledge practices. I can only speculate about this recalcitrance, but it perhaps derives from the high political stakes attendant upon medical knowledge and its claims to certainty about the body's operations. These claims to certainty are what protects medicine from relativisation as a historical practice, a relativisation which I will discuss in the next chapter.

6

CONCLUSION
Sexual identity and contamination

This text has interpreted AIDS as a symptom, not of the activity of a virus, but of a particular moment in the history of sexual politics. AIDS and its multifarious effects have without doubt been the most significant historical force at work in the field of sexual politics since the first strange signs of illness were explicitly linked to the homosexuality of its sufferers, and it will continue to exercise constitutive effects for some time to come. I emphasise my claim that it is a force *in* rather than *on* the field of sexual politics, because, as I have argued, the disease AIDS should not be regarded as a natural event with social consequences. Rather its conditions of emergence *as* a disease – as a describable, coherent entity with a name, an aetiology, a set of calculable symptoms and outcomes, rather than a nameless and random affliction – should be understood as socially located and politically interested. There is no point to which a naturally occurring phenomenon 'AIDS' can be tracked back, prior to its appearance in biomedical discourse and a field of sexual contestation. Studies which undertake to find 'AIDS cases' prior to 1981 may produce results, but these studies cannot dispense with the stable definition of AIDS which only emerged gradually out of its original sites of sexual contestation during the early 1980s. Like all historical enterprises these studies can only interpret the past from the point of view of the present.

There is then no point at which AIDS can be treated as a politically innocent or neutral entity which is misguidedly grafted onto a political field. This is so because biomedical discourse, which furnishes the representational conditions for the emergence of the disease, is an historical and political practice, and in the case of AIDS its practice is completely implicated in contestations of sexual power relations.

In biomedicine's own terms its representations of AIDS simply correspond to the natural categories and entities 'discovered' through study of the disease – the viruses, the cells, the 'transmission categories', and so on. It imagines itself able to describe these natural categories without being implicated in its own descriptions, able to penetrate to their essence while still only reflecting them in their natural intact state. However, I have demonstrated that biomedical discourse is constitutive of precisely the field of objects and relations that it

140

imagines itself only to describe. There is no 'outside' to this field from which it can adopt a neutral, asocial and panoptic point of view.

AIDS biomedicine's constitutive descriptions involve the translation of certain phallocentric concepts of social order into technical narratives, images and bodily practices. This translation strives to configure the 'reality' of AIDS, including the 'reality' of sexed bodies, according to the demands of that social order. The logics which inform biomedical knowledge – epidemio-logic, viro-logic, immuno-logic, sero-logic – are primarily concerned, it seems to me, with the ordering and government of the disease in these interests, an ordering which they *equate* with the generation of knowledge. In this sense they partake of the drive that Nietzsche attributes to all rational knowledges, the drive,

> Not 'to know' but to schematise – to impose upon chaos as much regularity and form as our practical needs require. In the formation of reason, logic, the categories, it was *need* that was authoritative: the need, not to 'know', but to subsume, to schematise, for the purpose of intelligibility and calculation.
>
> (Nietzsche 1968: 278)

The spectres of sexual infection, contagion and epidemic arguably present the greatest provocation to this schematising drive. They represent the limit case of its powers in the face of proliferating viral life, the erratics of human desire and the chaos of illness and death, the most profound challenge to the capacities of governance and the maintenance of social order.

Biomedicine is a useful discourse of governance *precisely because* of its capacity to translate social relations into 'neutral' technical discourses, and a set of practices and techniques which limit the effects of contagion and epidemic. This capacity enables it to intervene in detailed ways in a social field, to practise a micropolitics of the body and a macropolitics of the body politic, subsuming both domains of intervention under the flexible rhetoric of health. Biomedicine is able to articulate both domains because, as I have demonstrated, its representations of the body always involve the analogisation of the body to highly normative understandings of social order, and a reciprocal analogisation of the social order according to its normative representations of the body. This normative reciprocity allows biomedicine to readily conceptualise relationships between particular bodies and its hierarchical, hygienic programme for social order. Its arsenal of technical and behavioural technologies help it to reconcile particular bodily morphologies with the changing demands of that order.

The advent of AIDS has made this process of reconciliation more visible because it precipitated ambitious attempts to rapidly reinscribe sexual bodies according to the sacrificial order enshrined in and through the body politic, the order of 'Man'. This reinscription has been addressed to body boundaries, attempting to rechoreograph the subjective adoption of sexed boundaries in all sexual identity categories other than those of heterosexual men, whose access to a phallocentric sexuality, a sense of bodily integrity and cleanliness, and a right to sexual freedom have been largely preserved through the reconfiguration of these others. However, this privileging is not, I wish to stress, the outcome of a masculinist conspiracy so much as an effect precipitated by a particular way of *conceptualising order as such*. 'Order' is understood in biomedical discourse to mean a hierarchical, steady-state, closed system, a system whose self-preservation depends on its hermetic separation from its outside. This model of order is nevertheless phallocentric in the sense that historically masculine bodies have been understood to conform to its prescriptions, while feminine (or feminised) bodies appear more or less 'chaotic' and entropic. Biomedicine, it seems to me, deploys this model in relation to both social order and anatomical order, enabling each to be readily figured in terms of the other, and both to be figured in relation to implicit concepts of sexual difference.

My investigation of transformations in the 'immune system' in response to AIDS examined an exemplary instance of this capacity to refigure the social as the sexed anatomical. The immunological narrative which was elaborated around HIV infection can be seen to be a historical narrative, a way of refracting a moment in the political relations between masculinity and femininity, heterosexuality and homosexuality, through biomedicine's working concepts of the normal and the pathological. Immunological discourse allows the biomedical imagination to think HIV infection in relation to both the binaries of sexual difference and a concept of the national 'public health', through the creation of an ideal anatomy of immunological health. The 'immunocompetent' anatomy, while deployed as if it were simply a transparent representation of normal health, was seen to anatomise phallocentric concepts of bodily and social order, which privilege rational control over bodily processes, impermeable bodily surfaces and the maintenance of corporeal singularity. These concepts then form the basis for the government of the epidemic, determining the shape of public health intervention and the allocation of 'responsibility' for contagion according to the extent that bodily sex and sexuality was seen to depart from this anatomy.

In this way biomedicine's concepts of the normal and the pathological in AIDS discourse have mapped themselves onto normative categories of sexual identity, the categories *through whose bodies* the disease is governed. Biomedicine has ordered the field of AIDS through the classification and hierarchisation of sexually identified bodies, not because these bodies have a pre-given relationship to infection but because they serve as a means of giving predictability, calculability and shape to the amorphousness of epidemic, and hence a means of governance. The minimisation of uncertainty is a central strategy of governance, a political necessity which accounts for the relative inability of the biomedical sciences to come to conceptual grips with the operations of uncertainty in their discipline when compared with the physical sciences. While the play of uncertainty has been made central to the new areas of theoretical physics, that of quantum mechanics and chaos theory, it only provokes anxiety in the biomedical sciences. This anxiety lies behind the organisation of the HIV test that was discussed in Chapter 5. The practice of classifying people tested into 'transmission categories' is serology's way of adjudicating the uncertainty and ambiguity which characterise the test's results, a way of holding some variables constant, so that other variables can be measured. This exploitation of sexual identity as a stabilising 'constant' in fact characterises the entire field of AIDS discourse. I demonstrated its usefulness in the earliest classifications of the heterogony of symptoms which were to become 'AIDS', in the elaboration of distinctions between immuno-competence and immunocompromise, and in the specification of infectious distribution in AIDS epidemiology.

In all these instances, implicit or explicit concepts of sexual identity and the body, subjectivity and sexual practices which identity is said to denote are drawn upon to help give coherence to phenomena which constantly threaten to decompose, to escape the logical grids of calculability. Biomedicine uses normative categories of sexual identity as the means of organising and grounding its representations of the disease, and its way of conceptualising the control of infection. The categories of sexual identity provide biomedicine with a way to intervene in the chain of cause and effect, the keys to the control of transmission. Their usefulness as conceptual categories and stabilising 'constants' seems to me to furnish one answer at least to Butler's important question, cited in the first chapter, when she asks, '[What are] the political stakes in designating as *origin* and *cause* those identity categories that are in fact the effects of institutions, practices, discourses?' (Butler 1990: xi). My answer would be that posing identity categories as causes helps biomedical and other knowledge practices to elude acknowledgement of the constitutive role they play in these categories production. The political stakes in other words are their invaluable status as apolitical and neutral knowledge practices that simply describe and/or cure what is already there.

At the same time biomedicine's exploitation of the categories of sexual identity has highly contradictory effects that do not necessarily comply with its interests. The usefulness of these categories in the creation of biomedicine's logics, and in governance of epidemic, depends upon the extent to which the internal coherence of these categories, and the mutually exclusive, hierarchical nature of the binaries through which they are defined, can be enforced. Hence the classificatory violence wielded in AIDS discourse, attempting to enforce predictable, normative relationships between sexed body, sexual object choice, genital practice and identificatory subjectivity. In biomedicine's terms this classificatory violence is merely a description of the nature of sexual identities and their natural relationships to HIV infection. However, as I have argued, all biomedicine's descriptions are also *prescriptions*, and its use of these categories of sexual identity in governance of the epidemic depends precisely on their historical plasticity, their amenability to institutional manipulation.

143

Biomedicine has in other words made strategic use of particular identity configurations in an historical field of sexual relationships, relying to a large extent upon already established alignments between passivity, femininity, effeminacy and natural virulence to naturalise its interventions. It has tried to schematise these identity configurations in particular ways, but in doing so it has also precipitated unforeseen transformations, inadvertently helping to produce new configurations and meanings of sexual identity which do not necessarily conform to its logics. As Foucault (1980a) points out, the inscription of norms always provides the occasion for resistance and excess, the inculcation of the law always proliferates that which it seeks to contain. Biomedicine's attempt to enforce the borders and hierarchies of sexual identity as a means of epidemic control has produced multiple refusals to conform to these borders, refusals which reveal fractures in the normative binaries of sexual identity. This refusal is perhaps most evident in fragmentations of the masculine heterosexual/homosexual binary, a fragmentation which has, paradoxically, been precipitated by the concern of the AIDS public health authorities to shore the binary up. These fragmentations are the result of attempts by public health authorities to identify and moralise men who align themselves with the heterosexual side of the binary, while also engaging in sexual activity with other men. These men are highly problematic for public health authorities because, as I observed in Chapter 4, they are understood to form part of the conduit of infection from gay male bodies to heterosexual male bodies and infants, via the transmission bodies of women. Consequently public health education attempts to identify and address them as Men Who Have Sex With Men (MSM). The creation of this category represents an attempt, similar to that already commented on in the chapter on the HIV test, to protect the cleanliness of the category 'heterosexual' by excluding those who might introduce contamination into its ranks. However, while this strategy has made the relative lack of coherence between sexual identity and sexual practice publicly visible, it has not proved particularly successful in securing identificatory compliance. The group of men it tries to address have continued by and large to identify as heterosexual, and hence ignore exhortations addressed to them under the rubric of MSM. As Watney puts it:

> The main problem [for the public health authorities] is that the category of heterosexuality is proving stubbornly resistant to any acknowledgment of the sexual diversity which it so evidently contains.
>
> (Watney 1993: 23)

This constitutes a refusal to align sexual identity with sexual practice, a refusal presumably motivated by the psychic and political payoffs for men of identifying as heterosexual. These payoffs have moreover increased in value in the age of AIDS as the other side of the binary, the masculine homosexual, has succumbed to complete contamination. In a sense the refusal of some men to identify as anything other than 'heterosexual' is the price paid by public health discourse for its relentless defence of the cleanliness of this category, and its pathologisation of all who depart from it. The meaning of gay identified masculinity has been so thoroughly contaminated by AIDS that being 'out' now involves a willingness to defend an identity category which is regarded as isomorphic with the virus.

Another refusal provoked by public health categories can be seen in the assertion of the importance of lesbian identity in the framing of AIDS prevention education. I observed in Chapters 4 and 5 that lesbian identity is considered redundant by AIDS public health authorities, who continue to address all women as if they were heterosexual. Lesbian safe sex activists argue that, even if sex between women is not associated with HIV transmission risk, identifying as 'lesbian' does not imply that a woman never has sex with men, or that she does not have other possible routes of exposure. How you identify doesn't, they argue, have a very strong relationship to the contingencies of sexual object choice and practice.

These disjunctures between sexual identity as it is used in AIDS discourse and subjective sexual identification, coupled with the 'contamination' of gay male and various feminine identities in AIDS discourse, have also resulted in a different order of refusal, or perhaps more accurately a new shift or move in the history of sexuality. It has provoked the emergence of new queer and feminist critiques of the relationship between the organisation of sexual identity categories and the practices of governance. Queer theory and queer politics emerges directly out of the field of sexual identity politics so profoundly conditioned by AIDS during the 1980s. This is true both historically and conceptually. The organisation Queer Nation was founded at an ACT UP New York meeting in April 1990 (Berlant and Freeman 1993) and from this point the term 'queer' has been appropriated to designate a variety of intellectual and activist practices in English-speaking countries.

It seems to me that at least part of the impetus for the development of queer can be found in frustration with the strategies used by the generation of gay, lesbian and feminist activists initially involved in AIDS politics during the 1980s, strategies which framed their central task as the defence of the identity categories under attack. Queer works through a different strategic logic. It attempts to move beyond the binary logic of stable sexual identities, in favour of provisional identity practices which cannot be utilised in the interests of identification, classification and governance in the same way, and which enable new forms of political alliance. As Butler (1993) puts it, queer politics,

> still . . . pose[s] the question of 'identity', but no longer as a preestab-lished position or a uniform entity; rather, as part of a dynamic map of power in which identities are constituted and/or erased, deployed and/or paralyzed.
>
> (Butler 1993: 117)

Queer effectively rejects the normative coherence of sexual identity, arguing that relationships between sex, object choice, sexual practice and subjective identity are both historically and subjectively contingent. It recognises the extent to which the categories produced in the heterosexual/homosexual binary are mutually constitutive, purely relational categories which are completely implicated in each other. Complete identification with one side of the binary always involves a violent but unstable repudiation of the other side and queer is, among other things, an attempt to live out subjectivity in ways which are less inflected through defence against multiple or partial identifications. In this sense queer seems to be in at least potential alliance with that feminism which interrogates the coherence of the category 'woman' and 'heterosexual woman' and the constitution of the binary masculine/feminine, an interrogation also made more urgent by the discourses of AIDS.

Perhaps queer is also an attempt to rework relationships between identity, contagion and death, an ethical task of the self which the advent of AIDS has made so urgent. In Chapter 3 I argued that part of the psychic function of panic immunology, with its assertion of hierarchies, exclusions and borders, was to guard against the fragmentation of identity and self-coherence which from the perspective of 'Man' is precipitated by the processes of contagion and death. Stable concepts of identity work as prophylaxis for those who can claim them, but the more rigidly a claim to identity is asserted, the more prone it is to anxiety about the non-identity that it so fears. Contagion and the prospect of death are powerful provocations to this anxiety, but it seems to me that provisional concepts of identity are better able to accommodate the prospect of finality as well as the otherness of contagion. From the point of view of a claim to stable identity a person with HIV infection can only appear as, to quote Ellis Hanson, 'spectacular images of the abject, the dead who dare to speak and sin and walk abroad, the undead with AIDS' (Hanson 1991: 324). For those who struggle to live a stabilised identity, a positive self unperturbed by time, memory or desire, the prospect of death must be rejected in order for this sense of self-presence to be maintained. Fear of death is sequestered from identity as the unthinkable, an unthinkable which nevertheless returns to thought and is projected, made an effect of the body of the other. As representatives of the failure of prophylactic claims to stable identity, the infected can only be seen as abject anti-identity, as vampires or revenants whose very presence threatens others with absence and dissolution. On the arithmetic and paranoiac logic of identity, one is either a proper self or a threat to the proper self. Consequently, queer thinking about and valuation of uncertain identity might move towards reformulations of such stark and cruel antitheses between the living and the (un)dead, finding a way to accommodate death within a positive ideal of life.

Finally, queer could be considered an attempt to embrace and rework the meaning of 'viral' or hybrid identity, the identity which works within bio-medical logic as the rationale for AIDS surveillance. Biomedicine pathologises hybridity as the subjectivity of contagion, a subjectivity which departs from the fully 'human' through its alliance with duplicitous viral identity, and from singular, stable concepts of identity and subjectivity, through its erotic practices. Queer attempts to revalue these instabilities, to harness the contaminations that identity processes always court as the basis for a new political practice and coalitional identity. Queer subjectivity tries to interfere in the reciprocal constitutions between normative body and normative social order enabled by biomedical discourse, sending them out of alignment through its insistent adoption of the viral processes of rapid transformation and mutation, of chimerical, momentary identity, processes against which the normative subject wishes to defend itself. Queer uses these processes as a way to infect, and hence transform, the body politic.

NOTES

1 INTRODUCTION: TOTAL WAR

1 See, for example, the essays in Crimp (ed.) (1988), especially those of Bersani and Treichler, and Edelman's (1994) 'The plague of discourse'.

2 This acceptance of the truth of AIDS science is evident in even the militant AIDS activist group ACT-UP, which tends to frame its demands in terms of more funding for therapies or vaccine trials. Ariss's (1992) research indicates that PLWA groups and gay men generally have an extraordinarily complex technical knowledge of AIDS biomedicine, and are able to talk knowledgeably about T cell counts, seroconversion, antiviral therapies and the like. Everyday knowledge and media discourse about HIV/AIDS is of course also heavily medicalised. It shapes safe sex information and AIDS education generally, so that a large proportion of the population display some knowledge of the scientific explanation for HIV transmission.

3 A growing literature discusses the way that AIDS discourse is implicated in racial and post-colonial power relationships. See for example Treichler (1989) and Patton (1990), Chapter 4.

4 One very clear example of this exacerbation has been the escalation of 'poofter bashing' in large urban centres, where gay 'responsibility' for AIDS is used as an excuse for violence by young straight men.

5 To my knowledge only one AIDS education project addressed exclusively to straight men has been undertaken in Australia. This was based at the Family Planning Association of New South Wales, and was funded in 1992 after several years of lobbying on the part of feminist AIDS activists, including myself. It ran for six months and was not refunded.

6 At the same time straight men are free to position themselves within educational AIDS discourse according to their self-identification as heterosexual men, and hence as the 'general population'. This positioning has very real consequences for the ways that heterosexual men interpret 'safe sex' messages. For example, young straight men tend to use condoms only with women they feel may be an infectious threat to themselves, rather than considering the possibility that they themselves may infect someone else. For a discussion of this see Waldby *et al.* (1993a) and (1993b).

7 Microbiological textbooks now routinely devote a section of their discussion of the immune system to the idea of the 'homosexual patient' and his compromised immune system, due not only to AIDS but to a plethora of infections associated with the 'homosexual lifestyle'. See for example Masur (1990b).

2 THE BIOMEDICAL IMAGINATION AND THE ANATOMICAL BODY

1 Many other viruses and bacteria can live in various species or non-human reservoirs, in water, air, dust and so on, but the HIV is thought to only live outside human bodies for a very short time.

2 For a detailed 'textbook' account of biomedicine's understanding of the virus, see note 2, Chapter 3.

3 For an account of this association see Lloyd (1984).

4 This is somewhat paradoxical with regard to the representation of gay sexuality, which is of course regarded as the 'unnatural act'. The logic evident in biomedical texts which discuss the 'homosexual host' seems to be that homosexual suscept-ibility to infection is a kind of revenge taken by nature against such unnatural practices. Women's bodies transmit this revenge, however, because they are more implicated in the natural world than are heterosexual men.

5 See Ballard (1992) for an account of some crucial episodes of such contestation in Australia during the first years of the epidemic.

6 Some examples of this kind of literature would be most of the essays in Herdt and Lindenbaum (eds.) (1992), Kirp and Bayer (eds.) (1992) and O'Malley (ed.) (1989).

7 Biomedicine seems highly resistant to the kinds of epistemological sophistication which has developed in some of the 'hard' sciences, that of quantum physics or relativity, for example.

8 Martin (1990) reports both explanations from scientists she talked to about the recurrence of military metaphors in immunology.

9 This relegation of metaphor typifies logocentric interpretive practice according to Derrida (1982), in that it shores up the pre-existence of thought to its expression in language.

10 But as Le Doeuff points out, this pansexualisation occurs by virtue of a sort of oblivion of the actual female genitals, an oblivion which she argues is the corollary of the genitalisation of the entire body.

11 It is important to note here that specifying the process of transmission is of central concern in AIDS discourse. If a cure for HIV infection existed we might find that its distinction between the normal and the pathological would hinge upon a less sexually loaded imagery, that is an imagery derived more from the concerns of therapeutics. The absence of a prophylactic cure means that a large degree of AIDS biomedical discourse is addressed to the control of transmission, control at the level of sexual relations between bodies. It is this focus, and biomedicine's reliance upon naturalised concepts of sexual difference, that can be seen in allocation of degrees of 'risk' to different sexual 'identities'.

12 This is the sense evident in the seventeenth-century text, *The Anatomy of Melancholy*, for example (Burton 1971).

13 I am using Grosz's (1994) exegesis of Lacan's argument here.

14 Although not always successfully. The failure of medical pronouncements on the dangers of dieting for adolescent girls is a good example of the limits of medical intervention into fashion and popular culture.

15 Phallocentrism and the politics of the phallus have generated a huge feminist literature. For some recent discussions of the phallus see 'The Phallus Issue' of the journal *Differences*, 4 (1), 1992.

16 An order which Butler identifies with the Symbolic order of language.

17 Some examples of this include Butler (1990) and (1993), Grosz (1994), Hanson (1991) and Edelman (1994). In a slightly different register, Pateman (1988) and

Lloyd (1984) look at the circulation of phallically constituted notions of masculinity in political and philosophical discourse respectively.

3 THE PRIMAL SCENE OF IMMUNOLOGY

1   To call them microscopic is misleading because molecular action cannot be detected with a microscope, but must be inferred from other kinds of evidence.
2   Here is a slightly longer and more detailed 'textbook' account, which I have culled from a variety of technical sources. I include this not in order to present the 'facts' about HIV, but rather to present a coherent version of the biomedical narrative under discussion.

HIV infection could be described in the following way. The Human Immunodeficiency Virus is a cytopathic retrovirus – that is a virus which kills healthy cells, and which replicates itself 'backwards', in a reverse genetic order to that of other human viruses. Viruses rely upon the host cells of other organisms to reproduce themselves, and HIV targets particular cells of the human immune system as its sites of replication. These cells are the T4 lymphocyte cells and the monocyte/macrophage cells of the immune system, certain cell populations in the brain and spinal cord, and possibly other cells as well.

Once inside these cells the HIV begins its replicative cycle. HIV is called a retrovirus because unlike other viruses it has an RNA (ribonucleic acid) genome rather than a DNA (deoxyribonucleic acid) genome. This RNA genetic material is transcribed into DNA and inserted into the host cell's DNA, so that it functions as a new gene, able to instruct the host cell to produce HIV virions, rather than to replicate itself. This integration with the host cell is permanent, although the HIV may remain latent, that is it may not trigger the cell to produce virus for a long period of time.

A person with HIV infection can thus be asymptomatic for a number of years, although they register infection on an HIV test. The mechanisms whereby infection becomes activated are varied but the most common is thought to be infection with some other virus, which potentiates the HIV and causes it to begin replicating. Active HIV infection works to disable the immune system in various ways. The exact mechanisms of this disabling are controversial in immunology but are thought to include: a qualitative and quantitative deficiency in the T4 lymphocytes, that is a decrease in both their overall numbers and their efficacy in the many immunological tasks they carry out; defects in the immunological functions of the monocyte-macrophage cells, which normally work to alert the rest of the immune system to the presence of infection; functional abnormalities of the B lymphocytes, another major group of immune system cells. The net effect of these disturbances is the susceptibility of the HIV-infected person to contracting other infections, which eventually prove fatal.

Because HIV is a very fragile virus and cannot live outside of the appropriate kinds of cell it can only be transmitted in a limited and direct number of ways – through sexual contact, where it is carried in semen and vaginal fluids, through sharing of needles, needlestick injury or blood transfusion, where it is transmitted through blood cells, and through transmission from mother to infant either across the placenta, during birth, or through breast feeding.

3   This term is used in Montgomery (1991).
4   For important treatments of these founding concepts see Canguilhem (1994), Diprose and Vasseleu (1991) and Vasseleu (1991).

5   Current immunology textbooks acknowledge this, in the sense that they routinely refer to the 'revolution' in interest in and research upon the immune system since the advent of AIDS. This research has led in turn to new understandings of how the immune system functions.

6   This is evident in the explanation for cancer, for example, where aberrant genetic instructions are understood to send the reproduction of cells awry.

7   See, for example, Latour and Woolgar (1986), Amann and Knorr Cetina (1990), and Traweek (1988).

8   The symptoms displayed by a person with advanced HIV infection may include *Pneumocystis carinii* pneumonia, Karposi's sarcoma, a kind of otherwise rare skin cancer, oral candidiasis and other fungal infections of the mouth, diarrhoea, weight loss, tuberculosis, meningitis, cervical cancer and cervical thrush in women, and a number of other otherwise rare conditions.

9   See the discussion of Brandt (1987) in Chapter 4, pp. 91–2.

10 Thanks to Zoe Sofoulis for this term.

11 This logic is evident in the extent to which pregnant women have become the objects of public health surveillance since the advent of HIV/AIDS, a development discussed in depth in the next chapter.

12 The superior contagious powers of anal sex are treated as indisputable fact by biomedicine. It is a commonplace of epidemiological research, and studies repeatedly make statements like, 'There is ample epidemiologic evidence that during homosexual intercourse, the virus is transmitted from the penis of the insertive partner into the anus and the rectum of the receptive partner' (Kaslow and Francis 1989: 98).

13 For a longer development of this argument see Waldby (1995).

4 EPIDEMIOLOGY AND THE BODY POLITIC

1   The binary 'general population'/'risk group' is no longer in official use in epidemiological practice in Australia, the UK or the USA, although it is still current in popular media and some other more politically naive biomedical discourse. In epidemiological surveillance the idea of 'risk groups' has been replaced with that of 'transmission' or 'exposure' categories, which include heterosexuals as well as the previous risk categories. Nevertheless the idea of 'risk groups' still permeates this new terminology. While the categories of 'homosexual/ bisexual men' and 'IV drug users' are used in the *Australian HIV Surveillance Report* to simply designate rates of infection, a recording of HIV positivity for a heterosexual person must be further designated according to the 'risk category' of the person who 'gave' them HIV – IV drug user, bisexual man, person from a pattern two country, etc. This configuration is discussed in detail in Chapter 5.

2   Patton (1990) also makes the point that the terms 'general population' or 'heterosexual population' are often used to designate heterosexual men.

3   See Watney (1987) for discussion of the 'imaginary national family unit' as the subject to be addressed by the media's discourse about AIDS and the subject to be protected by public health policy.

4   In Australia women have been regularly appealed to in this way. In addition to the national 'If it's not on, it's not on' campaign, a television campaign depicting a couple in bed has the woman saying, 'Well, no condom means no sex.'

5   See Waldby *et al.* (1991) for a discussion of the significance of women's alleged sexual passivity in AIDS discourse.

6   For example see Guinan and Hardy (1987).

7   This is pointed out, for example, by Anastos and Marte (1991), Treichler (1992) and Gilman (1988).
8   There have been a number of publications designed to provide a feminine point of view on HIV risk, but these have generally been compiled by feminist AIDS activists. See for example Patton and Kelly (1987) and Richardson (1987).
9   See Chapter 2 for a discussion of some aspects of this contestation.
10 Haraway (1991) also refers to contemporary instances of the utilisation by the military of immune system discourse to describe itself. She cites the following recent extract from *Military Review*, a description of an elite corps of special strike force soldiers.

The most appropriate example to describe how this system would work is the most complex biological model we know – the body's immune system. Within the body there exists a remarkably complex corps of internal bodyguards. In absolute numbers they are small . . . . Yet they consist of reconnaissance specialists, killers, reconstitution specialists, and communicators that can seek out invaders, sound the alarm, reproduce rapidly, and swarm to the attack to repel the enemy.

(cited in Haraway 1991: n. 12, 254)

11 The epidemiological literature which links receptive anal intercourse and high numbers of sexual partners to both gay sexuality and HIV transmission is vast. For a comprehensive survey of this literature see Bolton (1992).
12 For a case study of this fantasy see Waldby *et al.* (1993b).
13 Foucault (1979) demonstrates that the strategies of individuation, which he nominates as the central feature of modern disciplinary subjectivity, receive their most detailed elaboration in the discourses of epidemic control. See particularly his account of the control of the plague town, pp. 195-9.

5 TECHNOLOGIES OF THE BODY POLITIC: THE HIV ANTIBODY TEST

1   Hanson (1991): 325.
2   This idea is developed in Foucault (1980a).
3   According to figures compiled by the Australian National HIV Reference Laboratory, over 800,000 HIV antibody tests were performed in 1991 (in a population of 17 million) (Kaldor *et al.* 1992). HIV tests are compulsory for applicants for migration to Australia, for donors to blood banks, for entry into the armed forces, and for prisoners upon admission and before release in some states. Of course it is possible in institutional contexts to 'encourage' voluntary testing in compelling ways, and there is considerable documentation of, for example, hospital patients whose general consent to treatment is taken to include consent to an HIV test, or whose access to medical services, particularly ante-natal services, is made conditional upon taking a test (New South Wales Anti-Discrimination Board 1992).
4   Reported in Kaldor *et al.* (1992).
5   Gallo is using his early nomenclature for what is now standardised as HIV. See Treichler (1988a) for an account of the professional struggles over the naming of the virus.
6   Some HIV seropositive people undergo what is termed a seroconversion illness, where the initial immune system reaction to the virus's presence produces flu-like symptoms. These symptoms are likely to be interpreted as a bad cold or mild influenza by the person concerned, and leave no symptomatic trace. A few people

develop permanently enlarged lymph glands (lymphadenopathy) without other symptoms.

7 This drive to mark the social or in this case infectious status of people so that it is instantly recognisable by all is identified by Garber (1992) as an enduring social dream, which at various times in history has been enforced. An example is the Hindu caste mark.

8 It is this general process of personification which is responsible for much of what is termed HIV-related discrimination, particularly against men who are identified as gay.

9 In several Australian state jurisdictions health authorities can compel an HIV seropositive person to reveal the names and addresses of their previous and current sexual partners (Patterson 1992).

10 The most notorious instance of this process in Australia occurred in 1989 when an HIV seropositive sex worker known as Charlene was incarcerated in Rozelle psychiatric hospital in Sydney on the basis of allegedly having unprotected sex with clients (at their request). She was incarcerated under a section of the Public Health Act.

11 This is not to suggest that this ethical idea of safe sex always obtains. Outside the politicised realms of gay-identified communities there is a great deal of evidence to suggest that in general 'safe sex' is a practice used only with casual partners, and that emotional intimacy and trust have become equated with 'unprotected sex' (Waldby *et al.* 1993a). Differential uses of safe sex are also frequently based on recent test result, even within gay communities (Patton 1990).

12 The ambiguity of number is deliberate here, so as not to foreclose upon Treichler's (1988a) question 'Do two names indicate two viruses?'

13 Specified countries are those where transmission is said to be predominantly heterosexual – sub-Saharan Africa, the Caribbean and some Asian countries.

14 In Australia education strategies addressed specifically to women involve among other things alerting them to the 'possibility that their sexual partners may be bisexual or IV drug users' (Intergovernmental Committee on AIDS 1992: 38). In the USA the National Institute on Drug Abuse (NIDA) has funded education programmes to target 'IV drug users and their sexual partners' (Kane and Mason 1992).

15 The assumption here it seems to me is that they were low risk before beginning this relationship, so in this way risk categories are themselves 'contagious'.

BIBLIOGRAPHY

Aggleton, Peter, Hart, Graham and Davies, Peter (eds) (1991) *AIDS: Responses, Interventions and Care*, Sussex: The Falmer Press.

Aggleton, Peter, Davies, Peter and Hart, Graham (eds) (1993) *AIDS: Facing the Second Decade*, London: The Falmer Press.

Albury, Randell (1985) 'Historical reaction to "new" diseases', *The Australian Journal of Forensic Sciences*, September: 5–12.

Allen, Judith and Patton, Paul (eds) (1983) *Beyond Marxism? Interventions After Marx*, Sydney: Intervention Publications.

Altman, Dennis (1992) 'The most political of diseases', in Timewell, Eric, Minichiello, Victor and Plummer, David (eds) *AIDS in Australia*, Sydney: Prentice-Hall.

Amann, K. and Knorr Cetina, K. (1990) 'The fixation of (visual) evidence', in Lynch, Michael and Woolgar, Steve (eds) *Representation in Scientific Practice*, Cambridge, Mass. and London: MIT Press.

Anastos, Kathryn and Marte, Carol (1991) 'Women – the missing persons in the AIDS epidemic', in McKenzie, Nancy (ed.) *The AIDS Reader: Social, Political, Ethical Issues*, New York: Meridian.

Anderson, Benedict (1991) *Imagined Communities. Reflections on the Origin and Spread of Nationalism*, London and New York: Verso.

Anderson, Roy and Johnson, Anne (1990) 'Rates of sexual partner change in homosexual and heterosexual populations in the United Kingdom', in Voeller, Bruce, Reinisch, June and Gottlieb, Michael (eds) *AIDS and Sex. An Integrated Biomedical and Biobehavioural Approach*, New York and Oxford: Oxford University Press.

Anderson, Roy and May, Robert (1992) 'Understanding the AIDS pandemic', *Scientific American*, 266 (5): 20–8.

Ariss, Robert (1992) 'Against death: the Sydney gay community responds to AIDS', Ph.D. Thesis, Department of Anthropology, University of Sydney, Sydney, Australia.

Armstrong, David (1983) *Political Anatomy of the Body: Medical Knowledge in Britain in the Twentieth Century*, Cambridge: Cambridge University Press.

Ascher, Michael and Kaslow, Richard (1989) 'The immune system: serology and applications', in Kaslow, Richard and Francis, Donald (eds) *The Epidemiology of AIDS. Expression, Occurrence, and Control of Human Immunodeficiency Virus Type 1 Infection*, New York and Oxford: Oxford University Press.

Australian Doctor's Fund (1992) 'AIDS – Have we got it right?' Unpublished conference proceedings. Sydney, Australia, 14–15 May.

Australian Medical Association (1991) *Policy on AIDS/HIV*, AMA.

Ballard, John (1993) 'Sexuality and the state in time of epidemic', in Connell, Robert and Dowsett, Gary (eds) *Rethinking Sex: Social Theory and Sexuality Research*, Melbourne: Melbourne University Press.

Ballard, John (1992) 'Policy-making on HIV in Australia', in Kirp, David and Bayer, Ronald (eds) *AIDS in the Industrialised Democracies: Passion, Politics and Policies*, New Brunswick: Rutgers University Press.

Bennett, Garrett, Chapman, Simon and Bray, Fiona (1989) 'A potential source for the transmission of the human immunodeficiency virus into the heterosexual population: bisexual men who frequent "beats" ', *The Medical Journal of Australia*, 151: 314–18.

Bennett, Marsha (1990) 'Stigmatisation: experiences of persons with Acquired Immune Deficiency Syndrome', *Issues in Mental Health Nursing*, 11: 141–54.

Berlant, Lauren and Freeman, Elizabeth (1993) 'Queer nationality', in Warner, Michael (ed.) *Fear of a Queer Planet: Queer Politics and Social Theory*, Minneapolis: Minnesota University Press.

Bersani, Leo (1988) 'Is the rectum a grave?', in Crimp, Douglas (ed.) *AIDS: Cultural Analysis, Cultural Activism*, Cambridge, Mass.: MIT Press.

Bloor, Michael, Goldberg, David and Emslie, John (1991) 'Ethnostatistics and the AIDS epidemic', *The British Journal of Sociology*, 42 (1): 132–8.

Bochow, M. (1992) 'Attitudes towards gay men in the East and West German population: has AIDS brought about a significant change?' Paper presented at the Second European Conference on Homosexuality and HIV, Amsterdam, The Netherlands, 14–16 February.

Bolton, Ralph (1992) 'AIDS and promiscuity', *Medical Anthropology*, 14: 144–223.

Brachman, Phillip (1990a) 'Epidemiology of infectious disease: principles and methods', in Mandell, Gerald, Douglas, R. Gordon and Bennett, John (eds) *Principles and Practice of Infectious Diseases*, 3rd edn, New York: Churchill Livingstone.

Brachman, Phillip (1990b) 'Transmission and principles of control', in Mandell, Gerald, Douglas, R. Gordon and Bennett, John (eds) *Principles and Practice of Infectious Diseases*, 3rd edn, New York: Churchill Livingstone.

Brandt, Allan (1987) *No Magic Bullet: A Social History of Venereal Disease in the United States Since 1880*, New York: Oxford University Press.

Brown, Norman O. (1966) *Love's Body*, New York: Random House.

Brown, Phyllida (1992) 'How does HIV cause AIDS?', *New Scientist*, 18 July: 31–5.

Burton, Robert (1971) *The Anatomy of Melancholy*, first published 1621, New York: Da Capo Press.

Butler, Judith (1990) *Gender Trouble. Feminism and the Subversion of Identity*, New York and London: Routledge.

Butler, Judith (1993) *Bodies That Matter. On the Discursive Limits of Sex*, New York and London: Routledge.

Caine, Barbara, Grosz, Elizabeth and de Lepervanche, Marie (eds) (1988) *Crossing Boundaries. Feminisms and the Critique of Knowledges*, Sydney: Allen & Unwin.

Canguilhem, Georges (1989) *The Normal and the Pathological*, first published 1966, translated by C. Fawcett and R. Cohen, Introduction by Michel Foucault, New York: Zone Books.

Canguilhem, Georges (1994) *A Vital Rationalist. Selected Writings from Georges Canguilhem*, edited by F. Delaporte, translated by A. Goldhammer, Introduction by P. Rabinow, New York: Zone Books.

Cannon, Walter (1963) *The Wisdom of the Body*, first published 1932, New York: W.W. Norton & Company.

Chaisson, Richard and Volberding, Paul (1990) 'Clinical manifestations of HIV infection', in Mandell, Gerald, Douglas, R. Gordon and Bennett, John (eds)

Principles and Practice of Infectious Diseases, 3rd edn, New York: Churchill Livingstone.

Chalmers, Alan (1982) 'Epidemiology and the scientific method', *International Journal of Health Services*, 12 (4): 659–66.

Chamberland, Mary and Curran, James (1990) 'Epidemiology and prevention of AIDS and HIV', in Mandell, Gerald, Douglas, R. Gordon and Bennett, John (eds) *Principles and Practice of Infectious Diseases*, 3rd edn, New York: Churchill Livingstone.

Chavigny, Katherine, Turner, Sarah and Kibrick, Anne (1989) 'Epidemiology and health policy imperatives for AIDS', in O'Malley, Padraig (ed.) *The AIDS Epidemic. Private Rights and Public Interest*, Boston: Beacon Press.

Cholodenko, Alan (ed.) (1991) *The Illusion of Life. Essays on Animation*, Sydney: Power Publications.

Clements, Mary Lou (1990) 'AIDS vaccines', in Mandell, Gerald, Douglas, R. Gordon and Bennett, John (eds) *Principles and Practice of Infectious Diseases*, 3rd edn, New York: Churchill Livingstone.

Coffin, John (1990) 'The virology of AIDS: 1990', *AIDS*, 4, Supplement 1: S1-S8.

Commonwealth AIDS Research Grants Epidemiology Advisory Committee (1990) *The Role of Epidemiology in Controlling HIV Disease in Australia*, Sydney: National Centre in HIV Epidemiology and Clinical Research.

Commonwealth Department of Community Services and Health (1988) *AIDS: A Time to Care, a Time to Act. Towards a Strategy for All Australians*, Policy Discussion Paper, Canberra: Australian Government Publishing Service.

Commonwealth Department of Community Services and Health (1989) *National HIV/ AIDS Strategy. A Policy Information Paper*, Canberra: Australian Government Publishing Service.

Connell, Robert and Dowsett, Gary (eds) (1993) *Rethinking Sex: Social Theory and Sexuality Research*, Melbourne: Melbourne University Press.

Corbin, Alain (1986) *The Foul and the Fragrant. Odour and the French Social Imagination*, translated by M. Kochan, R. Porter and C. Pendergast, New York: Berg Publishers.

Corbin, Alain (1987) 'Commercial sexuality in nineteenth century France: a system of images and regulations', in Gallagher, Catherine and Laqueur, Thomas (eds) *The Making of the Modern Body: Sexuality and Society in the Nineteenth Century*, Berkeley: University of California Press.

Crimp, Douglas (ed.) (1988) *AIDS: Cultural Analysis, Cultural Activism*, Cambridge, Mass.: MIT Press.

Crofts, N. and Hay, M. (1991) 'Entry of human immuno-deficiency virus into a population of injecting drug users, Victoria, 1990', *The Medical Journal of Australia*, 155: 278–382.

Daston, Lorraine and Galison, Peter (1992) 'The image of objectivity', *Representations*, 40: 81–128.

Davenport-Hines, Richard (1990) *Sex, Death and Punishment. Attitudes to Sex and Sexuality in Britain Since the Renaissance*, London: Fontana Press.

Dawson, Jill, Fitzpatrick, Ray, McLean, John *et al.* (1991) 'Gay men's views and experience of the HIV test', in Aggleton, Peter, Hart, Graham and Davies, Peter (eds) *AIDS: Responses, Interventions and Care*, Sussex: The Falmer Press.

De Certeau, Michel (1988) 'Tools for body-writing', *Intervention*, 21/22: 7–11.

Delany, Samuel (1991) 'Street talk/straight talk', *Differences*, 3 (2): 21–38.

De Lauretis, Teresa (1991) 'Queer theory: lesbian and gay sexualities', *Differences*, 3 (2): iii–xviii.

Derrida, Jacques (1982) *Margins of Philosophy*, translated by A. Bass, Sussex: The Harvester Press.

Derrida, Jacques (1987) 'Before the Law', in Udoff, Alan (ed.) *The Contemporary Critical Performance: Centenary Readings*, Bloomington: Indiana University Press.

Diprose, Rosalyn (1994) *The Bodies of Women. Ethics, Embodiment and Sexual Difference*, London and New York: Routledge.

Diprose, Rosalyn and Ferrell, Robyn (eds) (1991) *Cartographies. Poststructuralism and the Mapping of Bodies and Spaces*, Sydney: Allen & Unwin.

Diprose, Rosalyn and Vasseleu, Cathryn (1991) 'Animation – AIDS and science/fiction', in Cholodenko, Alan (ed.) *The Illusion of Life. Essays on Animation*, Sydney: Power Publications.

Douglas, Mary (1984) *Purity and Danger. An Analysis of the Concepts of Pollution and Taboo*, first published 1966, London: Ark Paperbacks.

Dwyer, John (1988) *The Body at War: The Story of Our Immune System*, Sydney: Allen & Unwin.

Dwyer, John (1993) *The Body at War: The Story of Our Immune System*, 2nd edn, Sydney: Allen & Unwin.

Edelman, Lee (1991) 'Seeing things: representation, the scene of surveillance, and the spectacle of gay male sex', in Fuss, Diana, *Inside/Out. Lesbian Theories, Gay Theories*, London: Routledge.

Edelman, Lee (1992) 'Tearooms and sympathy, or, the epistemology of the water closet', in Parker, Andrew, Russo, Mary, Sommer, Doris *et al.* (eds) *Nationalisms and Sexualities*, New York: Routledge.

Edelman, Lee (1994) *Homographesis: Essays in Gay Literary and Cultural Theory*, New York and London: Routledge.

Epstein, Steven (1988) 'Moral contagion and the medicalisation of gay identity: AIDS in historical perspective', *Research in Law, Deviance and Social Control*, 9: 3–36.

Fauci, Anthony and Lane, H. Clifford (1991) 'The Acquired Immunodeficiency Syndrome (AIDS)', in Wilson, Jean, Braunwald, Eugene, Isselbacher, Kurt *et al.* (eds) *Principles of Internal Medicine*, 2 vols, 12th edn, New York: McGraw-Hill.

Fee, Elizabeth and Fox, Daniel (eds) (1988) *AIDS. The Burdens of History*, Berkeley: University of California Press.

Fee, Elizabeth and Fox, Daniel (eds) (1992) *AIDS. The Making of a Chronic Disease*, Berkeley: University of California Press.

Feher, Michel (ed.) (1989) *Fragments for a History of the Human Body*, 3 vols, New York: Zone Books.

Fleck, Ludwik (1979) *Genesis and Development of a Scientific Fact*, first published 1935, edited by T. Trenn and R. Merton, translated by F. Bradley and T. Trenn, Chicago and London: University of Chicago Press.

Foucault, Michel (1975) *The Birth of the Clinic: An Archaeology of Medical Perception*, translated by A.M. Sheridan Smith, New York: Vintage Books.

Foucault, Michel (1976) *Histoire de la Sexualité 1: La Volonte de Savoir*, Paris: Editions Gallimard.

Foucault, Michel (1977) *Language, Counter-Memory, Practice. Selected Essays and Interviews*, edited and introduced by D. Bouchard, translated by D. Bouchard and S. Simon, Ithaca, New York: Cornell University Press.

Foucault, Michel (1979) *Discipline and Punish. The Birth of the Prison*, translated by A. Sheridan, Harmondsworth, UK: Peregrine Books.

Foucault, Michel (1980a) *The History of Sexuality. Volume I: An Introduction*, translated by R. Hurley, New York: Vintage Books.

Foucault, Michel (1980b) 'The politics of health in the eighteenth century', in Gordon,

Colin (ed.) *Power/Knowledge: Selected Interviews and Other Writings, 1972–1977 by Michel Foucault*, translated by C. Gordon *et al.*, New York: Pantheon Books.

Francis, Donald and Kaslow, Richard (1989) 'Prevention: general considerations', in Kaslow, Richard and Francis, Donald (eds) *The Epidemiology of AIDS. Expression, Occurrence, and Control of Human Immunodeficiency Virus Type 1 Infection*, New York and Oxford: Oxford University Press.

Freud, Sigmund (1955) 'From the history of an infantile neurosis', *The Standard Edition of the Complete Psychological Works of Sigmund Freud*, XVII, London: Hogarth Press.

Fultz, Patricia (1989) 'The biology of human immunodeficiency viruses', in Kaslow, Richard and Francis, Donald (eds) *The Epidemiology of AIDS. Expression, Occurrence, and Control of Human Immunodeficiency Virus Type 1 Infection*, New York and Oxford: Oxford University Press.

Fuss, Diana (1989) *Essentially Speaking: Feminism, Nature and Difference*, New York: Routledge, Chapman & Hall.

Fuss, Diana (ed.) (1991) *Inside/Out. Lesbian Theories, Gay Theories*, London: Routledge.

Gallagher, Catherine and Laqueur, Thomas (eds) (1987) *The Making of the Modern Body: Sexuality and Society in the Nineteenth Century*, Berkeley: University of California Press.

Gallo, Robert (1987) 'The AIDS virus', *Scientific American*, January: 39–48.

Garber, Marjorie (1992) *Vested Interests: Cross-Dressing and Cultural Anxiety*, New York: Routledge.

Gatens, Moira (1983) 'A critique of the sex/gender distinction', in Allen, Judith and Patton, Paul (eds) *Beyond Marxism? Interventions After Marx*, Sydney: Intervention Publications.

Gatens, Moira (1988) 'Towards a feminist philosophy of the body', in Caine, Barbara, Grosz, Elizabeth and de Lepervanche, Marie (eds) *Crossing Boundaries. Feminisms and the Critique of Knowledges*, Sydney: Allen & Unwin.

Gatens, Moira (1991a) 'Corporeal representation in/and the body politic', in Diprose, Rosalyn and Ferrell, Robyn (eds) *Cartographies. Poststructuralism and the Mapping of Bodies and Spaces*, Sydney: Allen & Unwin.

Gatens, Moira (1991b) *Feminism and Philosophy. Perspectives on Difference and Equality*, Cambridge: Polity Press.

Gilman, Sander (1988) 'AIDS and syphilis: the iconography of disease', in Crimp, Douglas (ed.) *AIDS: Cultural Analysis, Cultural Activism*, Cambridge, Mass.: MIT Press.

Gilman, Sander (1992) 'Plague in Germany, 1939/1989: cultural images of race, space and disease', in Parker, Andrew, Russo, Mary, Sommer, Doris *et al.* (eds) *Nationalisms and Sexualities*, New York: Routledge.

Goodman, Joel (1991) 'The immune response', in Stites, Daniel and Terr, Abba (eds) *Basic and Clinical Immunology*, London: Prentice-Hall International Inc.

Gordon, Colin (ed.) (1980) *Power/Knowledge: Selected Interviews and Other Writings, 1972–1977 by Michel Foucault*, translated by C. Gordon *et al.* New York: Pantheon Books.

Gostin, Larry (1992) 'The AIDS litigation project. A national review of court and human rights commission decisions on discrimination', in Fee, Elizabeth and Fox, Daniel (eds) *AIDS. The Making of a Chronic Disease*, Berkeley: University of California Press.

Gottlieb, M. (1981) '*Pneumocystis* pneumonia – Los Angeles', *Morbidity and Mortality Weekly Report*, (30), 5 June: 250–2.

Graubard, Stephen (ed.) (1990) *Living With AIDS*, Cambridge, Mass. and London: MIT Press.

Grossberg, Lawrence, Nelson, Cary and Treichler, Paula (eds) (1992) *Cultural Studies*, New York and London: Routledge.

Grosz, Elizabeth (1986) 'Language and the limits of the body: Kristeva and abjection', in Grosz, Elizabeth, Threadgold, Terry, Kelly, David *et al.* (eds) *Futur*fall: Excursions into Post-Modernity*, Sydney: Power Institute Publications.

Grosz, Elizabeth (1987) 'Notes towards a corporeal feminism', *Australian Feminist Studies*, 5: 1–16.

Grosz, Elizabeth (1989) *Sexual Subversions. Three French Feminists*, Sydney: Allen & Unwin.

Grosz, Elizabeth (1990b) 'Inscriptions and body-maps: representations and the corporeal', in Threadgold, Terry and Cranny-Francis, Anne (eds) *Feminine/Masculine and Representation*, Sydney: Allen & Unwin.

Grosz, Elizabeth (1994) *Volatile Bodies: Towards a Corporeal Feminism*, Sydney: Allen & Unwin.

Grosz, Elizabeth and Probyn, Elspeth (eds) (1995) *Sexy Bodies. The Strange Carnalities of Feminism*, London and New York: Routledge.

Grosz, Elizabeth, Threadgold, Terry, Kelly, David *et al.* (eds) (1986) *Futur*fall: Excursions into Post-Modernity*, Sydney: Power Institute Publications.

Grover, Jan (1988) 'AIDS: keywords', in Crimp, Douglas (ed.) *AIDS: Cultural Analysis, Cultural Activism*, Cambridge, Mass.: MIT Press.

Guinan, Mary and Hardy, Ann (1987) 'Epidemiology of AIDS in women in the United States: 1981 through 1986', *Journal of the American Medical Association*, 257 (15): 2039–42.

Gupta, Sunetra and Anderson, Roy (1992) 'Sex, AIDS and mathematics', *New Scientist*, 135, September: 34–8.

Gwinn, Marta, Pappaioanou, Marguerite, George, Richard *et al.* (1991) 'Prevalence of HIV infection in childbearing women in the United States: surveillance using newborn blood samples', *Journal of the American Medical Association*, 265 (13): 1704–08.

Hamburg, Margaret and Fauci, Anthony (1990) 'AIDS: the challenge to biomedical research', in Graubard, Stephen (ed.) *Living With AIDS*, Cambridge, Mass. and London: MIT Press.

Hamburg, Margaret, Koenig, Scott and Fauci, Anthony (1990) 'Immunology of AIDS and HIV infection', in Mandell, Gerald, Douglas, R. Gordon and Bennett, John (eds) *Principles and Practice of Infectious Diseases*, 3rd edn, New York: Churchill Livingstone.

Hanson, Ellis (1991) 'Undead', in Fuss, Diana (ed.) *Inside/Out. Lesbian Theories, Gay Theories*, London: Routledge.

Haraway, Donna (1991) *Simians, Cyborgs and Women. The Reinvention of Nature*, New York: Routledge.

Harvey, W. and Sladek, M. (1991) 'Ante-natal HIV testing', *Australian Nurses Journal*, 20 (6): 6–7.

Haseltine, William (1990) 'Prospects for the medical control of the AIDS epidemic', in Graubard, Stephen (ed.) *Living With AIDS*, Cambridge, Mass. and London: MIT Press.

Haverkos, Harry and Edelman, Robert (1989) 'Heterosexuals', in Kaslow, Richard and Francis, Donald (eds) *The Epidemiology of AIDS. Expression, Occurrence, and Control of Human Immunodeficiency Virus Type 1 Infection*, New York and Oxford: Oxford University Press.

Heng, Geraldine and Devan, Janadas (1992) 'State fatherhood: the politics of nationalism, sexuality and race in Singapore', in Parker, Andrew, Russo, Mary, Sommer, Doris and Yaeger, Patricia (eds) *Nationalisms and Sexualities*, New York: Routledge.

Herdt, Gilbert and Lindenbaum, Shirley (eds) (1992) *The Time of AIDS. Social Analysis, Theory, and Method*, London: Sage Publications.

Hesse, Mary (1963) *Models and Analogies in Science*, London: Sheed & Ward.

Ihde, Don and Silverman, Hugh J. (eds) (1985) *Descriptions*, New York: State University of New York Press.

Intergovernmental Committee on AIDS (1992) *A Report on HIV/AIDS Activities in Australia 1990–91*, Canberra: Australian Government Publishing Service.

Irigaray, Luce (1985) 'Is the subject of science sexed?', *Cultural Critique*, 1 (1): 73–88.

Jacobus, Mary, Fox-Keller, Evelyn and Shuttleworth, Sally (eds) (1990) *Body/Politics: Women, Literature and the Discourse of Science*, New York and London: Routledge.

Jaret, Peter (1986) 'Our immune system: the wars within', *National Geographic*, 196: 701–35.

Jawetz, Ernest, Melnick, Joseph, Adelberg, Edward *et al.* (1991) *Medical Microbiology*, 19th edn, London: Prentice-Hall International.

Juhasz, Alexandra (1990) 'The contained threat: women in mainstream AIDS documentary', *The Journal of Sex Research*, 27 (1): 25–46.

Kaldor, John (1992) 'Tracking the course of AIDS', *National AIDS Bulletin*, May: 41–2.

Kaldor, John, Elford, Jonathan and McDonald, Ann (1992) 'Monitoring heterosexually transmitted HIV infection in Australia', *Australian Journal of Public Health*, 16 (2): 202–5.

Kamani, Naynesh and Douglas, Steven (1991) 'Structure and development of the immune system', in Stites, Daniel and Terr, Abba (eds) *Basic and Clinical Immunology*, Prentice-Hall International Inc.

Kane, Stephanie and Mason, Theresa (1992) '"IV drug users" and "sex partners": the limits of epidemiological categories and the ethnography of risk', in Herdt, Gilbert and Lindenbaum, Shirley (eds) *The Time of AIDS. Social Analysis, Theory, and Method*, London: Sage Publications.

Kantorowicz, E. (1957) *The King's Two Bodies*, Princeton: Princeton University Press.

Kaslow, Richard and Francis, Donald (1989) 'Epidemiology: general considerations', in Kaslow, Richard and Francis, Donald (eds) *The Epidemiology of AIDS. Expression, Occurrence, and Control of Human Immunodeficiency Virus Type 1 Infection*, New York and Oxford: Oxford University Press.

Kaslow, Richard and Francis, Donald (eds) (1989) *The Epidemiology of AIDS. Expression, Occurrence, and Control of Human Immunodeficiency Virus Type 1 Infection*, New York and Oxford: Oxford University Press.

Kendell, Gavin and Wickham, Gary (1991) 'Health and the social body', unpublished paper, School of Social Sciences, Murdoch University, Perth, Australia.

Kippax, Susan, Tillett, Greg, Crawford, June *et al.* (1991) *Discrimination in the Context of AIDS: Disease and Deviance*, Monograph, National Centre for HIV Social Research, Sydney, Australia.

Kirby, Vicky (1989) 'The body unlimited', *West*, 1 (1): 8–11.

Kirby, Vicky (1991) '*Corpus delicti*: the body at the scene of writing', in Diprose, Rosalyn and Ferrell, Robyn (eds) *Cartographies. Poststructuralism and the Mapping of Bodies and Spaces*, Sydney: Allen & Unwin.

Kirp, David and Bayer, Ronald (eds) (1992) *AIDS in the Industrialised Democracies: Passion, Politics and Policies*, New Brunswick: Rutgers University Press.

Kitzinger, Jenny (1991) 'Judging by appearances: audience understandings of the look of someone with HIV', *Journal of Applied Social Psychology*, 1: 155–63.

Klein, Jan (1982) *Immunology: the Science of Self-Nonself Discrimination*, New York: Wiley-Interscience.

Kosofsky-Sedgwick, Eve (1990) *Epistemology of the Closet*, Berkeley and Los Angeles: University of California Press.

Kristeva, Julia (1982) *Powers of Horror. An Essay on Abjection*, translated by Leon Roudiez, New York: Columbia University Press.

Kroker, Arthur and Kroker, Marylouise (eds) (1988) *Body Invaders. Sexuality and the Post-Modern Condition*, London: Macmillan.

Kruger, Barbara and Mariani, Phil (eds) (1989) *Remaking History*, Seattle: Bay Press.

Laqueur, Thomas (1987) 'Orgasm, generation and the politics of reproductive biology', in Gallagher, Catherine and Laqueur, Thomas (eds) *The Making of the Modern Body: Sexuality and Society in the Nineteenth Century*, Berkeley: University of California Press.

Laqueur, Thomas (1989) *'Amor veneris, vel dulcedo appeletur'*, in Feher, Michel (ed.) *Fragments for a History of the Human Body*, 3 vols, New York: Zone Books.

Latour, Bruno (1990) 'Drawing things together', in Lynch, Michael and Woolgar, Steve (eds) *Representation in Scientific Practice*, Cambridge, Mass. and London: MIT Press.

Latour, Bruno and Woolgar, Steven (1986) *Laboratory Life: The Construction of Scientific Facts*, Princeton: Princeton University Press.

Le Doeuff, Michelle (1989) *The Philosophical Imaginary*, first published in 1980, translated by C. Gordon, Stanford: Stanford University Press.

Lefort, Claude (1986) 'The image of the body in totalitarianism', in Lefort, Claude *The Political Forms of Modern Society. Bureaucracy, Democracy, Totalitarianism*, edited and introduced by J. Thompson, Cambridge: Polity Press.

Le Goff, Jacques (1989) 'Head or heart? The political use of body metaphors in the Middle Ages', in Feher, Michel (ed.) *Fragments for a History of the Human Body*, 3 vols, New York: Zone Books.

Lilienfeld, Abraham (ed.) (1980) *Times, Places and Persons. Aspects of the History of Epidemiology*, Baltimore and London: Johns Hopkins University Press.

Lloyd, Genevieve (1984) *The Man of Reason. 'Male' and 'Female' in Western Philosophy*, London: Methuen.

Lynch, Michael and Woolgar, Steve (eds) (1990) *Representation in Scientific Practice*, Cambridge, Mass. and London: MIT Press.

Ma, Pearl and Armstrong, Donald (eds) (1989) *AIDS and Infections of Homosexual Men*, Boston: Butterworths.

MacDonald, M., Elford, J. and Kaldor, J. *et al.* (1992) 'Survey of antenatal HIV antibody testing in Australia: preliminary report'. Paper presented at The Australian Society for HIV Medicine Conference, Sydney, Australia, November.

McDougal, Steven, Mawle, Alison and Nicholson, Janet (1989) 'The immune system: pathophysiology', in Kaslow, Richard and Francis, Donald (eds) *The Epidemiology of AIDS. Expression, Occurrence, and Control of Human Immunodeficiency Virus Type 1 Infection*, New York and Oxford: Oxford University Press.

McKenzie, Nancy (ed.) (1991) *The AIDS Reader: Social, Political, Ethical Issues*, New York: Meridian.

McLaws, Mary, Brown, Andrew, Cunningham, Phillip *et al.* (1990) 'Prevalence of maternal HIV infection based on anonymous testing of neonates, Sydney 1989', *The Medical Journal of Australia*, 153: 383–6.

McMahon, Brian, Pugh, Thomas and Ipsen, Johannes (1960) *Epidemiological Methods*, Boston and Toronto: Little, Brown and Company.

Mandell, Gerald, Douglas, R. Gordon and Bennett, John (eds) (1990) *Principles and Practice of Infectious Diseases*, 3rd edn, New York: Churchill Livingstone.

Martin, Emily (1987) *The Woman in the Body: A Cultural Analysis of Reproduction*, Milton Keynes: Open University Press.

Martin, Emily (1990) 'Towards an anthropology of immunology: the body as nation state', *Medical Anthropology Quarterly*, 4 (4): 410–26.

Martin, Emily (1992) 'Body narratives, body boundaries', in Grossberg, Lawrence, Nelson, Cary and Treichler, Paula (eds) *Cultural Studies*, New York and London: Routledge.

Martin, Emily (1994) *Flexible Bodies. Tracking Immunity in American Culture from the Days of Polio to the Age of AIDS*, Boston: Beacon Press.

Masur, Henry (1990a) 'Therapy for AIDS', in Mandell, Gerald, Douglas, R. Gordon and Bennett, John (eds) *Principles and Practice of Infectious Diseases*, 3rd edn, New York: Churchill Livingstone.

Masur, Henry (1990b) 'Infections in homosexual men', in Mandell, Gerald, Douglas, R. Gordon and Bennett, John (eds) *Principles and Practice of Infectious Diseases*, 3rd edn, New York: Churchill Livingstone.

May, Robert, Anderson, Roy and Blower, Sally (1990) 'The epidemiology and transmission dynamics of HIV-AIDS', in Graubard, Stephen (ed.) *Living With AIDS*, Cambridge, Mass. and London: MIT Press.

Michaels, Eric (1990) *Unbecoming. An AIDS Diary*, Introduction by Simon Watney, Sydney: Empress Publishing.

Monger, Edith (1991) *Bibliography of Australian HIV/AIDS Publications*, Commonwealth Department of Health, Housing and Community Services, Australian Government Publishing Service.

Montgomery, Scott (1991) 'Codes and combat in bio-medical discourse', *Science as Culture*, 2, part 3 (12): 341–91.

Morbidity and Mortality Weekly Report (1981) 'Karposi's sarcoma and *Pneumocystis* pneumonia among homosexual men – New York City and California', 3 July, 30 (25): 305–8.

National Centre in HIV Epidemiology and Clinical Research (1990) 'The role of epidemiology in controlling HIV disease in Australia', unpublished paper, Sydney, Australia.

Nettleton, Sarah (1992) *Power, Pain and Dentistry*, Buckingham: Open University Press.

New South Wales Anti-Discrimination Board (1992) *Discrimination – The Other Epidemic*, Report of the Inquiry into HIV and AIDS Related Discrimination, Canberra: Government Printing Service.

Nietzsche, Friedrich (1968) *The Will to Power*, translated by W. Kaufmann and R.J. Hollingdale, New York: Vintage Books.

Nilsson, Lennart (1987) *The Body Victorious. The Illustrated Story of Our Immune System and Other Defences of the Human Body*, text by K. Lindqvist and S. Nordfeldt, translated by C. James, London and Boston: Faber & Faber.

Odell, David (1992) 'The politics of penetration', *Antithesis*, 5 (1/2): 6–20.

O'Malley, Padraig (ed.) (1989) *The AIDS Epidemic. Private Rights and Public Interest*, Boston: Beacon Press.

Oppenheimer, Gerald (1988) 'In the eye of the storm: the epidemiological construction of AIDS', in Fee, Elizabeth and Fox, Daniel (eds) *AIDS. The Burdens of History*, Berkeley: University of California Press.

Oppenheimer, Gerald (1992) 'Causes, cases, and cohorts: the role of epidemiology in the historical construction of AIDS', in Fee, Elizabeth and Fox, Daniel (eds) *AIDS. The Making of a Chronic Disease*, Berkeley: University of California Press.

Parker, Andrew, Russo, Mary, Sommer, Doris and Yaeger, Patricia (eds) (1992) *Nationalisms and Sexualities*, New York: Routledge.

Pateman, Carole (1988) *The Sexual Contract*, Cambridge: Polity Press.

Patterson, David (1992) 'The law', in Timewell, Eric, Minichiello, Victor and Plummer, David (eds) *AIDS in Australia*, Sydney: Prentice-Hall.

Patton, Cindy (1990) *Inventing AIDS*, New York: Routledge.

Patton, Cindy and Kelly, Janis (1987) *Making it: A Woman's Guide to Sex in the Age of AIDS*, Boston: Firebrand.

Perkins, Roberta, Lovejoy, Francis and Marina (1990) 'Protecting the community. Prostitutes and public health legislation in the age of AIDS', *Criminology Australia*, October/November: 6–8.

Phillips, D.C. (1970) 'Organicism in the nineteenth and early twentieth centuries', *Journal of the History of Ideas*, 31: 413–32.

Pontalis, J.B. (1978) 'On death-work in Freud, in the self, in culture', in Roland, A. (ed.) *Psychoanalysis, Creativity, and Literature: a French-American Inquiry*, New York: Columbia University Press.

Posner, Tina (1991) 'What's in a smear? Cervical screening, medical signs and metaphors', *Science as Culture*, 2, part 2 (11): 167–87.

Richardson, Dianne (1987) *Women and AIDS*, New York: Methuen.

Richmond, Phyllis (1980) 'The germ theory of disease', in Lilienfeld, Abraham (ed.) *Times, Places and Persons. Aspects of the History of Epidemiology*, Baltimore and London: Johns Hopkins University Press.

Richmond, Robyn and Wakefield, Denis (eds) (1987) *AIDS and Other Sexually Transmitted Diseases*, Sydney: Harcourt Brace Jovanovich.

Roitt, Ivan (1991) *Essential Immunology*, 7th edn, Oxford: Blackwell Scientific Publications.

Roland, A. (ed.) (1978) *Psychoanalysis, Creativity, and Literature: a French-American Inquiry*, New York: Columbia University Press.

Rompalo, Anne and Handsfield, Hunter (1989) 'Overview of sexually transmitted diseases in homosexual men', in Ma, Pearl and Armstrong, Donald (eds) *AIDS and Infections of Homosexual Men*, Boston: Butterworths.

Sacks, Oliver (1986) *A Leg to Stand On*, London: Picador.

Sattentau, Quentin (1988) 'AIDS: our defences are down', *New Scientist*, 7 April: 49–53.

Schaechter, Moselio, Medoff, Gerald and Schlessinger, David (eds) (1989) *Mechanisms of Microbial Disease*, Baltimore: Williams & Wilkins.

Schiebinger, Londa (1987) 'Skeletons in the closet: the first illustrations of the female skeleton in eighteenth century anatomy', in Gallagher, Catherine and Laqueur, Thomas (eds) *The Making of the Modern Body: Sexuality and Society in the Nineteenth Century*, Berkeley: University of California Press.

Schimpff, Stephen (1990) 'Infections in the compromised host – an overview', in Mandell, Gerald, Douglas, R. Gordon and Bennett, John (eds) *Principles and Practice of Infectious Diseases*, 3rd edn, New York: Churchill Livingstone.

Schleupner, Charles (1990) 'Detection of HIV-1 infection', in Mandell, Gerald, Douglas, R. Gordon and Bennett, John (eds) *Principles and Practice of Infectious Diseases*, 3rd edn, New York: Churchill Livingstone.

Scientific American (1987) Special issue on AIDS, January.

Sela, Michael (1990) 'Immunology in AIDS in 1990', *AIDS*, 4, Supplement 1: S9-S14.

Sell, Stewert (1987) *Basic Immunology. Immune Mechanisms in Health and Disease*, New York, Amsterdam, London: Elsevier.

Serres, Michel (1982) *Hermes: Literature, Science, Philosophy*, edited and translated by J. Harari and D. Bell, Baltimore and London: The Johns Hopkins University Press.

Shilts, Randy (1987) *And the Band Played On. Politics, People and the AIDS Epidemic*, London: Penguin Books.

Silverman, David and Bor, Robert (1991) 'The delicacy of describing sexual partners in

HIV-test counselling: implications for practice', *Counselling Psychology Quarterly*, 4 (2/3): 177–90.

Singer, Linda (1993) *Erotic Welfare: Sexual Theory and Politics in the Age of Epidemic*, edited and introduced by J. Butler and M. MacGrogan, New York and London: Routledge.

Sloand, Elaine, Pitt, Elisabeth, Chiarello, Robert *et al.* (1991) 'HIV testing: state of the art', *Journal of the American Medical Association*, 266 (20): 2861–6.

Sontag, Susan (1989) *AIDS and its Metaphors*, London: Allen Lane.

Stites, Daniel and Terr, Abba (eds) (1991) *Basic and Clinical Immunology*, London: Prentice-Hall International Inc.

Susser, Mervyn (1973) *Causal Thinking in the Health Sciences. Concepts and Strategies of Epidemiology*, New York and Oxford: Oxford University Press.

Susser, Mervyn (1987) *Epidemiology, Health and Society. Selected Papers*, New York and Oxford: Oxford University Press.

Tersmette, Matthijs and Miedema, Frank (1990) 'Interaction between HIV and the host immune system in the pathogenesis of AIDS', *AIDS*, 4, Supplement 1: S57-S66.

Threadgold, Terry and Cranny-Francis, Anne (eds) (1990) *Feminine/Masculine and Representation*, Sydney: Allen & Unwin.

Timewell, Eric, Minichiello, Victor and Plummer, David (eds) (1992) *AIDS in Australia*, Sydney: Prentice-Hall.

Tindall, Brett, Plummer, David and Donovan, Basil (1992) 'Medical management', in Timewell, Eric, Minichiello, Victor and Plummer, David (eds) *AIDS in Australia*, Sydney: Prentice-Hall.

Traweek, Sharon (1988) *Buying Time and Talking Space: The Culture of the Particle Physics Community*, Boston: Harvard University Press.

Treichler, Paula (1988a) 'AIDS, homophobia and biomedical discourse: an epidemic of signification', in Crimp, Douglas (ed.) *AIDS: Cultural Analysis, Cultural Activism*, Cambridge, Mass.: MIT Press.

Treichler, Paula (1988b) 'AIDS, gender, and biomedical discourse: current contests for meaning', in Fee, Elizabeth and Fox, Daniel (eds) *AIDS. The Burdens of History*, Berkeley: University of California Press.

Treichler, Paula (1989) 'AIDS and HIV infection in the Third World: a First World Chronicle', in Kruger, Barbara and Mariani, Phil (eds) *Remaking History*, Seattle: Bay Press.

Treichler, Paula (1992) 'Beyond *Cosmo*: AIDS, identity, and inscriptions of gender', *Camera Obscura*, 28: 21–77.

Tyler, Kenneth and Fields, Bernard (1990) 'Introduction to viruses and viral diseases', in Mandell, Gerald, Douglas, R. Gordon and Bennett, John (eds) *Principles and Practice of Infectious Diseases*, 3rd edn, New York: Churchill Livingstone.

Udoff, Alan (ed.) (1987) *The Contemporary Critical Performance: Centenary Readings*, Bloomington: Indiana University Press.

Vasseleu, Cathryn (1991) 'Life itself', in Diprose, Rosalyn and Ferrell, Robyn (eds) *Cartographies. Poststructuralism and the Mapping of Bodies and Spaces*, Sydney: Allen & Unwin.

Voeller, Bruce, Reinisch, June and Gottlieb, Michael (eds) (1990) *AIDS and Sex. An Integrated Biomedical and Biobehavioural Approach*, New York and Oxford: Oxford University Press.

Waddell, Charles (1993) 'Testing for HIV infection among heterosexual, bisexual and gay men', *Australian Journal of Public Health*, 17 (1): 27–31.

Waldby, Catherine (1995) 'Destruction: boundary erotics and refigurations of the heterosexual male body', in Grosz, Elizabeth and Probyn, Elspeth (eds) *Sexy Bodies. The Strange Carnalities of Feminism*, London and New York: Routledge.

Waldby, Catherine, Kippax, Susan and Crawford, June (1991) 'Equality and eroticism: AIDS and the active/passive distinction', *Social Semiotics*, 1 (2): 39–50.

Waldby, Catherine, Kippax, Susan and Crawford, June (1993a) 'Heterosexual men and safe sex practice', *The Sociology of Health and Illness*, 15 (2): 246–56.

Waldby, Catherine, Kippax, Susan and Crawford, June (1993b) '*Cordon sanitaire*: clean and unclean women in the AIDS discourse of young men', in Aggleton, Peter, Davies, Peter and Hart, Graham (eds) *AIDS: Facing the Second Decade*, London: The Falmer Press.

Ward, Frazer (1992) 'Foreign and familiar bodies', in *Dirt and Domesticity: Constructions of the Feminine*, New York: Whitney Museum of American Art Catalogue.

Warner, Michael (ed.) (1993) *Fear of a Queer Planet: Queer Politics and Social Theory*, Minneapolis: Minnesota University Press.

Watney, Simon (1987) *Policing Desire: Pornography, AIDS and the Media*, London: Methuen.

Watney, Simon (1993) 'Emergent sexual identities and HIV/AIDS', in Aggleton, Peter, Davies, Peter and Hart, Graham (eds) *AIDS: Facing the Second Decade*, London: The Falmer Press.

Weber, Samuel (1987) *Institution and Interpretation*, Minneapolis: University of Minnesota Press.

Weeks, Jeffrey (1991) *Against Nature. Essays on History, Sexuality and Identity*, London: Rivers Oram Press.

Wilson, Christopher (1990) 'The cellular immune system and its role in host defence', in Mandell, Gerald, Douglas, R. Gordon and Bennett, John (eds) *Principles and Practice of Infectious Diseases*, 3rd edn, New York: Churchill Livingstone.

Wilson, Jean, Braunwald, Eugene, Isselbacher, Kurt *et al.* (eds) (1991) *Principles of Internal Medicine*, 2 vols, 12th edn, New York: McGraw-Hill.

Winkelstein, Warren, Padian, Nancy, Rutherford, George *et al.* (1989) 'Homosexual men', in Kaslow, Richard and Francis, Donald (eds) *The Epidemiology of AIDS. Expression, Occurrence, and Control of Human Immunodeficiency Virus Type 1 Infection*, New York and Oxford: Oxford University Press.

Young, Iris (1985) 'Pregnant subjectivity and the limits of existential phenomenology', in Ihde, Don and Silverman, Hugh J. (eds) *Descriptions*, New York: State University of New York Press.

INDEX

anal sex 14, 41, 76–8, 79–80, 102–3, 105, 108, 136
anatomical atlas 27, 32, 35
anatomisation of culture 33 *ff*, 42 *ff*, 50
anatomy: imaginary anatomies 16, 42–6, 47–8, 50, 72; meaning of 33, 42

biomedical imagination 1, 4, 5–6, 15–16, 31–2, 33, 37, 39, 42, 54, 78, 79, 81, 122, 138, 139
biomedicine: attitude towards virus 2–3, 4, 40; biomedical discourse as discourse of culture 5, 6, 15–16, 32 *ff*, 57; 'bio-power', 7; discursive practice, as 24; epidemics and 7; human body and 26–7, 32, 33 *ff*; language of 28–9, 30–1; male homosexuality and 59–60; model of knowledge, 26; norm in 6, 13, 16, 36–8, 40, 41–2, 44–6, 50, 51, 52, 81, 83; panoptic aspirations of 15, 80, 96, 111; political philosophy and 58; political practice, as 20; 'real' of AIDS and 5, 7, 28; representations of AIDS, 40; 'science fiction', as kind of 27 *ff*; sexual difference/identity and 6, 20, 21–2, 23, 41, 50, 82, 140–7; violence of biomedical practice 4–5, 6
biomilitary metaphor *see* metaphor
bisexual men 18, 20, 41, 85, 86, 103–4, 106, 107, 108, 110, 112, 122, 136, 137, 144
blood donors 116, 130–1
body *see* human body
body boundaries 13–15, 41–50, 56, 57–8, 70–8, 80, 89, 104–5, 107, 141–2
body fluids 20, 40, 41, 49, 74, 75, 76, 80
body permeability 13, 14, 15, 17, 41, 46, 47, 48, 49, 74, 75, 76, 77

body politic 15, 18, 88–94, 109–10

cells: concept of 53, 58; personification of 70; 'sexual relations' between 66–7, 68, 70; *see also* T cells
clinical gaze 26–7, 28, 53–4, 80, 94, 95, 99, 117
condoms: women and 10

epidemic: body as social microcosm and 40; Case Reproductive Rate 97–8; declarations of 1–2, 7; feminine bodies and 20–1; legitimacy of biomedical knowledge and 7; nature/culture distinction and 19, 20; political nature of management of 9; sexual 7–8, 17, 98–9, 125; social order and 40; viral 1–2
epidemiology: body politic and 83 *ff*; clinical medicine and 97, 100–1; coherent narrative of 100; control of infectious flow 105–9; definition of 94; epidemiological surveillance 6, 9, 15, 94–100; generally 83; host factors, emphasis on 100–1; panoptic claims of 96, 111; reordering of bodies by 99; social power of 96–7; task of 84, 94, 95–6; topography of infection 100–1; violence of classificatory practices 9, 143
exposure categories 132, 135, 136–8

gay men: anal sex and 14, 41, 76–8, 79–80, 102–3, 105, 108, 136; association with AIDS/HIV 11, 13, 59–60, 62, 69, 74, 79, 87, 101; bodies of 14, 20, 48, 75, 76–8, 80–1, 83, 106, 110, 111; HIV